Sir Sundar Singh Majithia
and His Relevance in Sikh Politics

Sir Sundar Singh Majithia
and His Relevance in Sikh Politics

Gurnam Singh Rekhi

HAR-ANAND
PUBLICATIONS PVT LTD

HAR-ANAND PUBLICATIONS PVT LTD
E-49/3, Okhla Industrial Area, Phase-II, New Delhi-110020
Tel.: 41603490
E-mail: info@haranandbooks.com/haranand@rediffmail.com
Shop online at: www.haranandbooks.com

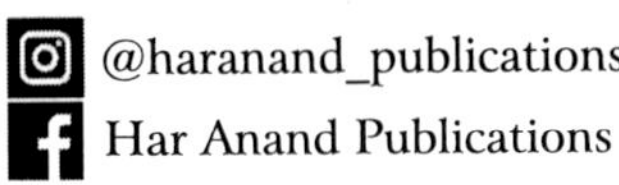

Reprint, 2025

Published by Ashok Gosain and Ashish Gosain for Har-Anand Publications Pvt Ltd

Printed in India

To
My Parents
who taught the meaning
of the word, "Gratitude"

Foreword

The ideals of social morality, if not anything else, require that each generation should continue to remember all those persons, men and women, who had during their life-times, added to the richness of human civilization, culture, polity and overall nobility of ideas which make successive generations better than before. Statesmen, scientists and sages all deserve our attention in this regard.

Shri Gurnam Singh Rekhi has done that by writing the historical biography of Sir Sundar Singh Majithia, a doyen amongst the Sikh reformist leaders of the Punjab during the last decade of the 19th century and first four decades of the present century. He put in his best efforts to spread education, to speed up socio-religious reforms among the Sikhs besides fighting, in his own way, the virus of communalism and class-hatred in a very difficult and challenging situation in which his community and nation were placed due to various factors.

The most significant factor was the attitude of the British rulers who used to swear by the sublimity of the Christian rectitude without understanding the basics of the Philosophy of the Vedas, the Quran and Guru Granth Sahib. They succeeded in breaking the cohesian among the Punjabis, Muslims, Hindus and Sikhs after the death of Maharaja Ranjit Singh in 1839 with the help of European Commanders, Mercenaries and some treacherous nobles and employees of 'Khalsa Sarkar' leading to annexation of Punjab not before the ferocious battles of Sabraon and Chillianwala which are memorable heroic deeds of loyalists like Dewan Mul Raj, Nazim of Multan, Sardar Mewa Singh and Surat Singh Majithia, General Kahn Singh Mann, Sardar Chattar Singh and Sham Singh of Attariwala, Sheikh Imam-ud-din, Governor of Kashmir, General Ilahi Baksh, Commander of Darbar's Artillery, Bhai Maharaj Singh and others. This is what a British Commander, who fought in the battle of Chillianwala, writes about his experience of the battle under the name of a British Subaltern:

"The Sikhs fought like devils.... Such a mass of men I never set an eye on and as brave as lion they ran right on the bayonets of the 24th (British Regiment) and struck at their assailants when they were transfixed."

This resulted in general despondency and indifference among the Sikh community to the (mutiny) of 'Poorbia' Sepoys of the British Indian armed forces in 1857 whereafter the British adopted more subtle methods of seeking the help of Indian princes alongwith, what they described as, constitutional reforms of 1907-1909, the Montague-Chelmsford reforms introducing dyarchy in the British ruled provinces and finally Provincial Autonomy introduced on the recommendations made by the Simon Commission in 1927. The system of franchise was on communal lines on the one hand and urban *vs* rural, rich *vs* poor educated *vs* uneducated, on the other thereby sowing the seeds of India's division into Muslim majority vis-a-vis Hindu majority Republics.

All these facts have to be fully grasped to understand the relevance of the policies suggested and pursued by leaders like Sir Sundar Singh Majithia, Fazl-i-Hussain, Prof. Ruchi Ram Sahni, Lala Lajpat Rai, Sir Gokul Chand Narang, Bhai Vir Singh and Harkishan Lal Gauba. But since the British were determined to undo their efforts, Punjabis had to undergo the "*Agni Pariksha*" again and again, whether at Jallianwala Bagh, Guru Ka Bagh morcha and other agitations related to Gurudwara movement.

Under these circumstances, we see that sober and moderate statesman like Sir Sundar Singh Majithia did his best to save the situation during his entire life-time, as unfolded in this book. The story, besides its historical significance, is worth recounting as the same is still very relevant, as the most appropriate title of the book suggests, even 58 years after his death.

M.L. AHLUWALIA

Preface

When late Dr. Fauja Singh Bajwa, then professor and head of the Department of History and Historical Studies, Punjabi University Patiala suggested to me in 1973 to work on the biography of Sardar Bahadur Sir Sundar Singh Majithia, the first natural reaction which could be expected from a young research scholar having been associated with the activities of Students union, was that of contemptuous refusal to dig out the history of an 'Aristocrat' who had worked for the British Government in various capacities and accordingly, I requested Dr. Fauja Singh to allot some other topic related to the Freedom Movement or the Gurudwara Reform movement for my dissertation. A gentle and affectionate person as he was, whom I always held in high esteem, Dr. Fauja Singh politely suggested to me to go through a small booklet which S. Mehar Singh 'Rawel', a former editor of 'Khalsa Advocate' had written on Sir Sundar Singh, before taking any final decision whether the great Majithia Sardar really deserved to be the subject of my research.

The study of the brief life-sketch was simply overwhelming which brought me face-to-face, literally, with one of the tallest leaders who, perhaps, wanted me to undo the injustice which the students and scholars of history appeared to have done to him so far. I could, thereafter, appreciate that among the leaders and reformers who guided the destiny of their community in socio-economic-religious spheres at the most critical juncture of its history during the beginning of the 20th century, Sardar Sundar Singh appeared to be an outstanding personality though, at the same time, the most misunderstood by his generation although his work has been consistently constructive and his activities covered, amazingly, almost every sphere of life stretched over a period of fifty years during which he initiated, guided, influenced and led so many institutions and events. To my mind the reason for this apathy on the part of his detractors was that he rationalized too much, whereas most of the self-imposed leaders of the

Sikh Community believed in extreme postures either way in matters of religion. In politics too, he preferred a balanced approach with a well entrenched foreign imperial power, which facilitated an era of 'fruitful cooperation' without ever compromising the interest of his community or the Nation. He was, in fact neither a stooge of the British, nor a fire-brand revolutionary. He comes out as a moderate leader and practical statesman, by all standards.

The result was that after submission of my dissertation on the life of Sir Sundar Singh Majithia in 1974, I became all the more involved in understanding the personality and perceptions of the most illustrious leader of the Sikhs—a great innovator and thinker—who was not only respected by his own community but by other communities as well as the British. In fact, this rare synthesis of qualities of Sardar Sundar Singh as a deeply religious person, an able administrator, a down-to-earth politician, economic reformer and a leader of the poor while simultaneously representing the aristocrats and the privileged landlords, made him an interesting and important subject for students of history, for his life raised and answered several questions which are significant for study of development of Sikh history in the pre-partition period besides its relevance in the present context of the Sikh psyche.

Source Material: Among important sources of material for this unattempted project were personal papers of Sir Sundar Singh Majithia which his sons had donated to Nehru Memorial Museum and Library, New Delhi, Legislative proceedings and other contemporary records preserved at National Archieves of India, New Delhi, Chief Khalsa Dewan records, Library of Khalsa College Amritsar besides other primary and secondary sources along with interviews of contemporaries of Sir Sundar Singh, some of whom like Dr. Bhai Jodh Singh, S. Mehar Singh Rawel, S. Nahar Singh Grewal, Dr. Sir Surendra Singh Majithia, S. Surjit Singh Majithia, the two illustrious sons of the Majithia Sardar, whom the author had the privilege to meet.

Among those who encouraged me to work on this biography of one of the great legends of Sikh History, have been late Dr. Fauja Singh, late Prof. Rajindar Singh and Dr. Kirpal Singh, all from the Deptt. of History and Historical Studies, Punjabi University, Patiala, beside my consistent source of inspiration, i.e. Prof. M.L. Ahluwalia, the eminent historian—archivist, whose dedication and contribution of Sikh history is a history itself.

I also take this opportunity to thank Sardar Dalip Singh Majithia son of late Sardar Kirpal Singh and Sardar Satyajit Singh Majithia son of late Sardar Surjit Singh, who gladly provided the required information, photographs etc., while the manuscript about their grandfather was being finalized.

Dedicating the biography of Sir Sundar Singh Majithia to the spirit of Khalsa, on the eve of tercentenary of its creation, I suggest to the students of history in particular and members of the Sikh Community in general, to go through the book dispassionately without any pre-determined bias or opinion, to facilitate proper appreciation of the role of an individual who provided leadership and worked for preserving and protecting the identity of his community during one of the most critical periods of its history.

While presenting my study on Sardar Sundar Singh Majithia at a time when the Sikhs find themselves once again, on the cross-roads between the sublime philosophy of Religion as espounded by the Gurus and conflicting postures adopted by its leadership, I also have to submit, most humbly, my apprehension that for the communities and the Nations which do not learn lessons from its Chapters, History repeats itself, often with a vengeance.

Gurnam Singh Rekhi

Contents

1

The Family and Heritage

While the entire majha region of Punjab could justly be proud of some of the brave generals who confronted the invaders from Alexander the Great to the British forces, the small village of Majitha[1] (near Amritsar)—which the family of Sir Sundar Singh, of Shergill clan among the Jat Sikhs—had adopted as their surname, could also be proud of its illustrious Sardars. With a view to discard the caste—system, most of the misaldars and other sardars took to distinguishing themselves by affixing names of their respective villages. For instance, the first to organize the Sikh 'dharvi derahs' in well-organized 'Misls' or Chiefships in the pre-Ranjit Singh period, Sardar Kapur Singh is known by the name of his Village, i.e., Faizalpur or Singhpur. Maharaja Ranjit Singh's family, also of Jats, adopted the surname of Sukarchakia from their ancestral village of Sukarchak, near Gujranwala Town, now in Pakistan. Under Maharaja Ranjit Singh, the two families of the Sardars who became most prominent were the Attariwalas and the Majithias. Though Majithias were first to rise to prominence from the period of Sardar Charhat Singh, the grandfather of Maharaja Ranjit Singh, yet the Attariwala family led by Sardar Sham Singh and Chattar Singh of village 'Attari', also near Amritsar, became equally important in the hierarchy of nobles in the court of the Maharaja.

The Majithias

The Majithias refer to their ancestors Izat Singh & Sahaj Singh who had followed the fortunes of Sukarchakia Sardars. Izat Singh had

[1]"The village of Majitha, situated ten miles to the North of the City of Amritsar, has given its name to one of the most distinguished families of the Punjab"—says Lepel H. Griffin in his book "Chiefs & Families of Note in the Punjab.

acquired a strip of the Dhani Country on his own account and held it with much difficulty and by dint of constant fighting, till his death in 1772. His sons, Fateh Singh and Jaimal Singh, were in their teens at the time of his death. Therefore, his brother Sahaj Singh took possession of the Estate. In 1781, Sahaj Singh died and Uttam Singh, his eldest son, succeeded to the entire property without any opposition from Fateh Singh and Jaimal Singh, who might have been reasonably expected to have claimed their Father's share. When Ranjit Singh rose to power and in 1803 -4 took possession of the Dhani Estate of the Majithia Sardars, then famous for its breed of horses, he settled a Jagir for the family. Uttam Singh was made Governor or Nazim of Rawalpindi. As Sardar Uttam Singh died interstate in 1827, so the Maharaja resumed the family Jagir and gave Sardar Attar Singh an estate of Rs. 28,000/- at Sayyadpur, Khasra and Ganjo-Mahal areas. After sometime, he was allowed to take management of his old family Ilaqa, though, he did not held it in Jagir, was killed in Hazara in 1843, and his only son Surat Singh succeeded him.

Raja Surat Singh

Sardar Sundar Singh's father, Raja Surat Singh was one of the brave generals of the Sikh Kingdom. He was stationed at Peshawar and during the first Punjab war in 1845-46, he was entrusted with keeping order about Nowshera which was in a state of turmoil at that time. Raja Surat Singh had successfully resisted the violent attitude of Misr Lal Singh who, on becoming a Minister, tried to force Surat Singh to exchange his Jagir in Jhelum for the one in Bari Doab. At the outbreak of rebellion in 1848, he joined it and took part in it. Because of that Sir Lepel H. Griffin, who held the charge of the Political Office of the English East India Company's government for the Chiefs and Rulers in Punjab, naturally criticised the conduct of Raja Surat Singh during this critical period. He writes:

"It seems that as early as July, 1847, he had talked treason with Sardar Chattar Singh and when he was summoned in July, 1848, to join Raja Sher Singh with five hundred horses, he had another meeting on the road with Chatar Singh and brought to Raja Sher Singh his father's injunctions to rebel. The defection of Raja Sher Singh appears to have been in a great measure owing to Surat Singh's influence. The evidence of Shaikh Imam-ud-din Khan is to the effect that at the meeting of Raja Sher Singh's Officers at Multan on the night of the 14th September, Raja Sher Singh tried to persuade his men to remain faithful; but that Surat Singh harangued the Soldiery, and by his arguments so inflamed their passions, that the Raja, could only receive his safety by adopting the popular side and going over to Mul Raj[2]. When Sher Singh left Multan, Surat Singh was placed in command of one division of his army, two thousand men and two guns. On the march to Jabalpur, in the Gujranwala district, this detachment committed many excesses[3].

After the battle of Gujrat, the Jagirs of Surat Singh, worth Rs. 22,500/ - were confiscated, and he was removed to Benares where he remained under surveillance on a pension of Rs. 720/- per annum.

But when a few years later Sardar Surat Singh after release from long captivity and perhaps more for the reason of concern for the safeguard of personal jewellery of maharani Jindan, as a matter of trust and loyalty to the much victimized widow of Maharaja Ranjit Singh, the one time rebel against the British took a stand against the mutineers of 1857-58 rebellion, the same Lepel H. Griffin showered praises on Sardar Surat Singh's loyalty to the British. The entire statement is worth quoting to be fully understood in this context. He writes,

"On the 4th June, 1857, the 37th native infantry was disbanded at Benares and some suspicious movement being observed in a Corps of Ludhiana Sikhs present on the ground. The guns, which were being served against the 37th, were turned against the Sikhs. 'The whole affair seems to have been a miserable mistake' and there is no reason to believe that the corps were anything but loyal. But it was not prepared for so severe a test for its loyalty, and accordingly charged the guns, but was repulsed with great loss and driven from the field. It happened that the Benares treasury, which

[2]After Maharaja Ranjit Singh's death in 1839 followed by a period of fratricide among the successors and nobles of the Khalsa Kingdom, the British succeeded in their manouvers and practically occupied the sovereign kingdom of Lahore by 1846 not before facing resistance from Khalsa Army led by some brave generals, among whom Diwan Mul Raj of Multan with a small but determined garrison "Kept General Whish at his wits' end for several months" (The Punjab's Pioneer Freedom Fighters by Prof. M.L. Ahluwalia and Dr. Kirpal Singh)

[3]"Chiefs and families of Note in the Punjab" by Lepel H. Griffin.

RAJA SURAT SINGH MAJITHIA

contained several lakhs of rupees and jewels of Maharani Jindan, valued at twenty lakhs, was guarded by a detachment of the Sikh Regiment which had been cut up, hand by the treasury was The Collectory's Court, a strong masonary building on the roof of which some twelve civilians had taken their stand to defend the treasure and their own lives in the event of an outbreak. When the Sikh guard heard the fate of their comrades, their agitation and rage were extreme, and they would certainly have mutined, seized the treasure and attacked the Europeans had not Sardar Surat Singh gone in among them and, by his personal influence and expostulations, kept them to a sense of their duty[4]".

At Jaunpur, another detachment of Ludhiana Regiment was stationed. They rose in rebellion, murdered the Commanding Officer, looted the treasure and marched to Lucknow. However, the situation at Benares was different where Sardar Surat Singh who, with his brave and tactful handling, did not allow the worse to happen. Sir Lepel H. Griffin describes Sardar Surat Singh's role in the following manner,

"Through that long June night, the Sardar, ably seconded by Pandit Gokul Chand, argued and entreated till, towards morning, the little party were escorted to the mint by the European force ... But for the gallantry and loyalty of Surat Singh, the same tragedy might have taken place at Benares*[5]."

On several subsequent occasions, he helped the British Government, and with his conspicuous gallantry, earned a good reputation. on 6th July, 1857, when engaged with a body of Rajputs who attacked Benares, he was severely wounded on the knees and was confined to bed for several months. Due to the effect of this injury, he became lame. Sir Lepel H. Griffin gives the following reason for Sardar Surat Singh's valuable assistance to the British Government at a critical juncture,

"Adversity had taught him wisdom; and he was now as warm in his loyalty as he had been before active in rebellion[6]".

However, this remark appears to be too sweeping and amounts to perversity of judgement, in so far as, it totally ignores the

[4]Ibid.
[5]Ibid.
*Incident at Jaunpur.
[6]&Ibid.

historical and psychological factors due to which the Sikhs had generally dissociated themselves from the mutiny in 1857-58. Sardar Surat Singh was, in fact, too great a general and a self-respecting Gursikh to have acted against his conscience. It could not have been possible for a man, who had taken a prominent and active part in the rebellian to safeguard the honour of the Sikh Kingdom a few years earlier, to have yielded to adversity, whatever might have been the circumstances. Some historians, no doubt, opined that the call of the Mutiny in 1857 did not arouse the national feeling among the Sikhs who, still fresh with the bitter memories of their kingdom being trampled under the feet of the Muslim Sepoys under the British Command, regarded this uprising with the contemptuous indifference. But more. than that, it was Sardar Surat Singh's emotional attachment and concern for the protection of Maharani Jindan's treasure which was the driving force for his spontaneous action. An additional reason could be that as a person of discerning mind, Sardar Surat Singh wished to win the confidence of the British who had already, by then, turned the tables on the Mutineer Sepoy Regiments, to be permitted to return to the Punjab to live in his village Majitha which his family and the Attariwala Sardars having been exiled, could not otherwise do. Sardar Surat Singh was thus permitted to return to his native place where he came in 1861 under the general clemency granted by the British, besides getting an additional Jagir at Dhumri in the present district of Gorakhpur in Uttar Pradesh (then United Provinces) alongwith a pension of Rs. 4800/- per annum. In 1875, he was appointed an Honorary Magistrate, and was invested with judicial powers which he exercised at Majitha where he constructed a big court-house. In 1877, the title of Raja was conferred upon him on the occasion of Imperial Assembly at Delhi. In the same year, he was awarded with Companionship of the Star of India. He lived at Majitha till his death in 1881. He was survived by his two sons, Umrao Singh and Sundar Singh, who were both minors at the time of their father's death. Their guardianship and management of their estates was entrusted to Captain Sardar Gulab Singh Attariwala under the supervision of "Court of Wards". On the death of Captain Gulab Singh in 1877, the charge was handed over to Gurmukh Rai, a Pleader of Amritsar. In November, 1882, the two brothers were entered on the rolls of Government School, Amritsar and later they both studied at Amritsar.

Sardar Umrao Singh

Sardar Umrao Singh had succeeded Raja Surat Singh as head of the family and held his father's seat in Provincial Darbars. In 1883, he was married to the daughter of Captain Gulab Singh. He and his wife visited Europe on several occasions. Balram Singh, the eldest son of Sardar Umrao Singh, was married to a cousin of the Maharaja of Patiala and was aide-de-camp to the ruler of Kashmir. He died in 1922 survived by two sons and a daughter. The two younger sons of Umrao Singh were educated at Aitchison College, Lahore. Sardar Umrao Singh's first wife had died in 1907. In 1911, he married a Hungarian Lady and had two daughters from her—one of whom was the celebrated Amrita Shergill. In 1912, he went to Europe and had to stay there till 1920 because of the First World War. In 1926, he went to Europe again and stayed in France for seven years for completion of education of his two-daughters.

According to Bhai Jodh Singh, Sardar Umrao Singh was "Jagirdar and he was a scholar of Sanskrit, Persian, Urdu and English. He wrote beautiful English. I have got some of his letters. He stayed at Lahore... I knew Amrita Shergill and her sister. Ultimately, he settled at Shimla. He built two houses there and when I became a M.L.C. and our meetings were held at Shimla, he asked me to stay with him. So I used to stay with him and his youngest daughter was incharge of the house because her mother had committed suicide... As for his influence. I have told you, that he introduced me to Leo Tolstoy, and through Leo Tolstoy I became an admirer of Gandhi. Then he gave me his own books on *Vedanta, Sankhya* and *Yoga* to study.... He was a great scholar. For me, he copied *Mandukiya* Upnishads, I have got that in his own hand. You know in Sanskrit, there is *Sandhi*. He just put these words separately, with an English translation over them, and he gave it to me. So I have got that with me as his souvenir[7]".

The fact that the visits of Sardar Umrao Singh abroad and activities, including contacts with Raja Mahendra Partap a revolutionary-were viewed with great suspicion by the British is borne by the contents of D.O. letter dt. 9th July, 1919 from Sir E.O. Maclagan to Sir William Vincent on the question of passage to

[7]Transcript of interview with Dr. Bhai Jodh Singh by Dr. Hari Dev Sharma (Nehru Memorial Museum & Library, New Delhi).

England for Sardar Umrao Singh and his family besides the issue of permission for remittances from his estates in India;

"I know the hero of this file quite well and speaking quite briefly, I look on him as guilty but harmless & have gone through these papers and our own file—and I think it would be fair to let him receive a sufficient remittance to keep him from starvation. I would look on £40 per mensem as more than is necessary, but if you suggest £20 I would agree[8]".

Sardar Sundar Singh

Born on Feb. 17, 1872 at village Majitha, Sundar Singh grew in Gursikh traditions of his family and loving father who died when he was only 9 years old. He grew in the care of Captain Gulab Singh and later Gurmukh Rai and had his schooling at Amritsar. Later he joined and graduated from Aitchison College Lahore.

At the age of 15, Sardar Sundar Singh was married to the daughter of Sardar Bishan Singh of Kandaula, maternal uncle of Raja of Faridkot, but she died soon afterwards. His second wife was a grand daughter of Sardar Attar Singh of Bhadaur. "The expenses of the ceremony were kept within reasonable bounds in terms with the new rules formulated by the bride's grandfather, which aimed at curtailment of marriage and betrothal expenses; this being the first marriage among the highest gentry in the province in which these rules were observed[9]". Partly due to family traditions, he had inherited and partly on account of the influence of Sardar Attar Singh of Bhadaur, Sundar Singh's personality started showing the signs of a great crusader whose perceptive mind helped him to analyze the challenges which his community and the nation were facing at that moment of history. Accordingly, Sardar Sundar Singh embarked upon a great mission of service at the young age of 20 years when he was attracted to promotion of education and the movement of religious renaissance among the Sikhs through Singh Sabha movement, which led to founding of Chief Khalsa Dewan in 1902. He became Secretary of Chief Khalsa Diwan and Khalsa College, Amritsar in 1902 and by the time he was nominated to Viceroy's Legislative Council 1909, where he successfully piloted

[8]Home-Political Files (Oct. 1919-No.5) National Archives of India, New Delhi.
[9]'Chiefs & Families of Note'—Lepel H. Griffin.

the Anand Marriage Act, he had influenced setting up of many important institutions like Central Khalsa Orphanage, Amritsar, Khalsa Advocate Paper and Punjab & Sind Bank Ltd. alongwith beginning of All-India Sikh Education Conference with the help and assistance of illustrious friends like Bhai Vir Singh, Sardar Tirlochan Singh, Sardar Harbans Singh of Attari and others. The list of his friends continued to grow with his age and expansion of spheres of activities and Majitha House at Amritsar acquired its status of centre-stage of many socio-political and religious activities besides proverbial hospitality to guests from all walks of life.

However, while centre of his activities essentially remained in Punjab, he did not neglect his ancestral Dumri estate with which he had nostalgic attachment as reflected in his following notings in his personal diaries:

"April 8, 1933 (Saturday). Received through registered post from S. Nihal Singh the title deed (in persian script) alongwith the list of villages in respect of Dumri estate under the signatures of Lord Canning and Khan Bahadur Mohammad Khan, Mir Munshi, dated Sept. 12, 1859[10]".

He took time off from his intense public life in Punjab and devoted considerable attention and energy to develop his estate. He succeeded in getting a Railway Station which was named 'Sardar Nagar' besides setting up a sugar factory in 1909 which was named 'Saraya Sugar Mills' thus making him one of the pioneers of Sugar Industry in India. His concern for promotion of education, as in Punjab, led him to patronize establishment of a university at Gorakhpur. His services for the development in the province won him recognition by the Government as early as 1901, which appointed him Honorary Munsif of the Gorakhpur district in the United Provinces. The following letter dt. 12th July 1901 from Sardar Sundar Singh Majitha to the Collector of Gorakhpur conveyed his acceptance of the assignment;

"I beg to acknowledge with thanks the receipt of a copy of the Government order no. 517 dt. 14th June 1901, regarding my election by the gracious Government as an Honorary Munsif of the Gorakhpur District sent to me by the Tehsildar Gorakhpur to know as to whether I would accept the office.

[10]Personal papers of Sir Sundar Singh Majithia—Nehru Memorial Museum & Library; New Delhi.

SARDAR BAHADUR SIR SUNDAR SINGH MAJITHIA
(Feb. 17, 1872 - April 2, 1941)

In reply I beg, humbly and heartily to thank the gracious Government for this honour and will be glad to perform the duties of the Honorary Munsif and will try my best to prove worthy of the honour conferred on me by this appointment[11]."

However, he was destined to playa greater and constructive role in the affairs of his community and the province to which he belonged. He became a member of Punjab Legislative Council and the Imperial Legislative Council after the Minto—Morley Reforms. In 1920, the title of C.I.E. was conferred on him by the British Government. He was knighted by the Government on his retirement from Punjab Legislative Council. He was Secretary of the Chief Khalsa Dewan since its inception in 1902 till he was appointed Revenue Member in 1921 the post he held till 1926. He remained president of the Chief Khalsa Dewan and presided over three Sikh Education Conferences. The Punjab University, in its Jubilee year in 1936, conferred the degree of Doctor of Oriental Learning (D.O.L.), 'honoris causa' on Sardar Sundar Singh. On 1st April, 1937, he became a member of the first cabinet of the Punjab Government, after provincial autonomy was granted to the States. He again held the port-folio of Revenue Department and was also the leader of Khalsa National Party in the Punjab Legislature party.

The study of the following Chapters reveal the unbelievable but true success story of an individual whose life and contribution to the Society deserved to be emulated by the leaders of the community besides a better place in the history of the Nation.

[11]Ibid.

2

Role of Sir Sundar Singh in Religious Renaissance Among the Sikhs

Ever since Guru Nanak Dev, the founder of Sikh religion-which was based on monotheism, universal brotherhood, tolerance, equality and freedom, denounced socio-cultural divisions as artificial creation of man-raised voice against exploitation of human-beings, the Gurus and their Sikhs were engaged in a constant struggle against the rulers and forces of oppression till Guru Gobind Singh, the tenth Guru, had to come out in an open struggle against the Mughals, as a matter of principle and difference of attitude towards the State.

While the period of persecutions after Guru Gobind Singh led this peaceful and religious faith into a military confederation ruled by Maharaja Ranjit Singh until 1849, when Punjab passed under the rule of British India, the post-Ranjit Singh era saw the decline of the Sikh faith facing the danger of extinction as pointed out by Dr. R.N. Cust, "Since the Sikhs have remained peaceful sectaries: their peculiarities have become very much softened by entire religious toleration and friendly contact with their orthodox Hindu brethren... With the Mohematans they are at peace, and it is quite possible that the sect *may die out* or merge into some religious development as many similar sects have done before.[1]" Dr. Ernest Trumpp, the scholar Commissioner of Punjab while reviewing 'The Adi Granth' or the sacred Books of the Sikhs' had prophesied in 1877 that "Sikhism is a waning religion that will soon belong to history."

Deprived of their kingdom, devoid of any political objectives, divided among themselves into various sects and schools of thought, the Sikh community was, indeed, facing threats from within and

[1]R.N. Cust-Linguistic & Oriental Essays, Third Series, London: 1891 p. 262.

outside at the end of the 19th century and beginning of the 20th century when Sir Sundar Singh Majithia and his associates in Chief Khalsa Dewan took upon themselves the task of providing leadership to the community for about three decades to fill the vacuum until in 1920, when SGPC carne into existence to exercise greater control over socio-political and religious affairs of the Sikhs.

However, before going into the role or contribution of Sir Sundar Singh and his associates in Chief Khalsa Diwan about resolving many volatile Sikh issues that suddenly confronted the community in rapid succession of developments during the early thirties of the 20th Century, it is interesting and pertinent to review the prevailing Sikh situation as visualized by the British Authorities in their Secret Report titled "The Sikh Question in The Punjab, 1919-1922", which reads as follows:

The Sikh Question in the Punjab, 1919-1922

"The Sikh Population: The Sikhs as enumerated in the Census represent a little less than 1 per cent of the population of India and a little less than 10.5 per cent of the population of the Punjab Province. They are recruited from various castes, the Jat Sikhs being most prominent in the country areas and the Khatri and Arora Sikhs in the town: and a large number of them, more especially the Jat Sikhs serve in the Army. Six of the Punjab States are ruled by Sikhs and the Sikhs represent some 18 per cent of the population in the Punjab States.

Its interests political and religious: The Sikhs speaking generally are a brave people and constitute a sturdy peasantry, but they are impulsive and prone to violence. These tendencies have shown themselves in two directions which may be classed roughly as the political and religious.

The *political aspect:* On the political side the agricultural Sikh being usually a prosperous yeoman has no innate tendencies towards change, but the urban Sikhs contain men who have the radical leanings of the times, and there are a number of Sikhs who have returned from work in the Colonies and these, more especially those who have returned from the Pacific Slope, have been infected with revolutionary and even anarchic ideas. An attempt at revolution by these latter was suppressed in 1915, but there are still a number of these men at large and there are extremist Sikhs who look openly for a removal of the present Government and the restoration of a Sikh Raj.

The religions question: The religious aspect of the present Sikh question has a long history behind it, but briefly speaking it may be said that the Sikh religion as practised under the first 9 Gurus underwent a marked change under the 10th and last Guru, which differentiated it sharply from its Hindu origin. The new type of religion has in the past tended to lapse into the older and more Hinduized methods, and the bulk of the Sikh shrines have been in the hands of the older or so-called Sanatan class of Sikhs. A purer type of the religion was maintained in Sikh regiments and was fostered from about 30 years back by a body known as the KHALSA DIWAN and the local associations known as Sikh Sabhas. With the progress of education, the desire for reform became more marked and a large number of Sikhs became filled with indignation at the Hindu characteristics of the ceremonial at many of their shrines and at the immorality and peculation practised by many of the Mahants or intendants of these shrines.

The *co-existence of the political and religious questions:* The difficulties presented by the Sikh problem in late years have been due to the synchronous advance and the frequent mingling* of these two currents of Sikh feeling."

It is also relevant here to understand the threat which Sikhism, as a faith, was confronted with, both from within and outside, at the end of 19th century before young Sundar Singh Majithia and his associates took upon themselves the task of leading a movement of religious renaissance.

The British Attitude

After annexation of the Punjab, Sikhism lost much of its old popularity and its members, uncertain of the attitude of the British Govt.. refrained from bringing their sons to baptism.

"The British adopted a very strict and rigid policy detrimental to the growth of Sikhism. After annexation, the Golden Temple Amritsar, alongwith 6 other Gurdwaras and the Gurdwara at Taran-Taran were practically controlled by the British authorities through a manager of these Gurdwaras appointed by the British Government. The Waqf Act of 1861 gave the control and

*Personal papers of Sir Sundar Singh Majithia—Nehru Memorial Museum & Library, New Delhi.

Management of the holy places of the Hindus and Muslims to the communities concerned, but in the case of Sikh Gurdwaras, the Act was not applied on political grounds. The properties of the Sikh places of worship were transferred and given over to the Udasi Mahants and others, throughout the Punjab[2]".

The Hindu Attitude

The fundamental principles of Sikhism, the monotheism, the absence of superstitution and denunciation of principle of caste; which is the foundation on which the whole fabric of Brahminical religion has been reared; had made orthodox Hindu leaders sceptical if not hostile to the new faith.

"The activities of Hindus have, therefore, been constantly directed to the undermining of Sikhism, both by preventing the children of Sikh fathers from taking Pahul and by reducing professed Sikhs from their allegiance to their faith. Hinduism has strangled Budhism, once a formidable rival to it and it has already made serious inroads on the domains of Sikhism[3]".

Hinduism, owing to its wonderfully assimilative character, reabsorbed a good part of Sikhism, as it has absorbed Budhism before it, notwithstanding that much of these religions is opposed to caste and the supremacy of the Brahmans. The militant Hindu Sect, known as Arya Samaj, was not content, like orthodox Hindu, to trust the slow process of time, but carried war into the Sikh domains by reclaiming certain low classes who were socially inferior to the rank and file of the Khalsa, but who were unquestionably outcastes and untouchables according to the caste classifications of the Hindu scriptures or Shastras".

The Sikhs, being educationally backward, began to play in the hands of Arya Samajis, who started criticising the Sikhs, their religion, their culture, and their Gurus. Swami Daya Nand, the founder of Arya Samaj, during his visit to Punjab in 1877-78, criticised the Sikh faith, its leaders and current practices. "For Daya Nand, Sikhism was one of the innumerable cults of Hinduism, to be noted, refuted and forgotten[4]".

[2]Development in Sikh politics (1900-1911) by D. Petrie footnote p. 7 (annotation by Nahar Singh).

[3]Ibid. p. 8.

[4]"Ham Hindu Nahin—The Aryan Sikh Relations 1877-1905" by Kenneth W. Jonnes (Punjab past and present) Vol. XI, Part II, 1977, Punjabi Univ. Patiala), p. 332.

The climax of Arya Samajists criticism of Sikhism took place at the Lahore Anniversary Celebrations on Nov. 25, 1888, when Pandit Guru Datta in a speech to the Assembly sharply criticised Sikhism. "The lecturer (Lala Guru Datta) trampled under foot the honour of the Khalsa community and in the course of his speech he said that the fact is that Keshab Chander and Guru Gobind Singh were not a hundreth part like our Maharishi Swami Dayanand Saraswati and it is difficult to say whether the Sikhs have any religion or not, but surely, they have no knowledge of any kind...[5]". The "Arya Samachar" of Meerut, the official organ of the Samaj, in its criticism of the Sikh religion, published many derogatory remarks and condemned Guru Nanak and his religion as mere hypocrisy. It also attacked the sacred book of the Sikhs, the Granth Sahib.[6]

Internal Factors

Apart from the above external forces at work, the internal factors were also responsible for decline in the popularity of the Sikhs and, as a consequence, their number was considerably reduced by the end of 19th Century. Contrary to the tenets of the Sikh Gurus, who attacked the authority of the priesthood and caste distinctions; there were Mahants, Sodhi and Bedi Sikhs who claimed special privileges attached with their quasi-sacerdotal position; the 'Mazhabis', 'Ramdasias' who, inspite of their theoretical social equality, were treated with the same contempt as Hindus had been treating their out-castes. The Brahamans reigned supreme in the social life of the Sikhs and they performed the rituals at important occasions of birth, marriage and death. They also flocked to Hardwar and other places of Hindu worship, though it was all repungant to the teachings of their scriptures.

Sikhism also had an inherent challenge not only to its opiscopal and sacredotal succession right from Guru Nanak, the first Guru, but a powerful claimant, in the form of udasi sect who, claimed their exclusive right over the management of most of the historical Gurdwaras and questioned the subsequent practices adopted and

[5]"Ham Hindu Nahin—The Aryan Sikh Relations 1877-1905" by Kenneth W. Jonnes (Punjab past and present' Vol. XI, Part II, 1977, Punjabi Univ. Patiala), p. 336.

[6]*A History of the Khalsa College*, Amritsar, p. 7.

enforced by Guru Gobind Singh. The philosophy and intentions of the udasi sect and its threat of Sikh religion, its practices and institutions is obvious from the following excerpts of the Memorandum which "All India Udasi/Mahamandal" represented by Mehant Harnarain Dass (First Talaqdar Hazari Bagh, Lucknow) President, Pandit Atam Swaroop Shastri (Guru Mandal Ashram, Hardwar) Vice President, Mahant Seetal Dass (Shanter Serai—Saharanpur) General Secretary and Mahant Basant Dass (Manak - Lahore Distt.) Asstt. Secretary, submitted to Sir RUFUS DANIEL ISSACS Viceroy and Governor-General of India:

"Most of the Gurdwaras and Dharamshalas, not only in the Punjab but in every part of the country, came into existence by the labour, and the efforts of the Udasis who wielded a great spiritual and moral influence over their followers. The entire management of all such shrines ever remained with the Udasis and they did and still manage them with unequalled proficiency".

"That as a matter of fact between the Udasis—who are an ascetic order of monks and who revere, and still revere Adi Granth, and the older school of Sikhs there was much in common. The Udasis, for the matter of that Dr. Trump says (vide his translation of Adi Granth Introduction XVII) imitate more closely the simple form of worship of Baba Nanak than any of its later developments. As Mr. Rose says in his census report for the Punjab 1901 Part I, page 126, Guru Nanak stood within the pale of Hinduism, and it is consistent with his tenets that followers of many Hindu sects should call themselves sikhs"... "The Udasis have clung to the ancient rites and usages, which had received the sanction of the previous gurus, and also of Guru Gobind Singh himself previous to the said Anandpur Mela, they are now poles assunder from an Akali in his rites, beliefs and religious ceremonies. Briefly the fundamental differences are:

(i) The right of charanpahul (drinking water touched by the feet of the Guru) is an essential adjunct of initiation among the Udasis; this was discontinued by Guru Gobind Singh Jee and Khanda-Ka-Amrit was substituted in its place;

(ii) The man who is thus initiated is called a Singh and all his previous castes are considered erased and thus there is no bar -to interdining or even intermarriage among all the Singh's—inter-se, Udasis do neither follow nor allow these rites to be performed in their shrines.

(iii) The Karaha Parshad (offering made to the Guru prepared by the Singh) is sanctified by crossing it with a kirpan, the Udasis do not follow this practice at all.

(iv) The Udasis venerate Baba Sri Chand Jee, and closely follow the rites introduced by him, while the Singhs follow the innovations made by the. tenth Guru to the entire exclusion of the rites and usages of old. Indeed the divergence between the two is vital and fundamental and is marked by no less distinction that exists between Shias, and Sunnis, among Mohammadans or Catholics and Protestants among Christians, or Sanatam Dharmis and Arya Samajists among Hindus[7]".

The rituals at the Golden Temple were considerably tinged with idolatrous practices, again contrary to the teachings of the Sikh Gurus. This state of affairs encouraged the aggressive Arya Samajisit to attract the Sikhs into its fold. "Young educated Sikhs reached to the Samaj with sympathy, interest, and for a few, enthusiastic commitment. Bhai Jawahir Singh worked closely with Swami Dayanand during his tour of the Punjab, serving as Secretary of the Lahore Arya Samaj from its inception, and as Secretary of the Dayanand Anglo-Vedic fund collection committed[8]". Jawahir Singh's leadership in the Samaj brought other Sikhs into the movement including Bhai Ditt Singh Gyani and Mayya Singh. Among others prominent Sikhs who joined it was Lakshman Singh. Arya Samjisit and 'reformist' Sikhs stressed the similarities of 'true' Sikhism and Arya Hinduism. Bhai Basant Singh, in a lecture delivered before a Sikh audience in Gujranwala on Sept 4, 1881, stated that ... the mission of Guru Nanak was simply to revive the vedic religion of the ancient Rishis of Arya Varta (the land of Aryas), that this religion consisted of the worship of one's incarnate, invisible and omnipresent God, that it had become degenerated and spoilt by ages of ignorance and oppression and that the evils which befell India were the natural consequences of Indians forsaking the true faith in the ancestors.[9]

There was no organisation to carry on the preachings of the Khalsa Faith, which had altogether stopped, as a result of which, the younger generation began to find the restrictions imposed by their religion

[7]Home Poll. Deptt. F. No. 179/111 /1922-National Archieves of India.

[8]Ham Hindu Nahin—The Arya Sikh Relations" 1877-1905 by Keneth W. Jonnes - Punjab Past and Present Vol. XI Part II, 1977 (Punjabi Univ. Patiala) p. 333.

[9]Ibid. p. 333.

irksome without realizing the pernicious effects which this relapse into Hinduism and re-adoption of its superstitious and vicious social customs had on their life. Mr. D. Petris while describing this effect writes,..." it is notorious that the Sikh loses much of his martial instincts and greatly deteriorates as a fighting soldier[10]".

Macaulifle also writes about the effect of the upbringing of Sikh youths in a Hindu atmosphere, "Such youths are ignorant of the Sikh religion and contract exclusive social customs and prejudices. It will thus be seen that the policy pursued in the Indian Army has been directly, and rightly directed to the maintenance of the Sikh faith in its pristine purity, for the reason that any falling off from orthodoxy detracts from the fighting value of the Sikh soldiers[11]".

However, a spirit of renaissance overwhelmed the Sikhs, who realized imperilling forces out to Destroy Sikhism, and started establishing institutions with a view to maintain their separate national individuality. Thus began "the struggle of the Sikhs since the third quarter of the 19th Century to maintain and to strengthen their position as a separate and fully independent religious community[12]".

The Singh Sabha

As explained, there were various dangers facing Sikhism and the Sikh population was dwindling. Apart from being reabsorbed into Hinduism, a number of people among the high and low caste Sikhs had been converted into Islam and Christianity through government patronage and missionary activities. Maharaja Duleep Singh, the last Sikh Sovereign of the Punjab, who had come under the British tutelage at the tender age of eight, had renounced the faith of his forefathers and embraced christianity.[13] This conversion took place at the instance of Lord Dalhousie.

However, there were three forces which worked for the revival of Sikh renaissance. They were, the Nirankari movement, the Namdhari movement and the Singh Sabha movement. Of these,

[10]Development in Sikh politics (1900-11) by D. Petrie, p. 11.

[11]Ibid. p. 11.

[12]"The British and the Administration of the Golden Temple in 1859" by Ian. J. Kerr "The Punjab Past and President", Vol. X Part. II, Oct. 1976, p. 306.

[13]Harbans Singh, Heritage of Sikhs (New York, 1964 Op. at pp. 138- 139) Maharaja Duleep Singh later made amends for his apostasy and re-entered the fold of Khalsa.

first two, because of their restricted scope and because of the schismatic character they acquired, failed to wholly absorb the Sikh people. But the Singh Sabha which followed them had a deeper influence. It penetrated the entire community and reoriented the outlook and spirit. Assuming its big role at the close of the 19th Century, it gave a new leaf to the Sikh history. The stimulus it provided has shaped their attitude and aspirations over the past several decades. The objects of the Singh Sabha were:

(i) to restore Sikhism to its pristine purity;

(ii) To edit and publish historical and religious books;

(iii) to propagate current knowledge, using Punjabi as the medium, and to start magazines and newspapers in Punjabi;

(iv) to reform and bring into the Sikh fold those who had diverged from the right path through heresy, anti-social activity or poli tical bias;

(v) and to interest the highly placed Englishmen in, and ensure their association with the educational programme of the Singh Sabha.

The first Singh Sabha was established at Amritsar in 1873. Due to its President and Secretary, having tried to secure absolute control of the society, the more disinterested members broke away and established another Singh Sabha at Lahore.

However, the Singh Sabha gained the quick support of the literate sections of the community and many Sikh Scholars and preachers were drawn to its orbit. The founders of the Singh Sabha at Amritsar included such names as Bhai Harsa Singh, Dhupia, Bhai Bur Singh, Bhai Agya Singh Hakim, Gyani Hazara Singh, S. Thakar Singh Sandhanwalia, Giani Gian Singh and Baba Sir Khem Singh Bedi.

Sardar Sundar Singh's Role

Sardar Sundar Singh Majithia, started his long career to the service of the community at the young age of 22. Youthful and sincere worker as he was, he became Secretary of Singh Sabha, Amritsar in 1894. He took a keen interest in the work of the Singh Sabha and devoted time and energy for its progress In the meetings of the Singh Sabha, education through the Gurmukhi Script among the children was emphasized.

"By its (Singh Sabha Amritsar) impact, the Oriental College of Lahore yielded to the demand of including the teaching of

Punjabi in the curriculum of its activities. This was a signal success ...[14]"

The Singh Sabhas at Amritsar and Lahore had their respective Diwans which soon indulged in quarrel over gaining superiority. The Lahore party was headed by Bhai Gurmukh Singh and had the support of the great majority of the Singh Sabhas of the Province, as well as comprising among the its members, the younger, better educated and more progressive members of the Sikh Community. The Amritsar party was headed by the Raja of Faridkot and Baba Khem Singh supported by the Amritsar, Faridkot and Rawalpindi Sabhas. The Lahore Diwan could be thus, regarded as the real controlling body of the Sikhs and as such it presented several addresses to various Viceroys and high officials on behalf of the whole Sikh community. "Its leading spirits were Bhai Gurmukh Singh and Bhai Jawahir Singh of the North Western Railway Manager's office and the energy of these two men seems to have made the Lahore Diwan the dominating factor in contemporary political and religious movements among the Sikhs[15]".

However, with the death of Bhai Gurmukh Singh, Bhai Jawahir Singh could retain neither the supremacy of the Lahore Diwan nor his position as Secretary of the Executive Committee of Khalsa College Council. Sardar Sundar Singh Majithia rose to the occasion and he not only took over as Secretary of the Executive Committee of Khalsa College Council, but also established the supremacy of the Amritsar Diwan and also gained the favour of Raja Hira Singh of Nabha and Sir Attar Singh of Bhadaur, both of whom had previously supported Lahore Diwan. The Sikhs, in general, were also becoming aware that communal interests of their community were but little advanced by dissension and disunion.

Inspite of the fact that the Amritsar party had gained considerably, in influence and importance, Sardar Sundar Singh Majithia made persistent efforts for the unity of Lahore and Amritsar Diwans and a happy result of these efforts and circumstances created by the death of prominent leaders of the Lahore Diwan, was that the internal gulf was narrowed down and the way was cleared for unity.

[14]A history of Khalsa College Amritsar (Amritsar, 1949) p. 2.

[15]Development in Sikh Politics (1900-1911) by D. Petrie. p. 14.

Chief Khalsa Dewan and Gurdwara Reform Movement

A special meeting of the Amritsar Singh Sabha, held in November, 1901 with the efforts of Sardar Sundar Singh Majithia, was attended by influential Sikhs from all over the Punjab and it was decided there" Amritsar branch was in future to be considered the ruling one in the Society and the leading Sikhs from Amritsar and elsewhere be invited to join; it was further decided to consult with the Lahore Branch and make known the results in the following February[16]".

The result of this meeting was the Chief Khalsa Diwan which was founded at Amritsar in 1902, and of which Sir Sundar Singh Majithia was the first secretary and Bhai Arjan Singh of Bagrian, Ludhiana, the first President.

The Chief Khalsa Diwan became a sort of central controlling Agency for the management of the numerous Singh Sabhas which existed all over the country wherever there was a large body of Sikhs. It came to assume, at a critical period of the Sikh History at the beginning of the reform movement, a representative character of providing leadership and guidance to the community besides safeguarding its interests through appropriate liaison with the Govt. of the day. There have been conflicting views about the stand taken by the Chief Khalsa Diwan over various issues concerning the community but there is no difference of opinion about the commendable achievements and influence it commanded vis-a-vis Socio-religious problems of the Sikhs. D. Petrie writes "The ostensible objects of the Diwan are religious and improvement of the Sikh community and the representation of its needs to Government[17]".

It was thus not only the self-constituted leader and spokesman of the Sikhs in all social and political matters, particularly till the formation of S.G.P.C. in 1920, but also it was able, through its organisation of preachers, to continue to wield great degree of influence in spiritual matters. Besides the community in general, its influence was considerable in all regiments of the Indian Army which enlisted sikhs and such regiments were visited from time to time by the Diwans Updeshaks (preachers). The impact was significant and far-reaching. "The supporters of the Chief Khalsa Diwan form essentially what is dubbed by the Hindus the

[16]D. Petrie-Development in Sikh Politics (1900-1911) published by Chief Khalsa Diwan, Amritsar, p. 14.

[17]Ibid.

"separatist" party among the Sikhs; that is, they dissociate Sikhs from Hindus, discourage the employment of Brahmans at Sikh social and religious ceremonies, and generally endeavour to keep their religion pure from the thialdom and grossness of Hinduism and is priesthood[18]".

Sardar Sundar Singh Majithia, alongwith S. Harbans Singh Attari, S. Tirlochan Singh, M.A, LLB. Bhai Vir Singh and other selfless workers, was associated with services which Chief Khalsa Diwan rendered for the amelioration of the Sikh Community. He was Secretary of the Chief Khalsa Diwan from 1902 to 1920 and again from 1934 to 1937. He was elected its President in 1932. He was closely associated with the efforts of the Diwan for social, religious and economic upliftment of the community. Following are some of the significant contributions of the Diwan and its role in important issues concerning the Sikhs.

Central Khalsa Orphanage and Blind Ashram

Establishment of the Khalsa Orphanage Amritsar was one of the most commendable and humane acts of the Chief Khalsa Diwan. This Institute was set up to look after the orphans and helpless children having lost their parents. It was established on April 1, 1904 and since then thousands of orphans and needy children have been brought up by it. The orphanage has a beautiful building on G.T. Road Amritsar. "The construction of this building was started with the efforts of Sir Sundar Singh Majithia in 1941 when he donated about thousand rupees which had been received from the Faridkot Darbar. Ashram for the blind was started in 1935 with the special effort of Dr. Bhai Vir Singh with arrangements for them to learn Hindi, Punjabi, English and to receive training in musical and religious arts. They were also taught to prepare certain handicrafts to earn their living[19]".

"Sundar Singh Majithia, with this wide human sympathies, took keen interest in the institution and worked for its efficient functioning and progress. He was its member Incharge from 1910 to 1920 and again from 1930 to 1937[20]".

Apart from his personal contributions, he was responsible for collecting large funds for the orphanage, using his influence with

[18]Ibid.

[19]Report (April 1968-1970) Central Khalsa Orphanage, Amritsar, p. 4.

[20]Ibid, p. 4.

the Sikh rulers and general Sikh Public. He begged for charity donations for this noble cause, which evoked good response from the community.

In an appeal on July 16, 1932 for funds for construction of the building, he said,

"As you know, the Chief Khalsa Diwan is running central Khalsa orphange at Amritsar for bringing up orphans and needy children of the Panth and this service is being rendered with the help of Panth-Lovers like you... For helping the children in the orphanage to learn the great and holy teachings of the Satgurus and to make their life religiously high, it is necessary to have a big Gurudwara in the orphanage... it will be a great and memorable service to the community[21]".

The orphanage has produced men who were not only able to earn their livelihood, but some of whom also won fame and rose to high offices, e.g. S. Tara Singh, Conservator of Forests (Retd.). Major Kartar Singh; Principal S.S. Amol: and S. Mehar Singh Rawel who was Editor of Khalsa Advocates for about forty years. Besides, it has produced a large number of Ragis who performed 'Kirtan: and served the community for many years. Among them Bhai Santa Singh, Bhai Surjan Singh and Bhai Gopal Singh are remembered for their melodious voices and unique styles in rendering 'Gurbani'.

Religious Preaching and Depressed Classes Movement

The activities of the Chief Khalsa Diwan were not confined to the Punjab only. It has been devoting its energies to other provinces as well in the matter of establishing Singh Sabhas and getting Sahajdhari Sikhs baptised as Singhs. Consequently, Singh Sabhas were established, for the first time, at places like Larkana, Shikarpur and Karachi (all in Sind) Poona, Sasaram (Bengal) Calcutta, Rangoon and several other important places. Preachers visited these outlying parts and delivered speeches on Sikh history and religion. They also collected money for educational and other causes of the community Parties of updeshaks and others were sent by the Chief Khalsa Diwan to Sind every year. Sundar Singh Majithia accompanied such teams on several occasions. It was during one of his visits to Karachi, in the winter of 1907 that the idea of establishing a Sikh Educational Conference carne in the mind of Sundar Singh. His magnetic personality

[21]Khalsa Advocate Amritsar July 16, 1932, p. 5.

made the stoutest hearts bend for him and his handshakes and embraces with the highest of the high and the lowest of the low, won their hearts. Moreover, he impressed the Sindhis with his sincerity and spirit of service[22].

Chief Khalsa Diwan used to publish thousands of booklets and pamphlets containing 'messages of truth' as expanded by the Sikh Gurus and Guru Granth Sahib. The leaders of the Diwan carried on the propagation of their religion and the cause of Gurdwara reform through the distribution of these tracts at various social gatherings. On the eve of celebrations from Jan. 1 to 6th at Delhi in connection with Coronation of the King of England in the year 1903, camps had been put by various states, Chiefs and Communities. These ceremonies coincided with the celebrations of birthday of Guru Gobind Singh and the leaders of the Diwan led by Sardar Sundar Singh Majithia and Sardar Trilochan Singh, made optimum utilization of the opportunity and distributed a lot of literature on behalf of the chief Khalsa Diwan and made considerable impact on the Sikh Chiefs and Sardars with their impassionate pleas.**

Sundar Singh also played a significant role in what is called depressed classes movement. Sikhs, inspite of the teachings of the Great Gurus, were not free from caste prejudices and the existence of Mazhabis, Ramadasias, Rehtias, Rangrettas and other classes of the Sikhs with whom the general body of the Khalsa neither interdined nor intermarried showed that cast distinctions existed amongst them as well. The Arya Samaj, theoretically at least, admitted all religions and all classes on terms of social equality and its attractions for low caste Hindus and Sikhs were strong.

"In consequence, many so-called low class Sikhs were 'reclaimed'

[22]According to S. Surjit Singh Majithia, Sardar Sundar Singh instilled a spirit of service in others by his practical example. On one occasion, the Sindhis were surprised and impressed by Sir Sundar Singh's selflessness when they found him squatting on the gate of the Conference and polishing the shoes of the 'Sangat'. The influence was amazing and instant. (As told to the author during one of the meetings)

**Personal Diary (for the year 1903) of Sir Sundar Singh Majithia-Nehru Memorial Museum Library, New Delhi. He has recorded his impressions about the coronation ceremony and various camps. Everyday the tracts and books were distributed on behalf of the Chief Khalsa Diwan and they persuaded all Sikh Chiefs and Sardars to participate in the birthday celebrations at Gurdwara Sis Ganj, which they did, with all the grandeur and splendour, a grand colourful procession to Gurdwara Sis Ganj and Lord Curzon and other officials also witnessed this procession quite enthusiastically.

by the Samaj and even shaved in public. Some of them publicity abjured the visible symbols of their faith[23]".

During 1907, there was formed in Amritsar a Society, known as the *'Khalsa Biradari'* which had as its object, "the levelling up of class distinctions in the way of interdining and intermarrying and which advocates the reception into the Sikh Brotherhood of all persons of whatever class who were previously; included in Sikhism[24]".

The Biradari soon attracted a large following. The actual promoters of this association were Sardar Sundar Singh Majithia and S. Mehar Singh Chawla of Lahore. The Majithia Sardar was always a source of inspiration for the 'Biradari' whose prominent leader was S. Mehtab Singh 'Bir'*, and it became the avowed policy of the Chief Khalsa Diwan to help these so-called low classes, and to accept them as their social equals. Accordingly, when it was announced that an Arya Samaj meeting was to be held at Jullunder in August, 1909 for the reclamation of Ramadasias and other low classes Sikhs, the Chief Khalsa Diwan issued a vigorous appeal asking its supporters to rally strong at Jullunder to save their brethern from the clutches of the Samaj. The most active man behind this move was Sardar Sundar Singh. "Arya and Sikh meetings were held the same day, the Chief Khalsa Diwan party outbidding the Aryas by receiving their low-caste brethern into the fold of Sikhism and eating food at their hands[25].

Resolutions were passed advocating more liberal admission of low-castes and asking Lambardars and Zaildars to interest themselves in the question. Among the persons were Sardar Sundar Singh Majithia, Kanwar Daljit Singh of Jullundur, Bhai Sahib Takht Singh of Ferozepur, Rai Bahadur Sadhu Singh a pensioned forest official of Amritsar, and Parduman Singh, a pleader of Jullundur. The leaders of Chief Khalsa Diwan had, thus, not only actively assisted in the reclamation of the low caste Sikhs on this specific occasion but had deliberately adopted it as their policy for the future.

[23]D. Petrie—Developments in Sikh politics, (1900-1911), p. 23.

[24]Ibid, p. 24.

*According to Dr. Bhai Jodh Singh, Mehtab Singh 'Bir' was son of Sant Lakhbir Singh, who converted from Islam to Sikhism but was subjected to prejudices by the Pujaris despite baptism (Transcript of Interview with Mr. Sharma-Nehru Memorial Museum and Library, New Delhi.)

[25]Ibid, p. 24.

Gurdwara Reform Movement

"Though probably originally aiming at nothing more than social and religious improvement, the depressed classes movement came to have at least as great political significance as it has social and religious significance[26].

The reform turned into a regular movement for reforms in the Gurdwaras resulting in the freeing of all the major Sikh shrines from the clutches of the Priests who had been exploiting their control over them. The credit to initiate the struggle goes to the Khalsa Biradari, already mentioned, which used to hold annual Diwans. On October 11 and 12, 1920 it held its annual Diwan at Jallianwala Bagh, Amritsar[27].

Thereafter, the newly baptised Sikhs, went in procession alongwith the students and preachers of the Khalsa College, to offer Karah Parshad at the Golden Tample. The Priests there refused to offer prayers for them. The Sikhs insisted on the right of every Sikh to get his prayer and sacred food at the temple.

The Holy Book was opened and by a miraculous chance the following words of Guru Amar Dass ji were read out by the 'Garanthi' who himself was among those who had raised the objections:

'Sorath Mahla III'

"Brother, He sends grace even to those who have no merit, and take from them the true Guru's service, which is most noble, as it turns out hearts to the love of God. He Himself forgives and brings us into Union with Himself. Brother, how worthless even, we, and yet the perfect and the true Enlightener took us into His followship. My

[26]Ibid.

[27]According to S. Mehar Singh 'Rawel', Editor Khalsa Advocates, the Khalsa Biradari Workers under Mehtab Singh 'Bir' who had organised the Diwan, were greatly discouraged since the priests of Akal Takhat and Golden Temple had called upon the people of Amritsar to boycott it and consequently, the attendance was very thin. S. Mehtab Singh sent a message expressing their distress to Sir Sundar Singh, who had always supported and helped them. Sir Sundar Singh, thereupon asked the students and teachers of the. Khalsa College to march in procession to the Jallianwala Bagh and, as a result, the Diwan came out to be a great success and the workers of the Biradri were greatly encouraged. This march of the students and teachers was something new and surprising for the citizens of Amritsar who began to think that they were going to take over control of the Golden Temple. It was a pointer towards shape of things to come subsequently, direction to a revolution (Interview with the author).

dear, what a lot of sinners He had forgiven by reason of His True word. How many He had ferried across the world-ocean in the Guru's safety-bark. By the touch of the Philosopher's stone, that is the Guru, the base metal has become gold. Selfishness has departed and the Name has come to live in the heart. Out light has blended with His Light; and we have become one with Him[28]".

These words had a wonderful effect.

Hundreds of men in the audience were visibly moved. The priests too were convinced and they agreed to offer the prayer and accept the sacred food from the hands of the newly converted Sikhs. This being done, the whole party proceeded to the Akal Takhat, the seat of the temporal power of the Sikhs just opposite the Darbar Sahib. Hearing of what had happened, the priests of Akal Takhat had fled from their posts, and those who remained refused to offer prayers or to accept their offerings, and then they too left the Takhat.

Founding of S.G.P.C.

It was for the first time in the history that the Akal Takht was deserted by the priests. The place being sacred memory of Guru Hargobind, the 6th Guru, was considered to be the highest temporal seat of the Sikhs and contained some of the weapons used by him and Guru Gobind Singh Ji and other Sikh Martyrs. It could not be, therefore, left vacant. "Assembly led by S. Kartar Singh of Jhabhar. called for 25 volunteers to sit and watch these temporarily without touching the money or the property29".

A 'Hukamnama' was issued from the Akal Takhat summoning a general assembly of the Sikhs' meet on November 15, 1920, in front of the Takhat for the purpose of electing a representative body of the Panth to control the affairs of the Golden temple and other sikh Shrines.

The inaugural meeting of the big committee, called the Shiromani Gurdwara Prabandhak Committee, came off at the Akal Takhat on Dee. 12, 1920 and the following office-bearers were elected:

1. Sardar Bahadur Sardar Sundar Singh Majithia-President

[28]A History of Khalsa College, Arnritsar, p. 91.

[29]Ibid, p. 92.

Bhai Mahendra Singh, Librarian of the Khalsa College, was placed on duty for religious services. Next day, on Oct. 13, the Deputy Commissioner of Amritsar formed a committee of nine Sikhs all reformers with the Official custodian, Sardar Sundar Singh Ramgarhia at its head to manage the affairs of the Darbar Sahib (Golden Temple) until a permanent one was formed (Ibid. p. 93)

2. **Sardar Harbans Singh Attariwala - Vice President**
3. **Sardar Sundar Singh Ramgarhia - Secretary[30].**

[30]The Gurdwara Reform Movement and the Sikh Awakening by TEJA SINGH, p. 115, 116 (published by SGPC Amritsar).

"When all had assembled, the Assistant Secretary read out the names of the members elected, who were taken to the upper part of the Akal Takht and subjected to a strict scrutiny as prescribed before. The *Five piaras* (i.e., (i) S. Teja Singh, M.A., LLB, AM., Hav., Principal Akal College, Mastuana, (ii) Bhai Jodh Singh, Principal G.N. College Gujranwala, (iii) Bawa Harkishan Singh, M.A. Professor Khalsa College, (iv) Bhai Teja Singh of the Central Majha Diwan and (v) Sardar Balwant Singh Reis of Kulla) who had been elected in the last meeting to conduct the scrutiny, asked each member as he came up, as to how far he fell short of standard prescribed. The scrutiny over, all the members headed by the 5 piaras, clad in black carrying their Kirpans on their shoulders, came down singing shabads and presented themselves before the sangat, which had been anxiously waiting for them.

The scene was most impressive when Bawa Harkishan Singh, the Asstt. Secretary, read out names of those who were declared duly inaugurated specifying the respective confessions of those who were found short in any respect. The attention became most rapt when the name of Sardar Bahadur Sardar Sundar Singh Majithia was announced. The Assistant Secretary explained in detail the position of the Honourable Sardar. He said that in view of the fact that certain members of the Panth were displeased with the Sardar Bahadur, he had been asked to say in the presence of the Guru, before His very throne, whether or not he had been prompted in all he had done, as secretary of the Chief Khalsa Diwan or as representative of the Panth by motives which in any way aimed not at the unalloyed welfare of his community. With perfect humility, calm and dignified serenity, Sardar Sundar Singh said that in the presence of the Guru he solemnly affirmed that whatever he did he did so to the best of his ability and understanding in the best interests of his community and was not all actuated by any selfish or unworthy motives that were attributed to him. Still, however, he said, he implored the indulgence of the forgiving panth in the words of the musician (Bhat) Kirat, whose verses are incorporated in the Holy Granth:

"I am full of defects and possess no merit. Forsaking nectar I drink the poison of evil, Led by false attachment and deluded by Superstition & fear, I have been engrossed in the worldly love of the wife and son, But I have heard of a noble panth and the Guru's sangat, By whose contact the fear of Death vanishes,I Bard Kirat, have to offer one prayer only: May Guru Ram Dass be my refuge."

On this, the five piaras had signified their satisfaction. *When* this *was announced* in *the meeting below, the whole audience was moved to tears.* This was the highest constitution of the spirit of democracy among the Sikhs. The very men, who had been loudest in crying him down in the past, proposed and supported his election to the presidentship of the Shiromani Committee. Sardar Harbans Singh of Attari was elected vice-president and Sardar Sundar Singh Ramgarhia - secretary. A suh-committee including the office - bearers was formed for drafting a new constitution and Dasturd-al-Amal of the Darhar Sahib.

The Shirornani Gurdwara Prabaridhak Committee was registered on 30th April, 1921."

While the Chief Khalsa Diwan did commendable job in socio-political life of the Sikhs and prepared the ground for an active movement, it was Shiromani Gurudwara Prabandhak Committee which took, upon itself the uphill task of religious reform beginning with seizure of various Gurdwaras from the clutches of Mahants followed by appointment of supervisory bodies to manage their affairs in accordance with Sikh tenets. The movement, which saw unprecedented enthusiasm on the part of Sikhs, provided the much needed impetus to Akali Movement and also saw violence, bloodshed and sacrifices by the Sikhs starting with the massacre at Nankana Sahib on 20th Feb. 1921. "The immediate effect of the massacre of Nankana Sahib was to accentuate the prejudices of the reforming party against the incumbent of Gurdwaras, with the result that numerous Sikh Shrines were seized in rapid succession[31]".

The movement aroused passions of the Sikh community and leadership of the S.G.P.C. passed on to the hands of firebrand Akalis who found themselves confronted by British oppression, Hindu opposition and moderate criticism. Although the British Govt. had doubts about their motives, they were, however, able to establish supremacy of the S.G.P.C. with regard to religious affairs of the Sikhs and management of Gurdwaras.

The British Govt. summed up this transaction thus:

"Hitherto the Gurdwara Reform Movement had proceeded on constitutional lines and the moderate element was sufficiently strong to discourage hasty action. With the New Year, however, the situation changed. A few desperate Akalis, the most notorious leaders of Reformist Akalis whom were Teja Singh of Chuharkhana and Kartar Singh of Jhabhar, renewed the campaign for the forcible seizure of Gurdwaras. At the same time politico-religious propaganda was started in rural areas and Sikh religious enthusiasm was assiduously nursed. Gurdwara reform became the dominant issue, and the committee of Sikhs originally appointed at Amritsar to deliberate on the management of the Golden temple was moved by its enthusiasm for the Sikh cause to enter a new and more comprehensive sphere of activity. It eventually emerged under the name of Shiromani Gurdwara Prabandhak Committee (the sacred shrine Management Committee), the professed objects of which were to obtain control over all sikh Gurdwaras and religious

[31]Horne Poll Deptt file no. 4S9/I1/1922, p. 13. (National Archives of India, New Delhi).

institutions and to provide for their management on the lines acceptable to the Sikh Nation. Its moderate members exercised little influence or authority and the Committee was in practice controlled by a class of extremists to whom the cause of religious reform differed from the extreme rationalism[32]".

Parting of Ways

Although this alliance also provided strength to the Gurdwara Reform Movement, as admitted by the British Government "the difficulty of ascertaining the value of the claim that this Prabandhak Committee accurately represented Sikh aspiration was accentuated by the acuteness of the general political situation. Under normal conditions, it is more than probable that the extreme demands of the gurdwara reformers would have aroused considerable opposition from the Hindu community, which had hitherto opposed the neo-sikh separatist policy. In the altered political conditions, however, the mere fact that these demands embarrassed the administration was sufficient to secure for them freedom from criticism. The opposition which the gurdwara reform movement encountered in its early stages soon spent itself and was not renewed. Conservative Sikhs were silent; they were either secretly supporting the movement or awaiting developments[33]". But it led to the parting of the ways between the Akalis and Chief Khalsa Diwan which had, until formation of S.G.P.C. commendably performed its role as representative body of the Sikhs in matters relating to social, religious, political and educational spheres with historical achievements. The new developments changed the situation and weakened its position vis-a-vis Sikhs affairs.

"The Chief Khalsa Diwan, formerly the official advisors on matters affecting the Sikh community, had been unable to maintain its position in the face of neo-Sikh onslaught, and was moribund. The Sikh League, itself an advanced political body, was comparatively inactive, but its most forceful members provided the driving power in the Gurdwara Prabandhak Committee... The political activities of the committee inspire less confidence among the conservative Sikhs, particularly the land-owning classes to

[32]Ibid.

[33]Home poll. Deptt. File No. 459/11/1922 (National Archives of India, New Delhi).

whom loyalty to the crown has always been an article of faith. Even in the ranks of the committee itself there are many who are opposed to the introduction of politics into an agitation which is essentially religious, and there are some indications that this moderate attitude will develop[34]".

Sundar Singh Majithia and his associates in the Chief Khalsa Diwan steadfastly and scrupulously adhered to this moderate attitude of selective and constructive cooperation with the British Government to the extent of safeguarding Sikh interests and securing their rights endeavouring to avert avoidable conflicts and bloodshed, wherever possible, while continuing their service to the community in various fields and capacities.

"The Chief Khalsa Diwan Amritsar is a religio-political association of the Sikhs established in 1902. Its leaders, headed by Sardar Sundar Singh Majithia, believed in the policy of political compromise with the government. This policy alone, they felt, could help the backward and predominantly rural community of the Sikhs to catch up in the social and educational fields with the rich and advanced Hindus and Government favoured Musalmans[35]".

Despite criticism from various quarters due to political developments in the coming years, including the formation of Unionist Party, Sundar Singh Majithia continued to enjoy overwhelming influence and respect among his friends and critics for his sincerity and dedication as a devoted Sikh, differences in approach notwithstanding. Like his colleagues in the unionist party, he was strongly opposed to alliance of the Akalis with Indian National Congress, as evident from political developments in subsequent chapters. This, sometimes, created an impression of Chief Khalsa Diwan being an anti-national body in so far as its leaders always attached first priority to Sikhs as a 'Nation'. In this context, Bhai Jodh Singh, another prominent worker of Chief Khalsa Diwan and Legislator in pre-independence era has replied to this insinuation about its leadership being pro-British and anti-nationalist "they were not anti-Nationalist... They wanted simply that the Sikhs should have. their own rights. When the first reform came and the communal representation came they said, we are also

[34]Ibid., p. 115.

[35]Some confidential papers on the Akali movement edited by Dr. Ganda Singh (SGPC Amritsar), Introduction.

a community'. They were helped by Hindus because they wanted to use them against the muslims in the Punjab ... they do not oppose the national movement under Gandhiji's leadership but did not actually joint it. They found themselves attracted to the activity of ed ucation[30]".

In the evenful and turbulent years of riots and violence that broke out in Punjab since 1919, Chief Khalsa Diwan, led by moderate leaders like Sundar Singh Majithia continued their relentless efforts to defuse the situation on various sensitive issues by contradicting false rumors, whenever necessary, which had a great restraining effect on the community besides serving the community in their own independent character. Some of the events deserve special attention.

Rowalt Act and Chief Khalsa Diwan

Immediately after Jallianwala Bagh Massacre which was consequence of anti-Rowalt Act Agitation in Punjab, rumours of bombing of Golden Temple, Amritsar shook the Sikh community and soldiers resulting in uprising and revolt at several places which perturbed the British Government. With a view to save the situation from taking an ugly turn, Sir Sundar Singh Majithia contradicted the false rumours in a telegram dated 25th April, 1919 to Indian News Agency, Simla.

"Rumour about bombing or firing any shots at the Golden Temple premises at Amritsar is absolutely baseless. Has already been contradicted. Chief Khalsa Diwan enjoins brethren in the country and abroad not to give any credence to it[37]".

A manifesto signed by following office bearers of Chief Khalsa Diwan was also issued-

Rai Bahadur Baghail Singh-*Rais-kulia* - President

Raghbir Singh Sandhawalia OBE-Vice President

Sardar Bahadur Sundar Singh Majithia—(Member Imperial Legislative Council)—Hony. Secretary—it stated-

"The passing of Rowalt Act has been made the occasion for starting agitation in the country under the name of passive

[36]Excerpts from interview with Bhai Jodh Singh by Dr. Hari Dev Sharma on Dee. 21, 1974 (Nehru Memorial Museum and Library, Oral History Section).

[37]Horne Poll Deptt. - File No. 184-B (National Archives of India, New Delhi).

Resistance. When the movement of Satyagraha was started by Mr. Gandhi, the representatives of the Punjab in the Imperial Legislative Council joined with their Honourable Colleagues Messers Banerji, Shastri and Dr. Sapru and others, in opposing this movement. They feared that this passive Resistance might turn into active opposition of law and order which was the duty and earnest wish of everyone to maintain in the country. Unfortunately for us this is what happened and atrocities have been committed which have given a bad name to the province. Even Mr. Gandhi from whom the idea of Satyagraha (passive Resistance) originated, has found that the peaceful movement which he started and which he intended it to be, has taken a form which probably he never dreamt of and has publicity declared that no hartal or demonstration is to be resorted to and himself has further declared to be ready to obey all orders of the Government.

The loyalty and services of the Khalsa in the past have shed lustre and added to the good name of the community and the country and in the gigantic war (world war I), our community has rendered meritorious services to the Empire. So it is the bounded duty of the sons of Satgurus to abstain from any such demonstrations and to keep themselves aloof from any movement against law and order[38].

That the British Government were more concerned with pacifying the Sikh community and soldiers by contradicting false rumours about the bombing of Golden Temple than the effects of massacre at Jallianwala Bagh, is obvious from the following telegram dated 25th April 1919 which the Secretary to the Govt. of India, Home Deptt. sent to the Chief Secretary to the Government of Punjab:

"It is stated by the Army Department that rumours are current all over the Punjab and are spreading elsewhere about the bombing of the Golden Temple at Amritsar. Could you obtain from the Chief Khalsa Diwan an authoritative public denial which might be communicated to Troops in India and Egypt if this has not already done[39]?

Besides the above manifesto of the Chief Khalsa Diwan which was widely circulated, following notice was also issued under the signatures of the office bearers of the Golden Temple:

[38]Ibid.

[39]Ibid.

"False rumours have been spread about the Durbar Sahib by mischievious persons. It has been said:

1. That an aeroplane touched the Durbar Sahib.
2. That a machine gun was planted in the Durbar Sahib and
3. That bombs were dropped in the Durbar Sahib.

Therefore, we the Managers, Granthis and Pujaris of the Durbar Sahib solemnly state that all these tales are false. No insult of any kind has been offered to the Durbar Sahib. On the contrary, civil and military officers of the Sirkar have taken every precaution to keep our holy place intact from pollution.

Sd/-S.B.S. Amar Singh C.I.E. Manager of Golden Temple and other shrines.

Sd / - Bhai Makhan Singh
Sd / - Bhai Karam Singh
Sd / - Bhai Sundar Singh
Sd / - Bhai Buta Singh
Sd / - Bhai Gurbachan Singh
Sd / - Bhai Partap Singh and
Sd/- Bhai Fateh Singh[40]".

These repudiations of false rumours saved the situation taking a violent turn and the British Govt. felt great relief. Accordingly, Sir William Vincent K.C.S.I. the Governor General of India thanked Sir Sundar Singh Majithia vide his D.O. letter 6th May, 1919:

"Many thanks for your letter dated 28th April, 1919 regarding contradiction of the false rumours about bombing of the Golden Temple at Amritsar. I have seen with great satisfaction that the Sikhs have kept practically entirely aloof from the recent disturbances and I am confident that you and all other Sikh leaders will recognize the importance of maintaining at the present juncture, as in the past, the traditional loyalty to the Government of the Sikh faith[41]".

Police Entry in the Akal Takht

However, the Sikh community soon found itself engulfed in the violent repercussions of repressive measures adopted in the province starting with application of prevention of seditious meetings Act, 1911 to declaration of Marital Law, with the Sikh leadership

[40]Ibid.
[41]Ibid.

particularly S.G.P.C taking active part in the anti-Government campaign. Accordingly, when a regular meeting of the S.G.P.C executive was taking place at Akal Takht on 7th January, 1924 the police officials entered it for the first time, to arrest them. There was widespread indignation and Sardar Udham Singh, the Jathedar Akal Takht issued a telegraphic notice:

"Indignantly condemn unprecedented desecrration perpetrated yesterday 7th January by Police officials with strong force in uniform who penetrated to shrine Akal Takht the highest seat of Sikh religious authority and attempted to mount the sacred steps. All this was done ostensibly to go and arrest members of Shiromani Committee who had already explicitly offered themselves to surrender whenever wanted. Sikh community holds government responsible for consequences of such wanton sacrilege[42]".

Mr. F.R. Puckle, the District Police Chief of Amritsar sent following detailed report to Mr. H. D. Craik, Esq. C.S.R., I.C.S. Chief Secretary to the Government of Punjab, Lahore on 8th January 1924 whose excerpts are reproduced below:

"I have already informed you by the telephone of the main facts of yesterday. The following is the full report -

We were informed that the meeting would begin at about 1.30 p.m. At 2.15 Jafferys after posting detachments at the Clock Tower and the Bazar entrances of the Golden Temple entered by the Thara Sahib entrance, about 100 yards from the Akal Takht with about 100 constables of whom 20 had muskets and the rest lathis. While this force was removing shoes the way was barred by 8 or 10 Akalis. These were brushed aside and the police reached the arched entrance to the Akal Takht at the bottom of the second flights by which entrance to the precincts is effected. Jaffreys entered the archway and was forcibly expelled. A scuffle ensued and in the meanwhile a column of Akalis appeared from the farside of the Akal Takht and attempted to expel the police. A struggle went on for about quarter of an hour. No blows were struck but short of that every violence was used and Jaffreys and the police were roughly handled. They were engulfed in the sea of Akalis. It was obviously impossible to effect the direct arrest of the committee without bloodshed. S. Nirmal Singh and Bhai Fateh Singh, members of the committee came out and succeeded in pacifying the crowd and

[42]Home Poll Deptt. File No.1 / 11 / 1924 (National Archives of India, New Delhi.)

asked Jaffreys to withdraw altogether. This he refused to do and formed up his force at the bottom of the steps, about 30 yards from the Akal Takht.

This was also the position when cocks and I arrived at about 3 p.m. We were in possession of the narrow approach to the Akal Takht round about and in front of the Akal Takht was a crowd of 2000 to 3000 of whom perhaps 600 were Akalis. It was impossible, I considered to effect any arrests without use of military force. I got hold of S. Jodh Singh M.L.C and sent him up to committee, which was meeting at the upper storey of the Akal Takht with the message that I had come to arrest all members present, if they did not surrender themselves. I should withdraw the police and report to Government that an open defiance of the law existed. They considered this message for sometime and then S. Jodh Singh returned and said that they were ready to give themselves once they know whom I wanted. Eventually I sent him with a complete list of the members of S.G.P.C and he called the names from the list and those who were there answered their names. There was of course a lot of delay and palavering but by 5.15 p.m. as it was getting dark and I did not wish to keep the police in the temple after dark, I withdrew, leaving a Magistrate and a guard at the clock tower about 6.30 p.m. 61 members of the S.G.P.C after having been garlanded and having visited Darbar Sahib, came out and gave themselves up to the Asstt. Distt. Magistrate. Jaffreys is sending a list of them to cocks. They are all member of the old committee and include some active members. Unfortunately we have not secured the men who have been directing affairs here, Amar Singh Chhabhal, Ranjit Singh Tajwar, Khazan Singh EAC, Waryam Singh, Secretary Local Committee and Arjan Singh, S. Mehtab Singh's nephew. These were either absent or slipped away at once.

Our first object to make arrests ourselves failed. Jaffreys and I miscalculated here. We only anticipated formal opposition as a protest, coupled perhaps with the attempts to involve the police in a charge of sacrilege by putting sacred objects in their way. We also underestimated the importance (this is probably a better word than sanctity) attached to the Akal Takht... I am told that it is said that never before has a force of Police gone upto the Akal Takht[43]".

[43]Ibid.

Thus the Chief Khalsa Diwan, the founder of the reform movement and the new S.G.P.C. leadership adopted divergent and contradictory stands over sensitive issues concerning the Sikhs with the latter having overwhelming influence over the community. However, Sardar Sundar Singh Majithia and his colleagues continued to serve the community in their own way, regardless of the criticism and opposition they encountered even to their sincere and wise efforts to secure interests of their community and prevent avoidable violence and bloodshed. In a handwritten letter dated 19.9.1932 from Majithia House, Simla E. Sardar Sundar Singh Majithia expressed these feelings to Sardar Shivdev Singh, about Akalis' attitude towards constitutional reforms and communal representation:

"In view of the fact that the council of action people do not wish to cooperate with us and use us for their own purpose the best course for us is not to be led by them but to carry on our own programme and let the community accept it or reject it. We would have done our duty to warn them against their hasty actions....

3

Sir Sundar Singh and Promotion of Education Among the Community

"The total worth of the person, or the total good he did to his community can be best judged by the results of his actions and achievements consequent on his efforts and toil in various spheres of nation-building[1]".

Judged from the services which Sundar Singh Majithia rendered to his community throughout his long public career spreading over five decades, we can say that his contributions touch almost every aspect of the Sikh community's life. His services were so zealous, so consistent and so sincere that one can assume that he had come to the world for no other purpose than to work and endeavour for the upliftment of his brotherhood, the Sikhs. Perhaps the greatest of his services to the Sikh community, is the part he played in the founding and developing the Sikh Educational Conference which, later on, became the fountain-head of education resulting in a great awareness among the Sikhs. The Sikhs, hitherto, had never paid adequate attention towards this essential aspect of life, for they had always been busy in fighting against tyranny and oppression. Education and knowledge are a necessary part of a nation. About knowledge, Napolean once remarked, "they must possess knowledge who wish to guide the destiny of the others".

The education during the Misl period and later under Ranjit Singh was confined to religious priests who knew Gurbani and the udasi saints who kept the pathshalas actively working and imparted education. With the advent of British rule in 1849, education entered a new period. The initial efforts for the spread of Western education were, however, made by Christian missionaries, who

[1]By Nahar Singh, M.A., Khalsa Advocate, Amritsar, October 9, 1943.

were, verily, "The pioneers of education in the Punjab[2]". They started schools with a two-fold purpose, viz, for instructing anglo-Indian and Christian children and for preaching Christianity. "Thus the missionaries used education not as an end in itself but as a means to evangelization[3]". As a result the conquest of the Sikh dominions was followed by several conversions to Christianity. One Daud Singh is recorded to be the first convert to Christianity in the Punjab. This conversion took place in 1853[4].

The Sikhs gradually began to realize the necessity of evolving means to impart education to their children in order to maintain their separate identity. The first man among the Sikhs who started educating the Sikh masses was His Holiness, Baba Khem Singh Bedi of village Kallar, District Rawalpindi who devoted most of his attention towards female education. The unique example of Babaji created interest among the Sikhs which was accelerated with the advent of Singh Sabha Movement in the Punjab in the year 1873 and a number of Sikh Schools were opened. Khalsa High School, Gujranwala was opened in the year 1889 and Khalsa Middle School Sukho was opened in 1894. Khalsa Middle School, Amritsar was raised to a High School in the year 1896 and to a college, in the year 1899.

Formation of All-India Sikh Education Conference

Sundar Singh Majithia who had been taking keen interest in the Khalsa College Movement, was mainly responsible for and instrumental in dissolving the disputes between the Lahore and Amritsar Diwans and the founding of the Chief Khalsa Diwan **in** 1902. He was, thus, one of those responsible and philanthropic members of the Sikh community who had organized a new forum where the Sikhs might assemble and sort out their common problems. Soon this forum, Chief Khalsa Diwan, became the main representative body of the Sikhs with many Singh Sabhas affiliated to it.

As mentioned earlier, one important socio-religious activity of the Chief Khalsa Diwan was to send preaching groups to various

[2]Mehta, H.R., A History of Growth and Development of Western Education in the Punjab. Monograph No.5, p. 15.

[3]Mukerji, S.N. History of Education in India (Baroda, 1955, p. 138).

[4]Harbans Singh, Heritage of the Sikhs (Newyork, 1964), p. 139.

provinces, particularly Sind where one such group used to go every year during X'mas holidays. During one such occasions in December *1907, the Muslims were holding their Educational Conference at Karachi.* Sundar Singh Majithia, a member of the preaching group for that year, went to see the Muslim Educational Conference. At once, this fired the zeal of Sundar Singh's genius to have a similar organization for the Sikh community as well. Sundar Singh and his companions pledged that they would themselves do the needful with the least delay.

Soon after returning from Sind, Sundar Singh Majithia invited 21 selected workers to a meeting at his house on January 9, 1908 at 4.30 p.m. Thirteen gentlemen belonging to Lahore, Gujranwala and Amritsar attended the meeting. S. Tirlochan Singh presided over the meeting and Bhai [odh Singh was appointed Secretary at that meeting. Sundar Singh Majithia explained to the audience the purpose of the meeting and expressed a desire to organise an All-India Sikh Educational Conference with a view to promoting education and literacy among the Sikh masses. The desire of the great Sardar was greatly appreciated by all those present there. It was decided that another similar meeting be called in which the matter might be further discussed and for which invitations be sent to more people. A notice to that effect was circulated under the signatures of the following five persons:

1. Sodhi Sujan Singh, B.A., Patiala,
2. Bhai Sahib Bhai Arjan Singh Bagrian,
3. Bhai Dan Singh, B.A. Lahore
4. Sardar Sundar Singh Majithia
5. Babu Gulab Singh Gujranwala

And the proposed meeting came off on January 19, 1908, at the house of Sundar Singh Majithia. In the meeting it was passed. that the proposal of Sundar Singh be accepted and given a practical shape at the earliest possible opportunity and the organisation called the Sikh Educational Conference be formed.

A sub-committee to frame the rules of the constitution of the conference was constituted consisting the following persons:

1. Sardar Gurcharan Singh, Bar-at-Law,
2. Sardar Kharak Singh, pleader, Lahore,
3. Bhai Dan Singh, B.A. Lahore,
4. Bhai Jodh Singh, M.A.,
5. Babu Gulab Singh, Gujranwala.

The draft constitution prepared by the above committee was sent to the Chief Khalsa Diwan for approval. After it was approved, it became the fundamental law of the Sikh Educational Conference. The following were the broad features of the constitution:-

Politics was to be excluded from the programme of the conference and from the Education Committees.[5] The conference was to hold its annual sessions regularly. For this, dates were to be determined by the Educational Committee three months before the session. If no dates were so determined, the session was to be held during the Easter holidays.

The most important committee of the conference was the Educational Committee. This committee consisted of 13 members to be appointed in the manner detailed below:

(a)	To be nominated by the Chief Khalsa Diwan	7
(b)	To be elected by the various Diwans and Singh Sabhas	1
(c)	To be elected by registered Sikh Graduates	2
(d)	To be elected by various educational institutions	2
(e)	To be elected by the Reception Committee of the place inviting the next conference	1
	Total	13 *[6]

Aims before the Conference

Realizing the economic backwardness, moral laxity and lamentable ignorance of sense of social responsibility among the Sikhs, the intelligentsia of the community envisaged the scheme of setting up the Sikh Educational Conference for spiritual elevation, social regeneration and material improvement of the Sikh community. The conception of education was to "produce citizens who should be able to raise the level of our people, who will convert this poor country into a prosperous one[7]".

The conference had a high ideal before it to achieve. It was to make a synthesis of the best of Western Education and the best of India Education alongwith religious flavour mixed with it.

Hundreds of Sikh youths after matriculating had to give-up their further studies perforce on account of poverty. The organisers

[5]The Report of the proceedings of the First Educational Conference (Appendix-D), p. 167.

[6]Proceedings of the Chief Khalsa Diwan, Amritsar Vol. I (1901-10). Meeting dated April 5, 1908, Item No.1, p. 213.

[7]Chagla, M.C. Education and the Nation (New Delhi, 1966), p. 19.

of the conference felt, unless we do something to bring about their glory, we shall be missing on the discharge of one of our duties[8]". Poverty was, therefore, another challenge to the conference.

Other items on the programme of the conference were:

(i) to start new educational institutions;

(ii) to help in getting the running schools recognized, to get state aid for them and also to sanction grants from its own funds to help these schools;

(iii) to establish cordial relations between the management and the staff of the schools;

(iv) To help in the admission of Sikh students in Govemrnents schools and institutions;

(v) To call for remission of tuition fees;

(vi) To organise National Fund to assist primary and mass education:

The objectives of the conference under religious education were:

(i) To undertake religious schemes under which religious books should be published.

(ii) To spread religious education in schools and other institutions.

(iii) To make arrangements for religious diwans alongwith the conference and singing of Gurbani;

(iv) To encourage private institutions to start panthic schools. Another grave problem before the Sikhs was how to make the message of the Sikh scriptures read, understood, appreciated and its inner meaning imbided in thought, word and deed. The knowledge of the Gurmukhi Script was fast dwindling. Out of 21,30,987 Sikhs only 88,558 were put down as knowing Gurmukhi[9].

As regards Female Education, the conference aimed at starting girls schools alongwith boy schools and to grant concessions to Sikh women seeking admission in training institutes. The conferences was expected to make efforts to abolish the evil of early marriage which was a great hurdle in the way of women's education and to establish boarding houses for them. It was to start widow ashrams where they could be given training to take up jobs

[8]The Report of the proceedings of the First Sikh Educational Conference held at Gujranwala, April 1908, p. 80.

[9]The Sikh Educational Conference held at Gujranwala on 18th & 19th April, 1908, p. 110.

of teachers, or they could be given nursing education to enable them to work in hospitals.

The aims before the conference were numerous, the task was gigantic fraught with all possible difficulties ahead. But the exponents of this great work like Sundar Singh Majithia, who had founded this conference, were equally spirited and ready to face all these difficulties. In fact, they had created a awareness among the Sikhs who had, by now, realized the urgency of the matter and they cooperated together for the educational amelioration of their community. "That the Sikhs are backward in education and that advancement is urgently needed are accepted as axiomatic truth by Sikhs of all shades of opinions who have, therefore, regarded the conference as a cause in respect of which all sectarian differences may be sunk in furtherance of the common goal; they have given not only moral support but also financial assistance[10]".

Working

When the conference is desired to be held somewhere, some respectable and responsible Sikhs of the place have to make a request to the Educational Committee and those whose request is granted appear in the open session with the request. The same is then granted in the open session with the shouts of Sat Sri Akal. This fixes the place for the next session of the conference.

Those responsible for taking the next session to their place hold a gathering of the important people of their district and form a Reception Committee with a Chairman, a Secretary and a Joint Secretary. To cope with the huge task of the session, the Reception Committee forms a number of sub-committees each with a convener.

The conference, extending over three days, included presidential procession, Kirtan Darbar, Dharmic Diwans, presidential address, some lectures, adoption of resolutions and 'kavi darbar'.

The regular annual sessions of the educational conference offered the Sikhs repeated opportunities to show their zeal of service, unity and keen interest in the' problems of the community. The first session held at Gujranwala in 1908 was landmark in the educational history of the Sikhs and it turned out to be a great success. The conference, since then, has been holding its annual sessions.

[10]D. Petrie, Developments in Sikh Politics (1900-1911-A report) Chief Khalsa Diwan.

If the sessions were marked by a high sense of maturity and discipline, it was in no small way due to the great wisdom and amazing capacity of Sardar Sundar Singh Majithia.

He laboured hard throughout his life for the success of the conference. He was associated with the educational committee from its very inception and he continued to work for its success till his death. Even about three months before his passing away in 1941, he attended the daily 'Dak' at his place, Estate Saraya, where he had been advised to proceed by the doctors for a change of climate. The Sikh Educational Conference in that year was to be held at Burewala, District Multan. Although Doctors had advised him complete rest yet he could not forget the conference and on a single day signed about 300 letters to different persons requesting them to join the conference and to make it a success, dictated many more and also gave instructions to be forwarded to the office of the committee[11].

"Without any discredit to his illustrious colleagues and co-workers in the field of the education like Bhai Vir Singh, Sardar Tirlochan Singh, Sardar Harbans Singh of Attari Sardar Shivdev Singh Uberoi, Sardar Sadhu Singh Dhupia, Sardar Gulab Singh Gujranwala, Baba Puran Singh of Dehradun, Bhai Sahib Bhai Jodh Singh, Rai Bahadur Wasakha Singh, and Sardar Shivdev Singh of Daska and others and also the Sikh princes, it may be safely asserted, that Sardar Sundar Singh Majithia, was the Chief pilot of the Sikh Educational Committee and he was ever ready to promote the cause of fighting against the demon of illiteracy and darkness among the Sikhs[12]".

Sundar Singh worked hard for the success of the first session of the conference which was held at Gujranwala on April 17, 18 and 19, 1908 under the Presidentship of S. Baghel Singh Rais of Kulha (Lahore).

At its third session held at Amritsar on April 10th, 11th and 12th, 1910, Sundar Singh worked as the Secretary of the Reception Committee. The President was Kanwar Sir Daljit Singh K.C.S.I. of Jullundur and Chairman of the Reception Committee was S. Raghbir Singh Rais of Rajasansi.

[11]S. Nahar Singh, M.A., Sir Sundar Singh and his Achievements, Khalsa Advocate, Oct. 9, 1943.

[12]Ibid.

At its fourth session at Rawalpindi in April 1911, Sundar Singh acted as President of the conference. The Chairman of the Reception Committee was Baba Ujaggar Singh Bedi of Rawalpindi. An appeal for the National Fund was made for the first time and Rs. 6730/- in cash and Rs. 45,000/- in promises were subscribed.

Sundar Singh Majithia again presided over the 15th session held at Patiala in April 1924. The Chairman of the Reception Committee on this occasion was Gen. Gurdit Singh of Patiala. The most notable event of the session was that the Maharaja of Patiala himself attended the conference and donated one lakh rupees for it and Rs. 14,000/ - for various schools.

For the third time, Sardar Sundar Singh Majithia presided over the twenty' fifth session, the Silver Jubilee Sikh Educational Conference held at Gujranwala on April 19, 20, and 21, 1935 and it proved to be a landmark in the Educational development of the Sikh community. The news of holding the Silver Jubilee celebration at Gujranwala created an unprecedented wave of ardent zeal, love and service to the community. 101 'Akhand Paths' were completed before the opening of the conference in which much importance was attached to divine thoughts, devotional songs and Akhand Paths. Another innovation in the usual programme of the conference was the hoisting of a flag by five Sikhs, *which was an indication of the victory of literacy over illiteracy.*

Sardar Mangal Singh who was the chairman of the Reception Committee explained the role played by the people of Gujranwala to make this conference a success like the first session which was also held at Gujranwala.

In his presidential address Sundar Singh Majithia, drew the attention of the people towards the step motherly treatment of the Education Department towards Sikh community. He quoted statistical data showing that the concessions granted elsewhere to important minorities were quite generous, whereas the Sikhs were not given share to which they were entitled by their numerical strength.

The figures which he gave showed that the Sikh representation in the Education Department carne only to 11.8 per cent, whereas according to their numerical strength they were entitled to about 14 per cent. "Under such circumstances, the Majithia Sardar added, "I have to urge the Ministry of Education to extend to us the same treatment as is given to the minority communities and we should be given the same rights and concessions as the minority communities enjoy in other provinces[13]".

He further drew the attention of the audience to the deteriorating condition of the *Sikhs who were blindly following the Western civilization.* He said, "*Both boys and girls are going away from Gurbani. Doing 'Nitname' is being regarded as a waste of time. Still they wonder why miracles do not happen for them. It* is *the same thing which has been so beautifully described by the Guru in the words, that the farmer sows the acacia tree and hopes to eat delicious grapes therefrom; he* is *using rough wools and wants to wear soft silk*[14]".

He also invited the attention of the Panth to the necessity of maintaining the existing schools in preference to the opening of new ones[15]. "So all our energies should now be devoted to consolidate what exists already, so that we have accomplished with our own efforts should rest on firm foundations and becomes permanent, and all our labour of the last twenty five years goes not in vain[16]".

The President also said, "Though there is a long way before the Sikhs to traverse amidst huge difficulties, yet the results they have gained after the establishment of the Sikh Educational Conference in 1908, are in no way a mean achievement. It is equally encouraging to note that the number of educational institutions has risen to 427 while it was only seven in 1908[17]".

In brief, the Sikh Educational Conference during the life period of Sundar Singh Majithia, had been what he had made it or intended to make it.

With his death in 1941, the conference lost a stalwart who was not only its founder but had always remained a force behind it for

[13]Presidential speech of S.B. Sir Sundar Singh Majithia, Kt. C.I.E., D.O.L. delivered on the occassion of silver jubilee celebrations of Sikh Educational Conference (Chief Khalsa Diwan), pp. 19-20.

[14]Ibid., p. 26.

"ਫਰੀਦਾ ਲੋੜੈ ਦਾਖ ਬਿਜਉਰੀਆਂ ਕਿਕਰਿ ਬੀਜੈ ਜਟੁ ॥
ਹੰਢੈ ਉਂਨ ਕਤਾਇਦਾ ਪੈਧਾ ਲੋੜੈ ਪਟੁ ॥"

[15]Golden Jubilee Book, (Educational Committee, Chief Khalsa Diwan, Amritsar, p. 119.

[16]Presidential speech of S.B. Sir Sundar Singh Majithia, Kt. C.I.E., D.O.L., delivered on the occasion of the Silver Jubilee session of Sikh Educational Conference (Chief Khalsa Diwan).

[17]Ibid., p. 8.

its success. After his death, his son, S. Kirpal Singh Majithia, presided over the 30th session held at Faridkot in 1943. After the sad demise of S. Kirpal Singh Majithia on February 25, 1944, S. Surjit Singh Majithia, the youngest son of Sardar Sundar Singh Majithia, came to serve the cause of the conference with the same sense of devotion as his father.

Achievements of the Conference

Sikh Educational Conference has done yeoman's service to the cause of education and its history is an admirable record of achievements of which Sikhs should be justly proud. It was through the constructive vision of its founders and the generosity of the Sikh people in those days when private funds were rarely devoted to education, that this conference started its network of educational institutions for eradicating illiteracy amongst the masses.

About the development of education among the Sikh community, the Government Educational Report of 1916-17 writes, "The activities of the Sikh community in the cause of education deserve special mention. No community shows such a percentage of increase in all branches of general education. About other commendable features of this activity was the founding of secondary schools in rural areas nither-to beyond the reach of anglo-vernacular education. Nor did the community neglect primary or female education[18]".

The following data of as early as 1944, shows the rapid progress made by the conference. Before the conference came into existence in 1908, there were only 1 college, 4 middle schools and 1 primary school for boys and 1 primary school for the girls. *But after a period of only 35 years, there were* 6 *colleges* (4 *for boys and for girls)*, 65 *high schools* (60 for boys and 5 for girls), 60 *middle schools* (34 for boys and 26 for girls) *and 300 primary schools and pathshalas*[19].

"The Educational Conference up to this time (1944) has donated Rs. 5,08,068 in the shape of grants-in-aid to the Sikh Institutions and Rs. 70,564/ - have been given to deserving students as scholarship for pursuing their studies. Rs. 34,000/- have been spent on elementary education and under this scheme 42 schools have been opened[20]".

"According to the last census of 1911, the population of the Sikhs in the Punjab, excluding the states is 14.91 per cent but the Sikhs are

[18]Educational Committee, 'Chief Khalsa Diwan Di Daswin Varshak Report' for the year 1917-18 (Amritsar), pp. S.H.

[19]Ibid.

[20]Ibid., p. 20.

ahead in literacy in comparison with the other sister communities. The following table reveals the fact clearly:

Community	Total percentage of Literacy	Male percentage Literacy	Female percentage Literacy
Muslims	6.97	5.52	1.45
Hindus	16.35	11.89	4.46
Christians	7.76	4.69	3.07
Sikhs	17.03	12.13	4.9 *[21]

Writing for the "Royal Asiatic Society" in 1917, Mr. Alfred Melvyn Davies, of Bishop's Straford College, in a prize winning essay "the Sikhs and their history" published in London, aptly remarked, "Alongside Government and other Educational Institutions in the Punjab, the Sikhs, with the approval and support of the Executive had developed an extensive system although they constituted but a minority of the population. They have a national residential college at Amritsar which is affiliated to the Punjab University. With a college in each Sikh state and over a 100 High Schools the number of which is continuously increasing, special attention is paid to female education and there are about 25 Sikh Girls Schools existing in the province. In the attention which they give to the education of women and girls the Sikhs rank highest amongst the people of India. Their schools which are managed and staffed by . the Sikhs are under the control of a 'Sikh Educational Conference' which meets annually. The aims and ideals of this conference as evidenced by certain speeches and papers given at it are remarkably fine and lofty, giving a clear proof that at any rate the religion of *Guru Nanak still holds sway in the hearts of a large and influential portion of the people*[22]".

The conference also paid adequate attention to agricultural and technical education. It also successfully worked for the introduction of Punjabi in Educational and government departments.

To sum up, we may say that the conference laboured hard to achieve success in every aspect of education. It started as a movement and the present state of education and the existence of various institutions particularly Guru Nanak Dev University Amritsar and Punjabi University Patiala, owe their foundation to

[21]Ibid., p. 20.

[22]By. S. Nanak Singh (Khalsa Advocate, Amritsar), March 31, 1934, p. 2.

the zeal fired by the conference amongst the Sikhs. But for the Sikh Educational Conference, the Sikhs would have lagged behind the sister communities in the hectic race of education. The Sikh community owes a great debt of gratitude to the great Sardar Sundar Singh Majithia and his friends for his hard work in the field of education.

4

Sir Sundar Singh Majithia and Khalsa College, Amritsar

Khalsa College, Amritsar, is the biggest and oldest Sikh institution founded as early as 1892. In fact the movement to open Khalsa College could be traced back to 1873 when Singh Sabha Movement came into existence. Sundar Singh Majithia, barring the first few years of his life till he came to the public scene, was associated intimately with the college affairs till death snatched him away from the community in 1941. The keen interest he took in the college affairs, the role he played for its development, the pains which he took, for its progress, the difficulties which he faced for this sacred institution of the panth, bears testimony to the spirit with which he was working for the upliftment of his community. In serving the college, he also had the aim of establishing a Sikh University, an ambition which however remained unrealized during his life period.

Founding of Khalsa College

As described in earlier chapters, a renaissance had occurred amongst the Sikhs who had awakened, as if from a deep slumber, and realized that their religion was imperilled by various internal and external forces. In this period of awakening, they had realized the importance of intellectual advancement of their community. In the absence of their own institutions, the Sikh boys had to go either to the Christian schools and colleges or to the newly established High Schools and Colleges of Arya Samaj which appeared to have launched an open and direct offensive against the Sikhs. "If the coming generation of educated Sikhs had then to be saved from absorption into the old fold, and if the religion of the Gurus had to be rescued from dissolution into the old heterogeneous mass of Hinduism, it could only be done through Sikh schools and colleges which could provide for their alumni all the amenities of modern education and satisfy their daily increasing thirst for knowledge, and, at the same time, educate them in the principles and practices of Sikhism and inspire them with the glorious tradition of their illustrious fore-fathers[1]"

The Khalsa College movement received a temporary set-back in 1886 when as a result of some difference of opinion in the Khalsa Diwan, Amritsar Bhai Gurmukh Singh established a new Khalsa Diwan at Lahore. Happily for the Khalsa College, both the Diwans had identical objects. One thing is, however, clear that in spite of all the acrimony brought on the surface by bitter controversies, the establishment of Khalsa College remained in the sharp focus of all the workers, to whatever party or group they belonged. Nay, Khalsa College became a passion and ideal, a unifying factor that provided a practical field for collective work and sense of collaboration on an organized level[2]. "All disputes between the Amritsar and Lahore workers and their respective Diwans were ultimately dissolved in 1897 through the intervention of Sardar Sundar Singh Majithia who had worked for it since long[3]".

In the Lahore Khalsa Diwans' address to Her Majesty the Queen presented to and read before His Honour Sir Charles Aitchison on February 16, 1887, the help of the Government was besought saying, "We pray your Majesty to bear us in your memory and assist us who are still behind hand in education and struggling against ancient prejudices". Sir James Lyall, who succeeded Sir Charles Aitchison to the Lieutenant - Governorship of the Punjab in the spring of 1887, promised to help the cause of Sikh education.

In February 1890, the aspirations of the Khalsa Diwan Lahore, assumed a more tentative form. Supported by all sections of the community and encouraged by the Government, the Diwan bya resolution passed in a meeting under the presidentship of "Mahamahopadhyaya" Sardar Sir Attar Singh K.C.I.E., the Chief of Bhadaur, entrusted the work of systematically carrying on the movement for a Khalsa College to a committee called the *Khalsa College Establishment Committee.* At its first meeting held on February. 22, 1890, the committee agreed, "to undertake the duties entrusted to them by the Executive Committee of the Khalsa Diwan..." A sub-committee was formed to consider the draft appeal for subscriptions,

[1]"A History of the Khalsa College, Amritsar", published 1949, p. 9.
[2]Ibid. p. 11.
[3]Khalsa Akhbar, VoL IV, No. 53, Editorial.

the draft for general outlines of the schemes of the college, and the rules for the conduct of business of the Establishment Committee.

The committee worked with amazing success and was soon able to collect donations of about five and half lakh rupees, of which more than four and a half lakhs were subscribed by the Chiefs and the people of the various Sikh States. The dispute about location of the college was also resolved and the foundation stone of the college was laid by Sir James Lyall, Lt. Governor of the Punjab on March 5, 1892 on the site of the college Gurdwara.

On April 3, 1892, Dr. William H. Rattigan took over the duties of the President of the Khalsa College Council, with 'Malazat-ulma-o-Fuzla-Mahamahopadhyaya' Sardar Sir Attar Singh, K.C.I.E., Chief of Bhadaur, as its vice President. The Executive committee from among the members of the Council was elected on December 18, 1892, and Bhai Jawahir Singh was elected as Secretary of the council. The first year class of the college was started on May 18, 1897, when the first admissions were made. The first boy to be admitted was Sohan Singh, aged thirteen years, son of Bhai Sunder Singh of Amritsar.

Sundar Singh Majithia's Role

By the year 1902, the college was facing a crisis "The college had lost the patronage of princes and the confidence of the public. It lacked in funds and friends... It was passing through a grave crisis and highest authority in the province had passed verdict for the total abolition of the college classes[4]".

"But this state of affairs was not to last long. The college had a great and bright future. It only needed the guidance of a master-mind which it soon discovered in its new Secretary, Sardar Sundar Singh Majithia[5]".

Considering the critical position of the Khalsa College as manifested at the annual prize distribution on January 22, 1902, Mr. William Bell, the Director of Public Instruction, Punjab and a member of the college council, under instructions from Sir William

[4]A History of the Khalsa College, Amritsar, p. 45.

[5]Ibid. p. 45.

According to Sir Surendra Singh Majithia (S/o Sir Sundar Singh), Sir Attar Singh, K.C.I.E., was influential behind Sardar Sundar Singh Majithia's starting taking interest in the educational field, particularly the Khalsa College.

Mackworth Young, Lieutenant—Governor of the Punjab, proposed in the meeting of the council, held in the Government college, Lahore, on Saturday, the 8th of March, 1902, the formation of Managing Committee of thirteen members, including a President. Sardar Sundar Singh Majithia was one of the thirteen members elected to the Managing Committee.

In its first meeting held on March 31, 1902, in the government college, Lahore, Sardar Sundar Singh Majithia was appointed its Secretary. The European members and the Secretary, Bhai Jawahar supported the proposal of the President, Mr. H.A.B. Rattigan, in favour of Mr. M.G.V. Cole, the Principal, while the other members insisted upon having a Sikh as the Secretary of the new Managing Committee. They proposed the name of Bhai Partap Singh, and, on his withdrawal, that of Sardar Sundar Singh, who secured seven votes out of eleven against four for Mr. Cole. This was a landmark in the history of Khalsa College. All powers were, since then, passed into the hands of the Managing Committee; and its Honorary Secretary, for all intents and purposes, became the master of the ceremonies' under the guiding control of the President. And the all powerful Khalsa College council became the constitutional head of the institution.

The youthful Secretary, Sardar Sundar Singh Majithia was comparatively free to devote himself whole-heartedly to the college. He marshalled all his energies and powers of organization to its advancement and before long signs of improvement became visible.

The first thing that Sardar Sundar Singh Majithia undertook was to remove the inconvenience of the students corning from the city. Amritsar city was then the main feeder of the college, and the day scholars coming from it felt great inconvenience for want of proper conveyance. All European schools at Lahore and Rawalpindi had their own buses, and if the Khalsa College could as well make similar arrangements, it would not only, the Secretary felt, remove the existing handicap but would offer the much needed convenience and add to the popularity of the college by attracting large number of students from the city. A Bus was therefore purchased for Khalsa College.

Sardar Sundar Singh Majithia, with the support of the Managing Committee, next devoted his attention to the improvement of the staff. An impression that the council was always divided had led to intrigues in the staff itself. It had become a common practice among them to see the Secretary and the members direct and to look their favours without caring much for the constitutional method of securing the recommendations of the Headmaster or the Principal.

"The collection of the funds for the main building and the necessary adjuncts, and for the creating of the an endowment Fund was a tough problem, but the perseverance of Sardar Sundar Singh Majithia and the far-sighted economic sagacity of S. Trilochan Singh, combined with the organizing capacity of Mr. Rattigan at last conquered all difficulties and succeeded in placing the Khalsa College on a strong permanent footing[6]".

All India Sikh Conference at the Khalsa College, 12 April, 1904

The holding of the All-India Sikh Conference at the Khalsa College on April 12, 1904, is the greatest event in the history of Khalsa College. The whole-hearted exertions and creative energy of Sardar Sundar Singh Majithia. the intellect of S. Tirlochan Singh and the creative art of Bhai Vir Singh worked behind the idea of All-India Sikh conference. The prince and peasant, the rich and the poor, all came forward in a spirit of service. With the interest shown **in** the movement by the venerable Chief of Nabha, His Highness Maharaja Sir Hira Singh, a grand and beautiful model of the old Sikhs, all Sikh rulers came forward with substantial donations.

The Baisakhi day, April 12, 1904 was fixed for the grand conference. The rulers of Patiala, Nabha, Jind, Kapurthala and Faridkot lent their Shamianas and tents and other equipage for the function. It was decided to hold two meetings on that occasion, one in the morning held to raise funds for the college and the other in the evening convened for the distribution of prizes to the successful students of the institution.

Among other things, the galaxy of Princes added to the splendour of the grand Darbar. The President of the morning Darbar, His Highness Maharaja Sir Hira Singh of Nabha came accompanied by His Highness the crown Prince (later on Maharaja) Ripudaman Singh and was received by the President Hon'ble Mr. H.A.B. Rattigan and others. Others present then were His Highness Raja of Kalsia, His Highness the Kanwar Sahib of Patiala, representatives from Patiala, Jind, Kapurthala and Faridkot states, the Sodhi Sahib of Kartarpur, Kanwar Partap Singh of Jalandhar and some prominent European and Sikh guests including his Highness Baba Sir Khem Singh Bedi, K.C.I.E.

[6] A History of Khalsa College, Amritsar. p. 48.

The Darbar opened with a sweet melodious hymn, from the holy Guru Granth Sahib,: "Ham Ghar Sajan Aye", sung by two groups of young students of the college, after which Sardar Sundar Singh Majithia, Secretary of the Managing Committee read, "appeal of the Khalsa college" issued under the signature of the President and the honorary Secretary, and printed copies of it were distributed to the gentlemen present. The appeal was a well-written document. After briefly narrating the, advantages of education, it regretted that after the annexation of the Punjab to the British dominions in India" *the Sikhs had been left behind. Though they possessed one of the sublimest religions* in *the world and a perfect code of ethics and had lofty ideals before them, and though they were the last ruling race in the land, from whose hands the reins of Government had passed into the hands of English rulers, still for some reason or the other, which may chiefly be ascribed to internal dissensions and crushed spirit, they kept on slumbering*[7]".

The appeal then referred to the help given by the Sikh States and to the apathy of the General Sikh Public, In fact the general Sikh public had not been appealed to "and having contributed almost nothing towards its funds they naturally feel no interest in its existence". "It is high time", said the Majithia Sardar, "that we should all make a combined effort and making the institution worthy of the name and a model one in the provinces[8].

The appeal then narrated the various needs of the college and the reforms which were intended to be carried out. "For the successful carrying out of these reforms about 28 lacs of rupees are required for funded capital which must come from the pockets of those who have the well being of Sikh community in their hearts and would like to see it flourish and prosper".

"No one will doubt", the appeal said in the conclusion, "that the Sikhs are most backward in education but not withstanding this they lack in none of the finer qualities of man-hood and posses traits in their character such as simplicity, straight-forwardness and truthfulness which, if developed, would make them ornaments of humanity. Would you suffer such a noble community to die for want of sound education? We believe, not. Hence it is that we count most upon your generous help and hope you will be liberal in response to our appeals. To us every gift, however, small, is most welcome. We are confident that our appeal will fall on willing ears, and

[7]A History of the Khalsa College, Amritsar, p.55.

[8]Ibid., p. 55.

God Almighty in His infinite wisdom will more than reward you".

Sardar Bahadur Bhai Kahan Singh, 'Mohtmid', Nabha, then addressed the audience on behalf of His Highness Maharaja Sir Hira Singh, and further appealed to all those present, the representatives of the Sikh states and the Sikh General Public, to do their best, for raising funds for the college. The speech of Bhai Khan Singh was supplemented by Sodhi Sujan Singh of Patiala.

The beautifully worded appeal had its effect on the audience. The Secretary, Sardar Sundar Singh Majithia, a great personality among the leading Sikhs of the period, then stood up and begged 'Dan' with stretched shirt. He requested the President, to ask the Patiala Darbar to announce the help from the state. The states then announced their contributions one after the other which amounted to about fifteen lacs of rupees. The cash collections at that time amounted to about fifteen thousand rupees.

In the evening, prize distribution was held which was presided over by Sir Charles Montgomery Rivaz K.C.S.I. Lt. Governor of the Punjab. Sardar Sundar Singh Majithia the Secretary of the Managing Committee, was presented with "Khilat of Honour" by the Lt. Governor for promoting the interests of the college. The Majithia Sardar truly deserved the honour for the services which he had rendered to the college and for his efforts in holding the great Darbar which indeed, was one of the most glorious events in the history of the Sikhs since the annexation of the Punjab.

Life-Long Association with the College

Sundar Singh Majithia first became member of the Khalsa College Council in 1895, when he was twenty-three only. He was Secretary of the Managing Committee of the college from 1902 to 1912. It was during this tenure that he organized a historic 'Darbar' at the college in 1904. He became the President of the Khalsa College Council in 1920 and remained in that office till his death, viz., April 2, 1941. *He was, therefore, at the helm of the affairs of the college for a period of about* 45 *years.* During all this long period, he worked ceaselessly for the progress of the institution. He never neglected his duties towards the college inspite of the fact that he was absorbed in other numerous socio-religious and political activities of the province.

But his tenure as Secretary and then President of the college was not without problems created by odd situations, including two strikes. The strike of January and May 1937, which occurred due to the students taking part in electioneering, resulted in much tension and led to disturbances. The Management dismissed several members of the college staff and in reply to a letter from S. Baldev Singh M.L.A. criticising the dismissal of Professors, Sardar Sundar Singh Majithia wrote:

"The Khalsa College is an institution belonging to the community and it must have a warm corner in every Sikh heart. So any attempts made from any quarter to harm this panthic institution, I know, could not have support from any Sikh, who has the best interests of the community at heart". He further said, "I can assure you that you would not find me and my friends and co-workers unmindful of the interests of the Sikh community which we all jealously guard and there could be no two opinions that united action at the present juncture is most desirable[9]".

The Patiala State had contributed a lot in the making of the college and was sending annual grants-in-aid from the state treasury. It had, therefore, keen interest in the affairs of the college. Sardar Sundar Singh Majithia had personal contacts with Maharaja Bhupinder Singh and met him on several occasion in this connection. Later on, Maharaja Yadvindra Singh was also intimately connected with the college affairs. In fact, he had been taking active interest in the college while he was still the Yuvraj. Criticising the working of the Managing Committee, the Yuvraj wrote to Sardar Sundar Singh Majithia who was then Revenue Minister of the Punjab, in a letter dated May 24, 1938, that:

".....while no doubt as chancellor of the institution and one whose house has contributed so generously to the setting up and development of this institution, I am keenly interested in the welfare of the Khalsa College. I am afraid, the Managing Committee as at present constituted, does not command the confidence of all sections of the Panth, which fact makes it difficult for me to actively associate with the institution ...[10]".

Sardar Sundar Singh Majithia, in his spirited reply of June 3,

[9]Paper on S. Sundar Singh Majithia, page No. 13, File No. 16 (Nehru Memorial Library, Delhi)

[10]Papers of S. Sundar Singh Majithia, p. 1, file No. 20 (Nehru Memorial Library, New Delhi)

1938, explained the matter to the Maharaja and added, "... Sometimes I feel disgusted at such machinations of these so-called Panthic leaders, but after all one has to do one's duty to the community. Moreover service is done for the sake of service with the object of cleansing oneself and with the hope that it will be acceptable to the Satgurus and not for any personal gain, and one should go on putting in his best endeavoures inspite of all misunderstandings".... ".... I am an old and humble servant of the Panth, and will go on doing my little bit inspite of what interested parties say about me[11]".

Paying tributes to Sundar Singh Majithia on the occasion of the unveiling ceremony of the portrait of the Majithia Sardar on October 19, 1938, the Governor, H.E. Mr. H.D. Craik, described him and the Khalsa College as two leading institutions of Amritsar, so indissolubly linked together that when one thinks of the Khalsa College the first personality that occurs to one is that of Sir Sundar Singh and when one thinks of Sir Sundar Singh one may be certain that the thought that is upper most in his heart is this College.[12]

Referring to the life-long association of Sundar Singh Majithia with Khalsa College, the Governor said:

> "My friend has been a member of the College Council now for 45 years and President of its Managing Committee for nearly 20 years. He has seen the College grow from a small and impoverished beginning with only a little over 50 students into the splendid seat of learning in which we are assembled today, with over a thousand students on its rolls and 50 professors, with an endowment fund of nearly 20 lakhs of rupees and equipped with seven hostels and thirty playing fields and generally with premises and facilities which would do credit to a public school in any country in the world".

The Governor further said:

[11]Papers of S. Sundar Singh Majithia, p. 5, file No. 20 (Nehru Memorial Library, New Delhi).

[12]Sir Sundar Singh Majithia, p. 81, Editor Mehar Singh Rawel, Published Amritsar, 1942.

"The Khalsa College is what Sir Sundar Singh has made it.* It was mainly by means of his influence with the Panth that the Sikh ruling Princes and other Sikh noblemen and associations have been induced to take a practical and benevolent interest in the College. It is not difficult to guess what time, industry and money he has lavished upon *it, will secure for him a permanent place in the memories of all who have the true interests of the Khalsa at heart.* I am reminded of that famous passage taken from the book, 'Ecclesiasticus', which is 'recited every year on the Founder Day of many a great English College and School - Let us now, the words run, praise famous men and the Father that begot us. ....All these were honored in their generation and were the glory of their times... Their names liveth for evermore.' Amid the company of those famous men will live for evermore in the memory of the Panth, the name of Sir Sundar Singh Majithia[13]".

@If the establishment of Guru Nanak Dev University owes its origin to Khalsa College, Amritsar, it is nothing but logical culmination of efforts of Sir Sundar Singh and his associates in Chief Khalsa Diwan who had studiously worked for development of the Institution into a full-fledged University, as obvious from the Resolution No. 15 adopted at 22nd Sikh Education Conference held at Lahore on March 25 - 27, 1932:

Resolution No. 15

"The Conference invites the attention of the Panth to give immediate consideration for development of Khalsa College into a Sikh University which is a great Panthic necessity and urges upon the community both Princes and people alike to cooperate with Khalsa College authorities to raise necessary funds for the purpose."

List of Donation for the Sikh University:

Some donors' Names are -

1. Rai Bahadur Sardar Basakha Singh, President, Sikh Educational Conference: Rs. 30,000.

2. Sardar Bahadur Sir Sundar Singh Majithia, Kt. CIE, Amritsar. Rs. 30,000.

3. Sardar Bahadur Sardar Mohan Singh, Rais-i-Azam, Rawalpindi, Rs. 20,000,

4. Sardar Bahadur Dharam Singh, Contractor, New Delhi. Rs. 15,000.

5. Sardar Balwant Singh, Superintending Engineer, Sargodha. Rs. 10,000, (Khalsa Te Khalsa Advocate, Amritsar, April 2, 1932, ps. 7 & 8).

[13]Ibid, p. 85.

5

Sir Sundar Singh and Gurdwara Bill

Sir Sundar Singh and Chief Khalsa Diwan had clear perception about the interests of the community and steadfastly worked for maintaining its separate identity without entering, to the possible extent, into confrontation with the Government or other leaders of their community. Based on Mont-ford Reforms of 1919, Punjab Legislative Council consisting of 71 elected members and 35 nominated members was constituted. It comprised 35 Muslims, 21 Hindus and 15 Sikhs in the elected category.

Proposing amendments on the Resolution on the proposal to appoint a Commission or Tribunal to go into the question of Charitable and Religion Endowments in the province, Mr. Ganpat Rai spoke at length to highlight different sects and divisions existing in the Sikh community. He said:

> "When I rise to speak on this motion, I do so in the first place, as a Sahjdhari Sikh, in whose family the Granth Sahib and the Gurus have been admired and worshipped as in other Sahjdhari families, recognised as Sikhs in the census papers and for all practical purposes in the social circle, in the second as an Advocate of the Keshdhari Sikhs and Sahjdhari Sikhs, represented in thousands of families in the sons of the same father and mother, in the other dearest relations of the blood and by ties of marriage lasting since centuries. No one would have questioned my authority, except for the differences which have been of late arising and have reached a stage, which everyone should regret and which has compelled the present motion to be placed before the Council.
>
> "Punjab, of all places, should be the last to give an occasion, when the first instalment of Swarajya has been given, for this to be said about it that those, who are leading its destinies in the

different sections of its varied community, are unable to look after the people and see order restored whence all order should spring to every other place, viz., in the House of God, where its people have been worshipping their Lord in peace, during the most troublous as well as peaceful times.

"The Act and the Ordinance, which the Minister in charge of Religious Endowments, is going to move, indicate that a condition of things has been brought about in the Punjab, which is extraordinary in its nature and requires exceptional legislation to stop the mischief which is going on. There can be no manner of doubt that the Government action is entirely justified. The Nankana tragedy, with all its horrors, for which every Hindu and Muhammadan has expressed sympathy with those who are killed, with its reports in the Press which have accentuated class differences, with what has been going on at the place and its neighbourhood by passions which became excited and by the unruly element, which then crops up, has not closed the chapter. There are reasons to believe worse things might happen in the case of other Gurdwaras. There is no knowing the Hindu and Moslem may not follow suit. Notices have been already received by some of those in charge of Hindu shrines.

"But is it not a case where the Council should be able to give assurances of restoring the normal condition of things, which existed before the law was taken in hand, with only one exception and that of improving the management in each shrine, not the method of worship, unless it were a recent introduction by any particular Mahant, according to his own will and pleasure. If, as is being alleged, the innovations were introduced by Maharaja Ranjit Singh, even if this were the case, it is hardly fair that a small minority of the worshippers at those shrines should introduce forms not acceptable to the majority. There have been reforms before this by the Nirankaris, Namdharis and others. They have set up their own places of worship and have not forced the reforms in the older ones. If, during the Moslem times, even now in some of the places, Hindu in others, and the Sikh in the Punjab, the lion and the lamb, the Singh and the humbler Sahjdhari or Hindu, could drink and can drink at the same fountain of truth, is there any reason why this should be made difficult in a more enlightened age. In Hyderabad, where His Highness Nizam rules, in Benares where a Hindu Raja rules, in Patna where an Indian Governor is ruling, and in every Indian State, the old methods of worship are going on and no disturbances have arisen, why then has such a thing happened in the Punjab, which is the home of the Stalwart Sikh as well as his humbler brother, a Sahjdhari? Go to Hardwar and you find above the Hari Ki Pohri the Maharajas of Patiala, Nabha, Jammu and Poonch owned their houses, where they and their Maharanis, when they come, and the common people allowed to reside there, carryon their worship of Ganga and the Granth Sahib simultaneously. You find similarly the Darbar Sahib at Amritsar, surrounded by Hindu deities and Hindu places of worship and the Samadh of the Fifth Guru ornamented by Hindu Gods and Goddesses and Hindu scenes, most of them, or perhaps all, taken from the Granth Sahib, where they were referred to. Such places with a common worship, going on side by side, will be found in the Punjab in large numbers. Did not the tolerant Hindu teach the Mogul Emperor to allow the worship of Hindu Gods and Goddesses by Hindu Princesses to go on within the fort? Did he not adopt some of the Moslem institutions and gradually influence the Muhammadan to adopt his? If the Hindu mind is shocked at what has been done without caring for it and his forms of worship and his deities have been desecrated no wonder even the Hindu has done things which offened the Sikh. Why should not a small party of Hindus and Sikhs go to every place to see normal conditions restored, take steps for improving the management in every shrine, leaving the form of worship as it is, to be improved, if necessary, by mutual love and not by force. I hope my friends will see that the dark spot on Punjab's fame is obliterated and that this Council may not be compelled to make it permanent in the records which it will leave for posterity.

"Sir, with these remarks I would suggest that, as some of the members have told the Council, because *there are four main divisions of Sikhs - Tat Khalsa, Sahjdharis, Sanatan Dharam Sikhs,* and *the sect represented by Sadhus, Udasis and Nirmalas* - there ought to be five members. If there are only three members it may not be an absolutely impartial committee. If there are five members every class of Sikhs will be adequately represented and there can be no grievance. In fact, I would go further and say that an orthodox Hindu and a Muhammadan should also be on the committee, because it is a well-known fact that to certain Gurdwaras large properties have been given by Muhammadan rulers. Similarly, there are other Gurdwaras to which orthodox Hindus have made valuable gifts of property and of money. Is it not fair that there should be representatives of those donors to help the Commissioners to arbitrate and to compromise but not to decide disputes. The spirit with which these Commissioners should be actuated is the spirit of compromise and conciliation and not the spirit in which criminal and civil courts decide cases. With these remarks, Sir, I move this resolution that this Council will accept and agree that instead of three, there should be five Commissioners with the object of promoting unity and not disruption, and with the object of bringing harmony between different classes of Sikhs and also to help our Sikh brethren in administering these Gurdwaras."

Strongly contesting Mr. Ganpat Rai's version on the subject, Sardar Bahadur Sardar Sundar Singh Majithia speaking in urdu said that -

"he wished to make a few remarks on this point, but his views were not those of the Government and were to be considered as his own personal views. He wished to make a distinction between Gurdwaras and Dharamsalas. A Gurdwara was the place of God and a Dharamsala was a school of religion. There were other terms also 'Akharas' and 'Deras' but he would deal first of all with the Gurdwaras. Gurdwaras were those places which the Gurus had founded while some had also been founded by their disciples subsequently. For instance, the Golden Temple at Amritsar had been founded by the 4th Guru. Now this Temple is open to all who profess the Sikh creed, whoever they may be, but not to those who do not believe in the tenets of the Sikh religion. And just as Sikhs and Hindus cannot enter the mosques of the Muhammadans, so no one who did not follow the teachings of the Gurus could enter a Gurdwara. But, "no one can say, as Mr. Ganpat Rai has said, that side by side with Gurdwaras they should worship images. I protest against that assertion by my friend and I take exception to the statement that in these places of worship any other creed can be taught."

"Proceeding, the Hon'ble Member said that the property belonging to these Gurdwaras had originally been bestowed for the general use and benefit of the whole community and was not meant for any particular man or Mahant. Some time later the Jagirs attached to the Gurdwaras were as a matter of fact offered to the Gurus, who refused to accept them as their personal property and passed them on to the Gurdwaras for the use of the general community. Still later some of the Mahants had this property transferred to themselves, and the present trouble is in fact the direct cause of this wrong on the part of those Mahants. He said, a true Mahant would never care for any property for his own personal use and he quoted the instance of Sant Attar Singh. He said that after the Sikh rule, the Mahants by surreptitious and foul means got the Gurdwara properties transferred in their own names and became their owners. This was in contravention of the principles of Sikhism. With this private ownership and greed for wealth, came the corruption and mismanagement of Gurdwaras which became the hot-beds of vice and corruption. He was opposed to the violent methods of reform adopted by a section of the Sikhs but said that it might be that those methods were adopted to attract the attention of Government. The Hon'ble Member proceeded to cite verses from the Sikh scriptures and historical instances to show the qualities that a Mahant must possess. He cited the instance of Guru Nanak, who had two sons Baba Sri Chand and Baba Lakhmi Das; but he did not regard them fit enough to succeed him and appointed Guru Angad as his successor. The principle was followed by all the Gurus.

"The Hon'ble Member denied the assertion that there were four classes of Sikhs with some warmth, and cited several texts from the Sikh scriptures in support of his position. He did not recognise any sect of Sikhs and strongly criticised the contention of Baba Hardit Singh Bedi that the 'gaddi' of a Gurdwara should remain in the same sect.

"He supported the resolution."[@2]

[@2]Punjab Legislative Council Debates, Vol. I, March 14, 1921 - National Archives of India, New Delhi.

The Sikh Gurdwaras and Shrines Bill

Before final adoption of the Gurdwara Act in 1925, the first attempt by the provincial Government to arrive at a settlement on the issue of control over the Gurdwaras was made as early as 1921 when Khan Bahadur Mian Fazl-i-Hussain. the Minister for Education, moved the Bill in the Punjab Legislative Council on April 5, 1921 elaborating the history and the necessity for enacting such a legislation in the light of ongoing Gurdwara Agitation. Diwan Bahadur Raja Narendra Nath speaking on the bill said:

"I look upon Sikhism as higher Hinduism. It is a reform of Hinduism as it existed at the time when Guru Nanak was born, i.e. about the middle of the 15th century. The Granth Sahib is nothing more nor less than the higher teachings of the Vedas and Upanishad as in popular language. I am aware of the fact that in the teachings of various founders of religions, separated from one another by time and space, there are many things in common But, in the case of the Gurus the fact cannot be ignored that they were Hindus born. They were brought up in the midst of Hindu associations and Hindu traditions. I need not dilate upon the close connection between the Hindus and Sikhs. It is well known that of two brothers one may be a Hindu and the other a Sikh and that the Sikhs and Hindus inter-marry freely. Khatri and Arora Sikhs living in towns are supposed to follow Hindu Law. In this connection, it would be interesting to peruse the Privy Council Ruling reported as No. 94-P.R. 1903 in which the learned Judges of the Privy Council held that Sikhs were Hindus.

"There is no wonder that a religion that has existed for the last five hundred years should be divided into sects. That the Sikhs are divided admits of no doubt. The main divisions ignoring the popuarly accepted nomenclature are the following:

(1) The advanced Sikhs well organised and well educated puritanic in their ideas.

(2) The orthodox Sikhs who conform to some of the old Hindu practices but who are strict observers of Sikh ritualism.

(3) Sahajdharis who revere the Granth and the Gurus but who are not strict observers of Sikh ritualism.

"Hindus in the Western Punjab and Sindh where the influence of Islamic monotheism has been felt more than in other places, mainly fall in the last category. I have personal knowledge as an official of the Western districts of the Punjab, and I can say that in rural areas of these districts there are more Dharamsalas where Granthis recite the Granth Sahib than temples dedicated to Shiva or Vishnu.

"To the question what is conducive to the maintenance and furtherance of Sikh religion, the last two classes will return on many points an answer absolutely different from that of the first. Whose answer is Government going to accept?

"Coming now to the question of the Board of Commissioners. How is this Board going to be constituted? I presume that there will be one board for the whole province. If each Gurdwara is going to have a separate Board of its own, I hope that the principle on which the appointment of the Commissioners is to be made will be fixed once for all and will be strictly adhered to in making appointments on the Board. The Board will inquire into the history and origin of Gurdwaras, and surely Government is not going to form an opinion about the history of each before the inquiry is held. Government should not therefore make appointments for each Gurdwara accordingly as Government thinks, that the history of the Gurdwara (unascertained and to be ascertained by the Board) requires. Are classes 2 or 3 who form the bulk of the followers of the Gurus to form a majority on the Board? If the Board is going to determine, as it will, the question what is conducive to the maintenance and furtherance of the Sikh religion, are the beliefs and articles of faith of the advanced class going to be forced, on the others or vice versa. Is not this interference with religion?

"In the first place, I seriously question the wisdom of putting for solution religious conundrums before a Board consisting of men whose views conflict with one another. Fancy a question relating to modes of worship on which Catholics and Protestants differ being put before a Board of Catholics and Protestants to decide which form of worship is conducive to the maintenance and furtherance of the Christian religion. If such a course would be unwise in the case of Christians, how could it be otherwise in the case of Sikhs? Religious belief admits of no compromises.

"The question what are the essential principles of a certain religion may come up before a court of law. As far as I am aware the question has arisen with regard to Hindus in certain cases and it has been decided negatively, viz., what does or does not militate against Hinduism but no court has yet defined in a positive manner what Hinduism is. I, however, contend that the frame of mind of a presiding officer of a court is and will always be different from the frame of mind which the Commissioners representing various sects and sitting on the Board of Inquiry will bring to bear on the questions before them. Each Commissioner will be on the Board not to administer impartial justice but to represent the views of his sect and to protect its interests. The result will be either a dead lock or a decision in accordance with the opinion of the majority. The crux of the problem is the constitution of the Board. How are the various sects going to be represented? Is the number of followers in each sect going to determine the proportion of their representatives on the Board? If so, will the advanced section be satisfied? If not, and if the advanced section is allowed to have its majority, is Government going to lend an aid to the reform of Sikh religion."[@3]

Despite being a member of the Punjab Legislative Council, Sir Sundar Singh had strong reservations about the Gurdwara Bill moved by Mian Fazl-i-Hussain, the Minister for Education, and subsequently recorded his minutes of dissent dated 7.11.1922 which reads as under:

[@3]Punjab Legislative Council Debates, Vol. I. (National Archives of India, New Delhi).

According to Prof. M.L. Ahluwalia (Select Documents - Gurdwara Reform Movement), the first Gurdwara Bill of the Unionist Party presented by Mian Fazl-i-Hussain, who was holding charge of Education and Religious Endowments in Punjab Government, was a compromise formula which according to Azim Hussain, son and biographer of Fazl-i-Hussain was opposed by Sikhs and the urban Hindus whereas, according to Azim Hussain, Mr. Malcolm Hailey, the British Governor, was anxious to strengthen the Sikhs so that they might serve as a counterpoise to the growing strength of the Muslim majority in the Punjab under the leadership of Fazl-i-Hussain. Sir Sundar Singh had reservations about the object and success of the Bill and worked for provisions more acceptable to different sections of the community till 1925 when it was finally enacted what Azirn Hussain describes as "British concession to politically active section of the Sikhs."

"The question of the Sikh Gurdawaras Bill was discussed in a meeting of the Executive Council at which the Hon'ble Minister of Agriculture was also present on Friday, the 3rd November 22. H.M. Eblingin disposed and there it was decided by a majority of votes to proceed with the Sikh Gurdwara and Shrines (Enquiry) Bill of the Hon'ble the Education Minister. I regret very much to have to dissent from this decision of my colleagues and therefore have the painful necessity of having to record my minute of dissent and to request that it be placed on the record of the Council proceedings and submitted along with them to the Government of India under Rule of Business of the Executive Council.

"2. The Council had to consider a very important question which has caused very anxious thought for its solution. From some time back the Akali movement has come into existence and is working under the guidance of the S.G.P. Committee. The ostensible basis of their demands are the reforms desired to be introduced in the management of the Sikh Gurdwaras and Shrines. The movement has spread so far that almost every Sikh whether living in rural or urban areas seems to be taking a very keen interest in it."

"To my mind, the best and the right way for solving the difficulty is to rightly analyse the causes which have created and intensified the agitation and having done so to meet them so far as they could be found legitimate and rightful at their source. This could mean, so to speak, the undermining the foundations of the undesirable part of agitation and leave the superstructure to take care of itself. To meet the demand of the Sikhs for the necessary Reform in the management of Sikh Gurdwaras, Government has devised three measures. Of these, the second Bill is known as the Hon'ble Sir John Maynard's Bill and was understood to have almost been accepted at a Conference between certain Government officials and certain responsible workers of the S.G.P. Committee, Changed circumstances necessitated some stronger measures being adopted against some undersirable activities of the Akalis and thus the Bill fell through. The Guru-Ka-Bagh incident followed and the forcible dispersal action of Government afforded the S.G.P. Committee their heartily wished for opportunity of spreading agitation. Their influence which was waning regained its equilibrium and the movement at once regained a popularity hitherto unknown. Money and sympathy flowed in abundance and after defraying a heavy expenditure of something like Rs. 2,500/ - a day, it left a heavy surplus in cash in the hands of the movement of many thousands of rupees. The Executive Government visited the scene and it was agreed to abandon the measures of forcible dispersal which had occasioned such strong agitation. Arrests have taken the place of former measures but the agitation has not subsided. Many hundreds of willing persons are offering themselves daily for arrest, each damouring to have precedence over the other to be sent up. All this could be possible with the Sikhs only in the name of religion. The remedy therefore lies in devising some means whereby the Government could convincgly show that it has not the least idea or desire of any interference in the Sikh places of worship and is sympathetic towards the Sikh religious reform.

"The Sikh members of the Punjab Legislative Council have refused to support the modified Bill while they have expressed their willingness to support the measure submitted by the Chief Khalsa Diwan which appears to be based on the least line of resistance. It does not disturb the present Mahants in their possession and does not interfere with their mode of succession. It adopts the system of the judicial Tribunal of H.M.F's Bill and provides the use of the Gurdwara funds exclusively to Gurdwara purposes; thus, it indirectly stops their being spent on political purposes. All that it provides is:

(a) To ensure a control of Committee over the Gurdwaras and Shrines (to which the Government has agreed), instead of leaving Mahants in their unrestricted uses;

(b) To ensure proper accounts being kept, audited and published;

(c) To ensure that Waqf properties shall not be converted into Mahants' private properties;

(d) To ensure that Mahants be of good conduct; and,

(e) that worship in the Sikh Gurdwaras and Shrines be in consonance with the teachings of the Adi Guru Granth Sahib.

"I do not think there is anything in these that the Government should feel interested to take objection to.

"The movement of Reform in the community is very very strong and the dissatisfaction appears to be spreading fast and I am afraid also in the Army. It may be straining the loyalty of the Sikh rank and file in the Army too much if we withstand this legitimate desire of the community for the reform of their places of worship. Already feelings have been embittered owing to certain action having been taken at Guru Ka Bagh and these may be growing worse, and it will be unstatesmanlike and extremely unwise to allow this feeling of disappointment and resentment to grow any more and let the loyal devotion of a community to be alienated and captured by others who will not hesitate to use it effectively. In other words, it will mean that in a statesmanlike strategy the real opponents of Government have beaten them on their own ground so far as Sikhs are concerned. Government ought to be generous with a community which has served them loyally from the time of their connection with the Empire and which has not hesitated on any occasion to shed their bluest blood in the service of the Empire wherever such service was requisitioned - whether in India or beyond the seas. The Sikh Gurdwaras and Shrines are after all Sikh places of worship and no other community has any right to inter fer in the management of these places by the members of the Sikh community and I want it to be realised that the Sikhs are the only persons concerned in this matter. The Sikh community will welcome any non-Sikh who wishes to drink the nectar at the fountain-head consecrated by the teachings of the Sikh Gurus, but it cannot for the matter of that allow their places of worship to become places of worship of other communities. They have withstood all such attempts and even now they appear to be ready to make all conceivable sacrifices to keep the purity of their places of worship in tact. No repression or strong measure will succeed with the Sikhs in the matter of religion. The Moghul Government adopted the policy of repression and failed to succeed in exterminating this community. The sacrifices they then made are writ large on the pages of Sikh history. Then why not deal sympathetically in the words of the Honble Sir John Maynard with a "generous community", in a generous manner and why alienate their sympathies for nothing to support bad Mahants who could never be of any service to Government.

"I am, therefore, constrained to advise very strongly that it is not right to push on H.M.F.'s present published Bill to which the Sikh M.L.Cs. have openly said to refuse to record their support and which will not be found acceptable to the Sikh community. I have not been able to convince my colleagues of my view of the case, but I have still hopes that time may not be far distant when on further thought they may findit possible to agree with me to eradicate the disease at its root by adopting the proposals of the Diwan and thereby to ease the situation on the one hand and to meet the legitimate demands of the loyal Sikh community on the other.

(Sd) Sundar Singh Majithia
Member
7.11.22.

While raising his moderate and restraining voice occasionally Sardar Sundar Singh Majithia and his colleagues in Chief Khalsa Diwan continued their crusade for the cause of their community in their own characteristic and dignified way, though in close association with the Govt. of the day but never at the cost of their religious sentiments which won them highest esteem from the Govt. and critics among the pro-Congress leadership of the Akali Dal.

Guru ka Bagh Agitation and Gurdwara Bill

While the agitation at Guru Ka Bagh Amritsar about the right of devotees to cut wood for Guru's free Kitchen, was in full swing, a conference was called by the Viceroy at Viceregal lodge at 6 p.m. on 3rd Oct. 1922 to discuss the Sikh situation and the Gurdwara movement where Sardar Sundar Singh Majithia presented broad outlines of his proposed bill which he proposed to introduce in consultation with the Sikh members of the council, in place of the Govt. Bill in order to defuse the situation. Those present were-

"His Excellency the Viceroy.
His Excellence the' Governor of Punjab.
The Hon'ble Sir William Vincent, Home Member.
The Hon'ble Sir Malcolm Hailey, Finance Member.
The Hon'ble Sir Tej Bahadur Sapru, Law Member.
The Hon'ble Sir John Maynard, Finance Member, Punjab.

[@@@]Personal papers of Sir Sundar Singh Majithia - Nehru Memorial Museum & Library, New Delhi.

The Hon'ble S.B. Sardar Sundar Singh Majithia - Revenue Member.

The Hon'ble Khan Bahadur Fazl-l-Husain, Minister of Education.

The Hon'ble L. Harkrishan Lal, Minister of Agriculture.

The Hori'ble Chief Secretary to Govt. of Punjab was in attendance:[4]

Following excerpts from the conference indicate anxiety and concern of the British Govt. and significance it attached to the early solution of the crisis by adopting Sardar Sundar Singh Majithia's suggestions instead of Govt's own bill on the subject:

"His Excellency the Viceroy explained the reasons for calling of the conference. The Government of India felt that some part of the responsibility for the existing Sikh situation fell on them and they desired to know what was the Punjab Govt. policy in the matter, and what were its proposals for dealing with the local situation at Guru-Ka-Bagh. It was clear that arrests at the rate of 80 a day could not continue indefinitely.

His Excellency the Governor explained that the beating of the Akalis had now stopped and the policy of making arrests had been substituted and consequently a good deal of excitement over Guru-Ka-Bagh had subsided.

His Excellency the Governor then explained the policy of the local Government as regards Legislation....

.......As regards the situation at Guru-Ka-Bagh, attempts to bring about a compromise by arbitration had hitherto been fruitless.....

Dr. Sapru asked if the right to cut wood had been claimed on behalf of the Sikh community or on behalf of the Akalis or the Prabandhak Committee, or by any other body.

Sardar Sundar Singh Majithia explained that the claim was on behalf of the Prabandhak Committee, to whom the Mahant had at one time agreed to surrender his rights.

Sardar Sundar Singh then explained the features of the bill which had been suggested as a permanent solution of the Gurdwara question. This Bill, he said, would very shortly be laid before the Punjab Government.... In reply to an enquiry by His Excellency the Viceroy as to what support this bill was likely to find, Sardar Sundar Singh stated that its main principles were approved by certain members of the Shiromani Gurdwara Prabandhak Committee

[4]Home Poll Deptt. F.No. 914/1922 - National Archives of India, New Delhi.

but that these members would not give their approval in writing. The bill was being drafted by the Chief Khalsa Diwan. Its basic idea was to disturb existing rights as little as possible. It would doubtless be opposed by the Mahants Party. The bill contemplated that where property is now registered in the name of a 'Mahant' it would continue to be the Mahant's property unless and until the special Sikh Tribunal decided otherwise. The decision of the Tribunal would be subject to appeal to the High Court.......

Sir William Vincent expressed the view that this Bill seemed to afford some hope of a permanent settlement of the question.

Sir William Vincent asked whether if the Bill explained by Sardar Sundar Singh was passed, the Akalis would not continue their attempts to seize forcibly the lands registered in the name of Mahants.

Sardar Sundar Singh replied he hoped that the Akalis would be ready to refer cases of such land to the special Sikh Tribunal which the Bill would set up. Sir William Vincent then pointed out the extreme desirability of an early settlement of the main Gurdwara question. The non-cooperators had placed all their resources at the disposal of the Akalis and the movement now had definitely an All India aspect. The information that reached the Government of India indicated that the movement was penetrating the Sikh regiments. Further delay would probably aggravate the situation and he suggested that there were very urgent reasons for legislating as soon as possible.... His Excellency the Viceroy enquired whether if the Bill explained by Sardar Sundar Singh had a better chance of acceptance, it would not be advisable to proceed with that Bill as quickly as possible and to discard the Government Bill.

Dr. Sapru pointed out the obvious objections to the confiscation of the property of individuals by legislative enactment.

Sardar Sundar Singh in reply to the observations explained his reasons for hoping that the bill which he had explained would be acceptable to moderate and reasonable opinion among both the parties. His Excellency the Governor agreed that this bill did afford some promise of a solution acceptable to moderate opinion and he was ready and indeed anxious to proceed with it as quickly as possible.

Lala Harkishan Lal when asked for his views, said that Shiromani Gurdwara Prabandhak Committee would accept no bill which would not give them complete control over the Gurdwaras and the property attached thereto. Each successive bill proposed to give them more than its predecessor and the committee probably considered that their best tactics were to refuse to accept any Bill in the hope that they ultimately gain the complete control.....

Sir John Maynard considered that nothing that Government could agree to would ever satisfy the Shiromani Gurdwara Prabandhak Committee. The Bill described by Sardar Sundar Singh, in his opinion gave some prospect of satisfying reasonable....[5]

Various Morchas

The position of the Chief Khalsa Diwan and Sir Sundar Singh was not much divergent from the others in so far as the rights of the community were concerned. These were rather instrumental, some times, not only in presenting the Sikhs' case in the right perspective but also had a sobering effect on the Government's reaction to challenge to its authority. The following note dated 13.2.1924[@] reflects strong views which Sir Sundar Singh conveyed to the British Government about the agitation at Jaitu:

> "I have read in the Indian News Telegram of the 10th February that the Nabha State Authorities are going to allow 50 members of the Jatha of 500 which has lately started from Amritsar to perform the Akhand Path at jaito and that they will ask them to give an undertaking that no political propaganda would be carried on and that the Jatha after performing the ceremony of Akhand Path would leave. The State territory, I am grad to find, that Government is taking a wise step in permitting the religious ceremony of the Akhand Path to be started in the Gurdwara, but I consider that the fixation of the number of 50 will be a wrong step. Every Sikh has a right to be present at the sacred ceremony of the Akhand Path, and I am strongly of opinion that we should not place any limitation on this. We must give in so far as the religious portion of the ceremony is concerned and must make a firm stand as regards political propaganda. No body should be permitted to carry on political propaganda in a Sikh Gurdwara which will be against the purposes for which the Gurdwaras

[5]Ibid.

[@]Personal Papers of Sir Sundar Singh Majithia. (Nehru Memorial Museum & Library, New Delhi).

have been established. Sikh Gurdwaras are established for the propagation of the Sikh religion and Sikh religious worship, and it is only right that nothing should be done to disturb the religious sanctity and traditions of the Gurdwaras by bringing in extraneous matters such as political propaganda.

"I send this note on to H.E. through H.M.F. and trust that necessary steps will be taken to advise the Government of India about it."

Question of Sikh Prisoners

In a confidential note dated 12th July, 1921 from Simla to Sir John Maynard, Finance Member of Punjab Government, Sir Sundar Singh strongly urged for suitable instructions to be issued to district officials while dealing with the agitators. He said:

"During the course of my tour in the last month while inspecting the jails, I have come across many people who have recently been arrested on account of the orders of the Government. Many of them appeared to be respectable and my conversation with them did not lead me to believe that they had criminal tendencies. In some districts, arrests of Akalis are being made some what indiscriminately. It is also stated that interested parties have taken this opportunity of settling old scores. I have seen the recent confidential letter of the 28th March addressed to D.Cs by the Home Secretary. Though it provides for the examination of cases of Hindus and Muhammadans, it does not at all provide that the cases of Sikhs should also be looked into. All subjects of His Majesty have a right to be equally treated and unless definite instructions for looking into the cases of all persons are given, I am afraid, it would focus the attention of district officers to Hindus and Muhammadans alone, and the cases of Sikhs including Akalis would not only escape their attention so far as careful examination goes but might give the District Magistrates an impression that Government intends to incarcerate the Akalis as a class. This is of course not intended. Stories are already circulated amongst the community that arrests of Akalis are being made somewhat indiscriminately, and are not confined to bad characters amongst them. The circular letter of the 28th March referred to above therefore requires some further amplification and instructions require to be issued to D.Cs to look into the cases of these people a bit more carefully, especially when the Gurdwara Bill is on the anvil and we are trying to bring round the Parbandhak Committee to a saner view. I feel that it is far better to deal with those persons who have done anything wrong than to deal with Akalis as a class as such. Amongst this class, there is a majority of people who are truly imbued with the spirit of religion and have nothing to do with political activities of the "so-called Akalis". If no instructions are issued, the cases of these people would remain unattended to, with the result that innocent would suffer along with the guilty, thus tending to increase bitterness of feeling which is bound to create acute discontent in the minds of the Sikh community. I would therefore strongly urge that another circular letter should issue to D.Cs asking them to look into the cases of Sikhs as well."

"In continuation of my note of yesterday (5.4.1922), I attach a cutting from the "Khalsa" based on a note from the Secretary, Gurdwara Parbandhak Committee in which it is complained that "Police unnecessarily interferes with religious meetings and the ceremony of the administration of "Amrit" (the baptismal ceremony of the Sikhs) and that the Sikhs are ready at all costs to maintain their religious ceremonies and rights in their Gurdwaras.

"If there is any foundation in this statement, then steps should at once be taken to set things right. I would, therefore, strongly urge and suggest that attention of D.Cs be drawn to this and they be asked to instruct Superintendents of Police to see that their subordinates do not in any way interfere with religious ceremonials in the Gurdwaras and particularly with the ceremony of the administration of Sikh baptism (Pahul of Amrit). (Note signed by S.S. Majithia on 6.4. 1922)

Communique in connection with the Gurdwara Bill.

"I see no objection to the issue of the communique which may issue. But, I am afraid, these will not get very far to meet the situation. The reformers wanted to be admitted that bad Mahants shall be removed and the establishment of custom which may be proved and disproved by counter evidence will not solve the difficulty. The last Government Bill was very nearly accepted by the reformers except that they wanted all the Commissioners to be Sikhs and this desire was, I have no hesitation in saying, a legitimate one. I would not like a non-Sikh to interfere what to have control of Sikh religious places of worship. If we could see our way to concede this point, then the Gurdwara Reform Movement, which is purely a religious movement, could be separated from the political colour that is being given to it by certain interested parties. I am strongly of opinion that we must be prepared to concede to the desire of the majority of the Sikhs and let them have all Sikh Commissioners (one Judicial Sikh Officer, two of the reformers and one of the old Sikhs) and then pass the Bill which is in a dormant stage at present, or, let another Bill be brought by the Council and lend our support in its passage. This is the only way to meet the situation and any amount of communiques—however well meant they may be—will not suffice to meet the legitimate demand of the community."

(Note signed by Sir Sundar Singh Majithia on 12.7.1921 and sent to H.M.E.)

As already stated, the Sikh Gurdwara Act was finally enacted in 1925 with a view to provide for 'Better Administration' at certain Sikh Gurdwaras and 'for Inquiries in to the matters connected therewith', after long drawn agitations and negotiations, reference to which has been made in these chapters.

6

The Akalis and Their Policy

For those who are conversant with the history of the Akali Dal which carne into existence during the Gurdwara Reform Movement will find that it had completely aligned itself with the policies and programmes of Indian National Congress and had even submitted undertakings to this effect, as evident from the correspondence between S.G.P.C. and Congress leadership. From what started as a purely religious struggle to take over Gurdwaras under the control of SGPC, the Reform Movement, for all practical purposes, became a political bandwagon comprising of the anti-British campaigners of non-cooperation and peaceful 'satyagrah' of the Congress Party and majority of the Sikh masses who responded to the popular slogans of the Akali leadership to fight the Government of the day on every issue without, sometimes, realizing the real interests of the community. Their gallant fight and sacrifices, no doubt, strengthened the Congress movement that brought them in the forefront of the freedom struggle as Prof. Ruchi Ram Sahni says in 'Gurdwaras Reform Movement and The Sikh Awakening'.

> "In the rapid march of events all over the country during the past two years, no where has Mahatma Gandhi's non-violent non-cooperation been so completely vindicated as at Taran Taran, Nankana Sahib and Guru Ka Bagh by the calm and cool courage, and the patient and even cheerful sufferings of the Akalis in the face of cruelties, inhumanities and death[1]".

The Akali-Congress Alliance

The simultaneous development of Akali movement, the Sikh Political force, together with the rapid succession in which various historical

[1]Foreword to 'Gurdwara Reform Movement and The Sikh Awakening' by Prof. Ruchi Ram Sahni.

and other shrines like Babe-Di-Ber' Sialkot, Punja Sahib Gurdwara, Sacha Sauda Sheikhpur, Taran Taran, Guru Ka Bagh, Amritsar, Nankana Sahib etc. were occupied gave a new direction to the Gurdwara reform movement which brought itself in the forefront of passive resistance launched by Indian National Congress whose Leaders like Nehru and Mahatama Gandhi were so much impressed and overwhelmed with the enthusiasm and spirit of sacrifice of the Sikhs in various morchas and Shaheedi Jathas that they came to Punjab with a view to encourage, adopt and lead the popular movement, as obvious from the following letter dt. 25.9.1923 from Central Jail, Nabha from Jawahar Lal Nehru, who also courted arrest in 'Jaito Morcha' "I rejoice that I am being tried for the cause which the Sikhs have made their own. I was in jail when the Guru Ka-Bagh struggle was gallantly fought and won by the Sikhs. I marvelled at the courage and sacrifices of the Akalis and wished that I could be given an opportunity of showing my deep admiration of them by some form of service. That opportunity has now been given to me and I earnestly hope that I shall prove worthy of their high tradition and fine courage. 'Sat Sri Akal[2]".

"Also luckily for the Congress, the people of the country had already become more restive and the now Congress did not find any difficulty to benefit from this mood of the nation and to launch a nation-wide struggle for freedom[3]".

Prominent Congress leaders visited Punjab and threw their lot with the Gurdwara Reform Movement. Although Mahatma Gandhi was first attracted to Punjab immediately after Jallianwala Bagh massacre at Amritsar in April 1919, when he issued an appeal by reproducing Swami Shiv Shardhnana's report about casualties and sufferings of the victims for donation and help, he soon found himself completely involved in various morchas launched by the Akalis despite the violence and bloodshed, which invariably accompanied such agitations, being contrary to his professed non-violence. Some of his letters bear testimony to this.

"If I am entirely satisfied so as to the nature of and implications of the present Akali movement and the methods adopted to gain the end, I should have no hesitation in throwing myself heart and

[2]The Akali Movement - by Mohinder Singh

[3]Select Documents - Gurdwara Reform Movement - Introduction by M.L. Ahluwalia - p. IV.

soul into it and even burying myself in the Punjab if it becomes necessary in order to guide the movement. The satisfaction that I require is on the following:

1. The strength of the Akalis.

2. (a) A clear manifesto publicly stating the minimum which I understand to be the performance of the Akhand Path ceremony in the Gangsar Gurdwara, the Sikhs openly and sincerely declaring that it has no political end that they do not desire, through the Akhand Path Movement in any shape or form, to carry on an agitation directly or indirectly, for the restoration of Nabha Maharaja...

(b) In connection with the movement for control of Gurdwaras in every case of disputed control or possession the matter should be referred to arbitration... In the event of the party in possession of such Gurdwaras declining the surrender of control of the S.G.P.C. or to refer the matter in dispute to arbitration the Akalis would be free to take such direct action that as is consistent with non-violence in the strictest sense of the term.

3. Full assurance and, therefore, a document intended for publication signed by all the Principal leaders or on behalf of the S.G.P.C. giving a description of the methods which will clearly set forth the all implications of non-violence. By the term I do not wish to convey that no violence is to be regarded in the document referred to above as final creed of the Sikhs which I know it is not...

4. That the movement is neither anti Hindu not anti any other race or creed.

5. That the S.G.P.C. has no desire for the establishment of Sikh Raj and as a matter of fact, the committee is purely religious body[4]".

"I learnt from Pandit Moti Lal after you had gone, that the S.G.P.C. was actually defending the accused in the matter of prosecution of Akalis. I learnt too that a Hindu temple within the precincts of the Golden Temple had been destroyed by the Akalis and that the latter took stand upon religion. In your letter which you had promised I would like you to please deal with all these questions[5].

In a letter dated April 20, 1924, the S.G.P.C. duly complied with Mahatama Gandhi's letter and submitted to his clarifications and conditions for supporting the movement:

[4]Letters dt. 4th March 1924, by M.K. Gandhi - some confidential papers of the Akali Movement· edited by Dr. Ganda Singh (53 to 55).

[5]Ibid.

"Dear Mahatma Ji,

... We have discussed the issues raised in your letter and we wish to state that on all those points our position is very clear. We are glad that on these points our views concide with yours and we can request to at once declare them on your behalf again, if you like-

1. Yes, we agree that in the matters of disputed control or possession, arbitration should first be tried and if you study the facts about our movement so far, you will find that we have been following this practice. As you say, it should be assured that all historical Gurdwaras must remain in the control of the S.G.P.C the onus of proving the historical character of a Gurdwara, when questioned, will be on the S.G.P.C With reference to all Gurdwaras, all the facts in dispute should be a matter of arbitration. Satyagarah to be resorted to by the Akalis only in the event of arbitration and other attempts at amicable settlement being rejected by the incumbents. Satyagrah is to be practised in the spirit of perfect non-violence ...

2. Our movement is neither anti-Hindu nor anti-any other religions in spirit. And objectives, it is thoroughly national in out-look. We have, therefore, all along endeavoured to carry with us the sympathy, approval and good wishes of all that is best in India or elsewhere; and we take pride in the fact that we have been successful in it.

3. The movement is purely religious and has no secular object or intention. The S.G.P.C is a purely religious body and has no desire, for the establishment of Sikh Raj... It is exactly because ours is a religious movement that although we have sought and received sympathy and support from non-Sikh friends and non-Sikh national workers; yet our people have been jealous of keeping the control and guidance of the Gurdwaras movement in purely Sikh hands, and we are glad to note that our friends have appreciated this view and approved of it... Of course, we can not repay the deep debt of gratitude that we owe to Hindu and Mohammadam friends like Pandit Dina Nath, Swamy Shardha Nand, Swami Vishwa Nand, Pandit Jawahar Lal Nehru, Gidwari Onkar Nand, Santanam, Kitchlew and others who have suffered for sympathising with us. If for no other reason, the love of these friends and of Malviyaji, Swami Shankercharya, Ali brothers, Mr. C.F. Andrews and yourself would prevent us from becoming anti-Hindu or anti any other community or entertaining any dreams of dominating other communities.

II

As for the significance of the Jaito struggle and its implications we wish to state as follows:

Right of free congregation and free worship by holding religious diwans is the birth right of the Sikhs. Not the deposition of the Maharaja but the invasion of these rights at Jaito by the Nabha Administration was the cause of the going of jathas to Jaito. The S.G.P.C. supported the protest of the Sikhs of the state against this action but the authorities turned the deaf ear to the legitimate demand of the Sikh community and further aggravated the position of closing the Gurdwara and interrupting the Akhand Path by forciby breaking the congregation. This and this alone was the cause of the sending of the Jathas, to re-establish the rights assailed... It is our intention that when the Gurdwara is thrown open to us we should depart within a few days after establishing our rights and making necessary arrangements for the fulfilment of our vow of completing 101 Akhand Paths there. We do not wish to make any unnecessary delay in completing the above number of paths there ...

We hope the above statement will make our whole position clear to you and convince you. If you have any further views on the matter kindly communicate them to us... As for the suggestion about making Nabha deposition an All India question and as a preparation for that securing certain announcements from His Highness, it requires much consideration and there is no immediate pressing need of coming to a decision on the matter.

As for the query about the strength of the Akalis we have the satisfaction that the whole 'panth' is with us except a few individual 'Mahants' who are opposed to us for selfish ends. *The number of Akalis and 'Satyagrahis' depends upon the intensity of repression.*

We agree with you in principle on the question of non-violence and in its methods and implications too. We mainly agree with you ....

III

Pandit Moti Lal Nehru was right in informing you that many of the Akali leaders are defending themselves in the present conspiracy case against them. They are doing so in this case because the charge is extraordinary i.e. that they want to seize the Punjab. They want to combat that wicked charge/positively instead of by the negative method of denying it in their statement...

As for the demolition of a Hindu Temple within the precincts of the Golden Temple the facts are these:

There was a Hindu image, 'Shiva-Lingam' in a comer of the parikarma of the Golden Temple, which had been introduced in the recent times. The Sikhs are not idol-worshippers and the S.G.P.C had always worked forward to an amicable removal of the image in consultation with Hindu leaders. In fact this matter had been brooked with Pandit Malviya [i and Swami Shankercharya, both of whom had agreed with the Sikh view. Before the S.G.P.C could achieve this consummation or had at all set about it, some irresponsible and misguided men, most probably Sikhs, demolished it in one night in April 1923 without even the knowledge of S.G.P.C or any person connected with it. When it was discovered next morning the S.G.P.C hastened to condemn this action and expressed deep regret in public and its readiness to make amends to injured Hindu sentiments in consistency with the principles of Sikhism. While we resent to be called idol-breakers, we dare not figure idol-rectors. So the restoration of the image by the S.G.P.C the trustee of religious reform was out of question... By a strange irony of fate the image was demolished on the same night, April 12, when about 1600 Akalis were patrolling the streets of Amritsar to protect the life and property of Hindus and their temples and Thakurdwaras. This combination of circumstances pained the S.G.P.C most.

IV

Most of the suggestions made in your first letter have already been adopted and carried out by us and we have bee? trying to act in the spirit which you are anxious to inculcate....[6]"

While the spirit of sacrifice and momentum generated by the Gurdwara Reform Movement thus attracted the National leaders and their sympathy, this association of the Akalis and Indian National Congress which strengthened their respective campaigns against the British, had far-reaching consequences in the history of the country and the Sikh community, with Indian National Congress having obvious advantage of seasoned leaderships which subjected these movements to its professed principles and

[6]Ibid, p. 56 to 62 (Excerpts from letter dt. April 20, 1924 from S.G.P.C. Amritsar).

objectives. "It was in this context that we find that Indian National Congress sought to neutralise, as far as possible, the virus of communalism, by providing selective support to the two contemporary movements, which were basically anti-British and anti-imperialist. One was the Khilafat movement and the other was the Gurdwara Reform Movement in the Punjab launched by the newly formed Akali Party and the Shiromani Gurdwara Prabandhak Committee, later being a society formed under the Indian Societies Act[7].

"In return for the help extended to the Akali movement, the Congress leadership was able to establish a good deal of influence with the Akali leaders and through them the Congress programme was carried to the Sikh masses[8]".

"The Akali movement became a part of the national movement, in effect a branch of the Congress programme of non-cooperation at the provincial level and in return received sympathy and support from the Congress leadership in its struggle against the Government[9]".

In fact, the India National Congress could not expect a better province than Punjab or a valiant community than the Sikhs to execute its non-cooperation movement more effectively. Prof. Ruchi Ram Sahni has given following historical description of the struggle and sacrifices made by the Akalis:

I cannot help remarking that simple rustics, who mainly composed the Akali Jathas, appeared to us as heroes of a twentieth century Epic before the story of their heroism inspired by a sublime idealism, is immortalised in verse by a poet of eminence. It certainly deserved to be cherished in our memories with the same love, regard and admiration as the ancient Epics are treasured today[10].

These heroes of the Gurdwara Reform Movement by forming an alliance with Indian National Congress and joining 'Satyagraha' not only strengthened the latter's crusade against the British Govt. but also took to distinct approach of confrontation than that of

[7]Select Documents - Gurdwara Reform Movement By M.L. Ahluwalia (Introduction page VI).

[8]The Akali movement by Mohinder Singh, p. 141.

[9]Ibid, p. 142

[10]Select documents - Gurdwara Reform Movement by M.L. Ahluwalia (Introduction page XXX).

fruitful cooperation hitherto pursued by the Sikh Organizations, including Chief Khalsa Diwan.

However, swayed by their enthusiasm to confront the British Government in the wake of ultimate successes in various morachas, facilitated by the overwhelming public response of the masses, influence of the moderate leaders and ultimate acceptance of realities by the authorities, the Akalis many times overstepped their objectives at the cost of avoidable misery to innocent common man and even loss of human lives.

The intrasigent attitude adopted by the Akali leaders over some of the issues would reveal to the students of history a striking similarity which those events of the past have with the incidents happening at present—as the policy of confrontation with the Government of the day goes on along with the never-ending in-fighting, rather the fratricidal war—which has been another hall-mark of the Sikh history. Some of the instances and the British assessment of this trend and the factors responsible for it, offers an interesting reading.

The Birdwood Committee: With the on-going struggle of the Sikhs to gain control over the Gurdwaras, the British Government had been making serious efforts ever since introducing the first Gurdwara Bill in 1921 to arrive at an acceptable settlement. **In** this connection, in the early months of 1924, Sir Malcolm Hailey, the Horne Member of the Government of India, suggested to His Excellency Lord Reading, the Governor-General, to invite Sir William Birdwood, the Commander-in-Chief of India, to help restore friendly relations between the Government and the Sikh community and to draft, in consultation with the members of the Punjab Legislative Council, a bill for the control of the Sikh Gurdwaras that may be acceptable to both the parties. General Birdwood was also authorized by the Governor-General to promise that if the Akalis cooperated with him in his work; those of them imprisoned under trial for offences in connection with the Gurdwara Agitation would be released. Sir William was known for his friendship for the Sikhs. During thirty five years in the Indian Army, he had seen much of the Sikhs and knew them well. It was, therefore, hoped that he would be able to overcome the hostility that had come to be created between the Government and the Sikhs. With the help of Bhai Jodh Singh and Sardar Narain Singh of Gujranwala, General Birdwood entered into negotiations with the Government of the Punjab, represented by Sir Henry Craik and the Akali leaders detained in the Lahore Fort and working outside... Both sides worked with mental reservations and suspicions and looked more to their prestige than to the solution. and settlement of the problem before them. Thus, the efforts of the Birdwood Committee failed to achieve its objective and it was dissolved[11].

General Sir William (later Field Marshal Lord) Birdwood has in autobiography 'Khaki and Crown', thus summarized the failure of his negotiations:

"The more extremist Akalis obstructed progress with quite unreasonable demands. They tried to make it a condition that, in addition to those detained for simple Gurdwara offences, all Sikhs undergoing imprisonment or awaiting trial-even for murder or manslaughter resulting from the seizure of Gurdwaras - should be released before they would cooperate. To this stipulation, it was of course quite impossible to agree, and after a whole month's discussions, I had reluctantly to inform the Viceroy that the appointment of my Committee appeared to have been premature[12]."

That the General was substantially correct in his conclusion is borne out by Sardar Raja Singh, then a Member of the Working Committee of the SGPC, in his letter of resignation dated August 28; 1924. Writing to the President of the SGPC, he said:

> "As I do not believe in the policy and actions which actuated in breakage of Birdwood negotiations so far as our side is concerned (and on the day the rejection of the settlement was finally decided in Lahore Fort Jail, I stood against the rejection) and as the present policy of the S.G.P.C. (only one General Committee has met after 13th October, 1923 and one Executive, and these two considered the policy) and policy and actions of its very powerful and important instruments are unduly dominated by outside influence and consequently, under the circumstances, not in the interests of the Panth,... I have been obliged to hereby submit my

[11]'Some Confidential Papers of the Akali Movement'—Introduction by Dr. Ganda Singh (p. XIX).

[12]Ibid, p. XX.

resignation from the Working Committee, which please accept and oblige[13]".

If the Akali leaders had accepted the proposed basis for cooperation with the Negotiations Committee, the draft of the Bill for, the management of Gurdwaras would have been immediately taken up by a Committee of six members, with Sir William Birdwood as president, set up for the purpose. The majority of the members were Sikhs-Bhai Jodh Singh, Sardar Narain Singh and Sardar Tara Singh—with two Hindu Members, Raja Sir Narendra Nath and an eminent lawyer from Madras. The lawyer had actually arrived at Lahore. But, the Akalis insisted that such of the Sikh soldiers as had been convicted by the Military Courts for wearing Kirpans should as well be released. Bhai Jodh Singh was of the opinion that when the negotiations were successfully concluded, the release of those soldiers could be easily secured. But, the Akali leaders prompted mainly by emotion, rigidly stuck to their demand being fulfilled as a preliminary condition for their cooperation. And, the Birdwood negotiations broke down[14].

While the Gurdwara Legislation was finally enacted by Punjab Legislative Assembly on July 7, 1925 and it came into force with effect from November 1 1925[@]. Dr. Ganda Singh opines that—

"This refusal to cooperate with the Birdwood Committee by the extremist Akalis is considered to be one of the greatest blunders committed by them. The passage of the Gurdwara Bill at that stage would have ended the struggle of the community with the Government much earlier and saved it from the rot into which it fell as a result of the mutual split and acrimony created by the accentuation of differences by the extremists[15]".

That the differences indeed existed among the Akali leaders themselves, apart from divergent views of other sections of the

[13]Ibid.

[14]Ibid. p. XXI.

[@]The Gurdwara Act, whose provisions significantly omitted any minimum educational qualification or number of terms for office bearers of the Committee, has become centre-stage of politico-religious affairs of the Sikh community, ever since its enactment in 1925.

[15]Ibid, p. XXI.

Sikhs including moderate leaders of Chief Khalsa Diwan[@@], Namdharis and other sects not only compounded their difficulties but also confused the community about possible safeguards to preserve and protect their separate identity resulting into an unending era of confrontation, even after freedom of the country for which they had shed so much of blood, to the extent of imprisonments and subsequent Morchas which made the Akalis an object of suspicion about even their loyalty and patriotism. As Dr. Gokul Chand Narang states—

[@@]That the Chief Khalsa Diwan had played an important role in securing the release of Sikh prisoners is borne out from the letter dated 15th September 1921 from Sir Sobha Singh (Khushwant Singh's father) from Raisina, New Delhi, which reads as follows:

"Copy of Telegram 16th Sep. 1921
Delhi C 15.15.15 p. 37
Reomem Simla

Khalsa Diwan highly appreciates your services in releasing Sikh prisoners offering heartfelt thanks.

Sobha Singh
Secy.
Raisina
Delhi dated 15th September 1921

My dear Sardar Sahib,

I confirm my telegram on behalf of the Khalsa Dewan of today offering heartfelt thanks for your services rendered to the Sikh community in securing release to our brethren convicted for enthusiastic zeal in the cause of religious reform of our Gurdwaras. You have, no doubt, proved yourself worthy of the trust vested in you by the province and these sincere efforts of your for the Sikh cause will, I am sure, endear you and the Government of which you are such a prominent member, to the Sikh Community.

It will not, moreover, be out of place here to request you to convey the Diwan's sincere thanks to your worthy colleague Sir John Maynard, KC.S.I.C.I.E. whose services in the cause have been equally praiseworthy.

Thanking you in the end and wishing you success.

I am yours very sincerely
Sd/ - Sobha Singh
Honorary Secretary

To
The Honourable
Sardar Sundar Singh Majithia Sardar Bahadur C.I.E.,
Simla.

"This two-nation theory was started by the Muslim League Leaders. Jinnah said, 'We have nothing in common with the Hindus except the country; we are a separate Nation by ourselves; we should be prepared for all sacrifices, for the division of India which would give us a separate Nation.' This is what the Sikhs are doing now. If the Government does not take precautions, a time may come when the Sikhs may demand a separate nation for themselves. There is no difference between Master Tara Singh and Sant Fateh Singh, though Sant Fateh Singh speaks against Tara Singh. At heart, all the Sikhs want a Sikh State, an autonomous State. Master Tara Singh wants a sovereign Sikh State, not only an autonomous Sikh State[16]."

The British Assessment of Akali Movement and Its Support Base

The following secret notes of the British officials about the Akali movement, the composition of its support-base and its representative character form an interesting and relevant reading for any student of history:

The Akali Dal

(Its origin and growth)

"The genesis of the present Akali movement is vague and obscure. The Nihangs or Akalis were originally a band of devotees founded by Guru Gobind Singh after the siege of Chamkaur. Dark-blue garments and a peculiar head-dress' emblematic of the martial characteristics of Sikhism were ordained for them. They were regarded as the custodians of the Akal Takht at Amritsar and the directions of religious ceremonials. Turbulent and fanatical and addicted to intoxicating drugs, they later on became a constant source of terror to the more peaceable classes of the community. Maharaja Ranjit Singh endeavoured with some success to reduce them to a state of subjection but for many years they were the most troublesome element in the Khalsa[17]".

[16]Transcript of interview with Dr. Gokul Chand Narang. (Nehru Memorial Museum & Library, New Delhi).

[17]Home-Poll. Department, File No. 914/1922 (National Archives of India, New Delhi).

Support Base of Akalis

The following secret notes of the British officials about Akalis support-base amongst the Jat Sikhs affords an in-sight into their view point about the agitation on the Gurdwara issue:

> "The illiterate Jat Sikh, easily. misled by heated talk of a tyrannical encroachment on his cherished religious rights needed little encouragement at a time when plain speaking was the general rule, to join the crusade and denounce his oppressors. The facts of the case were generally unrepresented or misrepresented to him; he was too uneducated to grasp the points at issue and preferred to be led by those whose volubility indicated superior knowledge. This inflammable material, when untouched by political or religious propaganda, is by nature obedient to established authority; it has martial traditions and forms the backbones[@] of many of the Punjab battalions. As far as can be ascertained, the trained Sikh sepoy has so far not succumbed to the mischievous influences at work in his village, though there is ample corroborative evidence that soldiers on leave are vigorously assailed by propagandists who wish to shake their attachment to their regiments and their loyalty to the Raj. In Cantonments, open propaganda is almost impossible but there is good reason to believe that the Publicity Bureau of the Parbandhak Committee has despatched to various regiments posters and printed statements bearing on the subject of the "keys affair" and attacking the action of the Government[18]..."

[18]Home Poll. Department File No. 459/11/1922 (National Archives of India, New Delhi).

[@]The Jats indeed formed the backbone of Guru Gobind Singh's Khala, Banda Bahadur's crusade and Maharaja Ranjit Singh's "Khalsa Fauj" followed by strong band of Akali 'Jathas' in the Gurdwara Liberation Movement till partition of the country and thereafter-all in the name of religion - till the end of 20th Century when signs of frustration started becoming evident because of what they feel is their consistent exploitation in the name of religion as also due to other socio-economic factors and ideological propaganda by other socio-political groups. With about 58.2% literacy rate in Punjab, they still constitute most vulnerable group prone to exploitation for narrow electoral . and petty gains by various unscruplous leaders.

\- Author

SGPC Established Supremacy

The position as to how the S.G.P.C. established its supremacy is explained in a document published by the British officials, as follows:

> "The difficulty of ascertaining the value of the claim that the Parbandhak Committee accurately represented Sikh aspirations was accentuated by the acuteness of the general political situation. Under normal conditions, it is more than probable that the extreme demands of the Gurdwara reformers would have aroused considerable opposition from the Hindu community which had hitherto opposed the neo-Sikh separatist policy. In the altered political conditions, however, the mere fact that these demands embarrassed the administration was sufficient to secure for them freedom from criticism. The opposition which the Gurdwara Reform Movement encountered in its early stages soon spent itself and was not renewed. Conservative Sikhs were silent; they were either secretly supporting the movement or awaiting developments .... Gurdwara reform is no longer an academic question but has passed into the field of practical politics and is making a strong appeal to all classes of Sikhs. The political activities of the Committee inspire less confidence among the conservative Sikhs, particularly the land-owning classes to whom loyalty to the Crown has always been an article of faith. Even in the ranks of the Committee itself, there are many who are opposed to the introduction of politics into an agitation which is essentially religious and there are some indications that this moderate attitude will develop[19]".

[19]Ibid.

7

Sir Sundar Singh and Provincial Autonomy

The annexation of the Lahore Kingdom founded by Maharaja Ranjit Singh by the British authorities in India in 1849 has been, without doubt, single most important event that has remained uppermost in the minds of Sikh leaders-irrespective of their divergent view—as also the British rulers while framing and amending their policies vis-a-vis each other.

While the Minto - Morley reforms of 1909 and Mont-ford Reforms of 1919 gave limited autonomy to the provinces, the question of communal settlement in Punjab activated Sir Sundar Singh Majithia and his associates in the Khalsa National Party to press for adequate representation to the Sikh community in the Muslim dominated province. After a great deal of consultations with his colleagues, Sir Sundar Singh Majithia wrote a letter dated 8th July 1932 to Sir Geoffery de Montmoraney, the Governor of Punjab, enclosing therewith a representation to be forwarded to the Viceroy. He wrote:

> "I am forwarding herewith a note which we have taken the liberty to submit in the hope that it may be forwarded to His Excellency the Viceroy with a view to its communication to His Majesty's Government. We thought it our duty to bring to your kind notice the views held by Sikhs of all shades of opinion in this matter, and to say that if His Majesty's Government pronounce an award favouring any particular community placing the Punjab at the mercy of such community inaddition to the separation of Sindh and North West Frontier Province at the request of the favoured community which would cost the Central Government nearly two crores a year, it will be regarded an unjust act by vast population of other religions and have far reaching effects, which cannot be

conducive to a better understanding between the communities, which is essential for the working of the New Government."

Copy of the Note Annexed:

"May we take the liberty even at this stage to place the Sikh position before Your Excellency in the hope that you may be pleased to place our final representation before His Majesty's Government so that the communal award on which depends the future peace and prosperity of the Punjab may be given not only on political considerations but on principles of justice and in conformity with the declaration made by Her Majesty Queen Victoria in her proclamation solemnly promising equality of treatment to all the people of India.

"2. We claim nothing more than that a single principle, in the giving of weightage, to all minorities in the Provinces be applied and the Sikh community should not be singled out and deprived of its rightful weightage in the Punjab. This is the only Province which we call our own and in no other Province our numbers are not such as to exercise any counter-balancing influence. The weightage given to the Muslim community in other Provinces should be the guiding principle in awarding the weightage to the Sikhs in the Punjab. We have heard, and we have no reason to disbelieve the rumour, that after reserving 51 per cent of the seats in the New Council for the Muslims in the Punjab, the rest are to be distributed amongst other communities. We respectfully beg to point out that this entirely reverses the principle followed in other Provinces where minorities have been given weightage and their interests safeguarded without extending protection to the majority community.

"3. We may be permitted to say that territorial position and the distribution of population in the Punjab needs careful study. The Punjab proper, which extends from the borders of Delhi to the banks of Chenab, shows no dominance of Muslim population, and the bulk of the revenue of the Punjab is paid by the Central Punjab. It is trans-Chenab districts which carne into the Punjab as a result of conquest by Sikh Maharaja Ranjit Singh, and have remained ever since attached to the Punjab, which gives Muslim population its majority. Is it reasonable then to expect that people of the Central Punjab with their large vested interests, their tradition and their stake in the country would submit quietly to an award which would place their destinies in the hands of a population, which has done so little to add, to the wealth of the Province or to win confidence of the majority communities. It is an irony of fate that those whom Sikhs conquered should now rule the Central Punjab, by means of an award given by British Government in whose service we have shed our best blood and have never hesitated in making every sacrifice in the service of the Empire. In addition to our continuous record of service in the Army we gave during the Great War the biggest number of fighting men. Indeed, the Muslim population in the Central Punjab consists largely of labouring classes and establishment of Muslim majority would amount to transferring the large interests of landowning classes to their tenants and others who have no stake and pay no direct taxes. We beg to say that we shall accept no such award which places us in a position of subordination and exalts a sister community also in other Provinces. It is not with any idea of self-aggrandisement that we seek protection but to secure for the Punjab by opposing a communal rule, which is bound to fail a good Government capable of safeguarding the interests of all communities. We faced the might of the Mughal Empire with no other purpose but to prevent a communal Raj and today again if we are called upon to do so, we shall consider no sacrifice too great to defend our honour, our hearths and homes—so help us God.

"Lastly, we shall be failing in our duty if we refrain from mentioning the impression that is gaining ground that the award is going to be influenced not by the justness of the claims of communities, but on other political , grounds. We would humbly say that His Majesty's Government may as well take measures of the resentment of other communities, and the consequences of their permanent alienation, if the award singles out anyone community for a favoured treatment[1]".

[1]Personal Files of Sir Sundar Singh Majithia. (Nehru Memorial Museum & Library, New Delhi).

The Three Alternatives

Sir Sundar Singh Majithia and his associates suggested three alternatives to the Punjabis for the proposed settlement on the basis of existing geographical position. These were as follows:

> "There are two or three alternatives open to Punjabees to come to a settlement. The Punjab naturally falls into three zones-(i) Punjab Proper; (ii) Northern Punjab; (iii) Southern Punjab.
>
> "In the Punjab proper, the Muslim and non-Muslim population is almost equal; in the Northern Punjab, Muslim population dominates; while in the Southern Punjab, Hindus are in the majority. The Punjab proper would be well served if it had joint electorates, with plural member constituencies with single non-transferable vote. In the North Punjab, separate electorate could be given to Hindus and Sikhs and in the Southern to Muslims. This will produce a good House free from the taint of communalism.
>
> "Another solution would be to form the Province into three cantons and federate them in the same way as cantons are federated in Switzerland. Each canton governing its affairs with the exception of such subjects as require central control sending representative to the federated House according to the revenue and population of each canton.
>
> "The third solution can be: Supposing that the New House is to have 175 members, we may allot equal number of seats, say 75, to Muslims and 75 to non-Muslims from separate electorates but the remaining 25 to be from special constituencies with common electorates. The special constituencies already exist only, the landlords const: the largest interact in the Punjab may be increased to 16. This will provide equality of opportunity and meet the demand of communities, that no community should be placed in domination by statute. It will give the House some stability by increasing the representation of Landlords and at the same time given an incentive to Muslim community to win the confidence of sister communities and secure its majority[2]".

[2]Ibid.

The Simon Commission and Sundar Singh Majithia

Sir Sundar Singh Majithia, ex-Executive Councillor to the Punjab Government, gave evidence on behalf of the Chief Khalsa Diwan. He claimed a fair and equitable treatment for Sikhs who, he said, would never submit to any subordinate position in the constitution of the country. The Sikhs have been a separate community from the time of the Gurus. Their interest was not identical with that of any other community[3].

He said, "Sikhs should get 30 per cent of representation in the Legislature. Sikhs are a small consolidated community centralised in the Punjab. We want that our hearths and homes should be safe. The other communities have a majority in one province or the other. Hence, they can counteract each other's activity, protect the respective interests and keep the balance of power. Further, Sikhs have a large number of Gurdwaras which require protection. We are a military community. We have fought for the Empire not on Frontiers alone but in Africa and the Great War. Taking the question of revenue, Sikhs are paying 40 per cent of the total of the canal and land revenues in the province. Hence, unless the Sikhs are given adequate representation, they cannot protect themselves. No minority should be at the mercy of the majority allowed to be tyrannised over[4]."

Motilal Nehru Report and Sundar Singh Majithia

The Nehru Report of May 29, 1928 rejected the separate communal electorates on the ground that they perpetuated communal antagonism and proposed joint electorates with reservation of seats for the minorities but without any weightage. The Report was not acceptable to the Sikhs and Sunder Singh Majithia along with 32 other leading Sikhs presented on behalf of Chief Khalsa Diwan an address to Sir Geoffery Fitzhervey de Montmorancy, Government of the Punjab. The address said:

> "Since 1919, the year of introduction of Reforms, the Sikhs have not been having their full share in the administration of their country which is due mainly to the fact that they are in a hopeless minority and those in whose hands lay the

[3]"Khalsa Te Khalsa Advocate", Amritsar: November 20, 1928, p. 1.
[4]Ibid. p. 1.

distribution of patronage, belonged to other communities. Under the influence of the communal wave, the claims of the Sikhs have more often than not been ruthlessly ignored[5]".

"The Address added: "The Nehru Report has kept communalism fully recognized though cleverly screened but in its wise diplomacy, has passed over the Sikh claims as a strong minority in the Province by a mere word of praise.... The Sikhs cannot be satisfied as long as their due share is not given to them in the Province... The Sikhs have as great a stake in the country as any other community and their political importance is admitted by each and all. Nothing less than 30 per cent share in the Legislature and Administration of this Province will satisfy them[6]".

The Address also requested the Governor to release those who had been arrested in connection with the Gurdwara Reforms Movement, which it regarded as a purely religious matter pertaining to the community and asked the Governor to release the prisoners.

The Communal Award (August 8, 1932)

The Macdonald (communal) Award was grossly unfair. to the Hindus and Sikhs in the Punjab. They were not given weightage on the same scale on which Muslims received it in provinces wherein they were in minority. While Hindus and Sikhs in the Punjab were dismissed with a formal pat, Indian Christians, Anglo-Indians and Europeans literally basked in the sunshine of British patronage. They received 300%, 3,000% and 25,000% patronage respectively[7].

The Sikhs opposed, with a unanimous voice, the Communal Award which gave Muslims 52% seats while Sikhs were to get 19% and Hindus 27% with Christians more than 2%. In a letter from the Majithia House, Simla, on July 8, 1932 addressed to Sir Montmorancy, the Punjab Governor, Sardar Sundar Singh Majithia, asked the Government not to pronounce an award favouring any particular community placing the Punjab at the mercy of such a community[8]. A note was attached to the letter which was to be sent to His Majesty's Government. The note said:

[5]"Khalsa Te Khalsa Advocate": Amritsar: December 8, 1928, p. 1.

[6]Ibid, p.2.

[7]Bombwall, K.R., Indian Constitution and Administration: p. 54.

[8]Papers of Sundar Singh Majithia: Nehru Memorial Library, New Delhi: File No. 48, p. 23.

> "We claim nothing more than that a single principle in giving of weightage to all minorities in the Provinces be applied and the Sikh community should not be singled out and deprived of its rightful weightage in the Punjab[9]".

After the Award was announced, the Sikh leaders—Sir Sundar Singh Majithia, Sardar Jogendra Singh, Raja Daljit Singh, Sardar Ujjal Singh, Sardar Sampuran Singh, Sardar Sant Singh, Bhagat Jaswant Singh and Giani Kartar Singh issued a joint statement on August 17, 1932 from Simla. Criticising the Communal Award of the Prime Minister, they said:

> "The decision of His Majesty's Government has shaken the faith of the Sikhs in the British Government's sense of justice and fair play. It establishes a Muslim communal majority in a province like the Punjab where other communities pay about 2/3rd towards the revenues of the Province. The small Muslim majority in population is the result of Northern districts which came into the Punjab, as a result of Sikh conquest. The promises held out to the Sikh community have not been fulfilled, We have not even been given the benefit of our increase in the population and the weightage that automatically accrues on it. While the Muslims not only retain their considerable weightage in the six Provinces, but have been given more than they asked for in the Punjab. They asked for one seat more than the combined representation of all other communities, but they have been given seven. (Sir Fazl-i-Hussain's Resolution of November 1918; Note prepared for the Simon Commission by Sir Fazl-i-Hussain and Malik Feroz Khan Noon and the Recommendations of the Provincial Reforms Committee).
>
> "At the first Round Table Conference in private negotiations with the Prime Minister in the Chair, Muslim delegates were willing to accept 50 per cent representation for their community in the Punjab, but the decision of the Government ensures them 91 seats, i.e. 52 per cent, as they are likely to secure two seats from the Lahore constituency, which the award has left out of account-an ommission which is not worthy of a Government.
>
> "The Europeans in Bengal, with less than *1/2* per cent population are given 10 per cent representation in Bengal

[9]Ibid., File No. 48, p. 27.

Council and are allowed to hold the balance; while the Sikhs with 13 per cent of the Punjab population and paying about 40 per cent of provincial revenues, with unchallenged record of loyal services, with hundreds of their educational institutions and thousands of their religious shrines, are reduced to a position of subordination in a province which they ruled and in which they have the largest stake in the country.

"By establishing an absolute religious communal majority of 52 per cent, the Government have permanently banished the possibility of the formation of parties on non-communal lines and all chances of communal agreement by communities themselves. The decision cuts at the very root of democratic system of Government. *The Sikh community is anxious* to *secure a national Government not only for the Punjab but the whole of India, and can never submit to such a decision and would rather tolerate the existing constitution than accept the new, which in the name of democracy aims at perpetuating communal differences by setting a single community in permanent authority; thus, putting the clock of progress back by several decades.*

"The award has an air of finality about it, but in the name of democracy and self-determination, it can never be the purpose of British Government, we believe, it can never receive the approval of the world to force half the population of the province, against its wishes, into a position of subordination or to enforce a new constitution without its consent. We are confident that the British Parliament with its traditions of democracy and sense of justice and fair play will never consent to the coercion of a large population against their will into such a one-sided constitution.

"We would, at the same time, appeal to our community to exercise control and act in a constitutional manner and prepare itself:

(i) To secede from the Northern districts of the Punjab.

(ii) To organise opinion to exercise self-determination, and,

(iii) To maintain peace and good relations with sister communities[10]".

Sardar Ujjal Singh and Sardar Sampuran Singh, Barrister sent in their resignations from their Advisory Committee and the Round Table Conference.

[10]"Khalsa Te Khalsa Advocate", Amritsar, November 10, 1928, p. 1.

Sir Sundar Singh Majithia and Sardar Jogendra Singh refused to accept the membership of the third Round Table Conference to express their resentment against the Communal Award[11].

Sir Sundar Singh Majithia and S. Jogendra Singh also wrote a joint letter to the Governor of Punjab threatening to stall other reforms in the Province if the Communal Award was not changed[12].

The Majithia Sardar along with Sir Jogendra Singh and Raja Daljit Singh also sent the following telegram dated August 15, 1932 from Simla to London which was addressed to the Prime Minister of England, the Secretary of State for India and Sardar Shivdev Singh, Member Council of State for India. The telegram reads as follows:

> "Negotiations to reach communal settlement broke down, as Muslim leaders believe that they are getting from the award, many seats in excess of the combined representation of all other communities. Muslims asked for only one seat in excess of combined representation of all other communities which the Sikhs never accepted-See Sir Fazl-i-Hussain's Punjab Council Resolution 21st November, 1918 Note 22nd August-Recommendation of the Punjab Reforms Committee, 1929. If Muslim anticipations about the award are correct, it would create grave situation and we request that unless willing cooperation of all the communities is forthcoming, it would be dangerous to introduce new constitution with communal majority of one community over the ~ombined representation of others and against the wishes of Sikhs and Hindus who form half of the population of Punjab, paying almost 2/3rd of the revenue of the province. Under the circumstances, we consider that new constitution with fixed communal majority would be worse than the present constitution and we would request that existing constitution of Punjab should continue to function till communal agreement is reached."[@]

[11]"Khalsa Te Khalsa Advocate", Arnritsar, October 8, 1932, p. l.

[@]Personal Papers of Sir Sundar Singh Majithia. (Nehru Memorial Museum &: Library, New Delhi).

[12]Ibid., October 15, 1932, p. 2.

Majithia's Action Plan

In a letter dated 19th September, 1932 from Majithia House, Simla, Sir Sundar Singh wrote to Sardar Shivdev Singh in reply to his letter dated 17th September, as follows:

"In view of the fact that the council of action people do not wish to cooperate with us and want to have their own programme and wish on every occasion to take advantage of our first statement and thus use us for their own purpose, the best course for us is not to be led by them but to carry on our methods in a peaceful way or we may give our programme and let the community accept it or reject it. We would have done our duty to warn them against their hasty actions and if they persist in their method and lead the Panth astray, then the responsibility will be theirs and not ours. In a nutshell, our method is:

"(1) A walk-out from the present Council as a protest and in this I believe we can prevail upon Hindus to join hands with us.

(2) Abstention from actual meetings of the Council but members to be present in Lahore during sessions to attend if needed with a view to obstruction on constitutional lines. (3) Ministers not to resign their seats and carry on and thus not allow dummies to take their places.

(4) Members not to resign at present but only act as in (1 & 2) above.

(5) To take a plebiscite of the Hindu and Sikh voters saying they don't want reforms but wish present constitution to continue. If we can do this, Government cannot force reform upon 45% of Punjab.

(6) Press for distribution of Province if we do not succeed. Plebiscite to include cessation from Frontier districts which are prominently Mohammedans.

(7) Meeting of protest to be held monthly to record protest.

(8) Formation of Sabhas in towns and villages for propagation of programme.

(9) Special instructions to keep non-violent and to propagate brotherly feeling between different communities[13]".

[13]Ibid.

Formation of Khalsa National Party

When the Akali Oal was finally transformed from religious reform movement to a political party with extreme views on various Sikh issues, often at variance with Chief Khalsa Oiwan and other moderate leaders, Sir Sundar Singh Majithia and his associates decided to form a separate party Which was named as 'Khalsa National Party'. However, the circumstances and bitterness that appear to have preceded the formation of this new party is evident from Sir Sundar Singh's letter dated 19th July, 1936 to Sardar Bhag Singh, B.A., LL.B., Advocate, Gurdaspur which reads as follows:

> "You must have learnt from the papers that on the refusal of the Akali Party to join hands with us for the formation of a joint Board, we had to form a new Party to call the 'Khalsa National Party'. We are now anxious to. enlist the sympathy and support of all of our friends for carrying on the work of this party in different districts of the Province. You have hitherto attended two meetings that we convened. Now I shall be happy if you could join us in the work that is before us. You know that the future of the Sikhs in this Province depends a good deal upon the united action and though a new party has been formed, we are keeping our door open for coming to understanding between the different groups who are working during the coming elections. I hope you would give us the benefit of your cooperation by joining us in this matter."

Constitution of the Khalsa National Party

Students of the Sikh history will find the following aims, objects and the constitution of the Khalsa National Party quite interesting:

> **"Creed of the Party**
>
> 1. To work for the realisation of the ideals of Sikhism, i.e. the promotion of truth, tolerance, individual freedom and brotherly feelings.
>
> 2. To work for the attainment of Swaraj, i.e. full responsible Government.
>
> 3. To work for the abolition of the Communal Award and its replacement by a just and national solution.
>
> 4. *To work for the unification of all communities into a united Indian Nation.*

5. To work for raising the social and economic standard of the masses.

Programme of the Party

1. To promote communal concord as a prelude to development of Nationality and National self-respect.

2. To develop the resources of the Province by harnessing Urban and Rural effort.

3. To raise the standard of living in the villages—

(a) by improving the methods of marketing agricultural products and by raising agricultural prices;

(b) by developing cottage and large scale industries;

(c) by exploring all the resources of the Province with the object of opening new avenues to provide employment for the unemployed.

4. To protect the interest of all minorities including those of the depressed classes.

5. To safeguard civil liberties and to secure abolition of all civil disabilities to which any section of the people may be subjected under the existing political, social or religion systems.

6. The Khalsa National Party without merging itself in any communal Party till the Communal Award is abolished, will cooperate with any Party that works for similar aims and objects.

7. As a preliminary to formal understanding with other communities, the Party will require that absolute freedom should be given to all communities in the performance of religious ceremonies, e.g. taking of processions, possession of religious places of worship, to eat and drink according to one's custom and inclination.

8. The Party will protect the interests of Sikhs in service and secure the community's full share of representation in the recruitment to services and representation on local bodies etc.

9. The Party will work for relieving the burden of taxation including land revenue and water rates.

10. The Party will work for the relief of indebtedness and for the creation of agricultural credit.

11. To work for strict economy in public expenditure and to reduce the cost of Administration.

12. The Party will endeavour to unite all sections of the

Panth to save the Punjab from the establishment of communal tyranny and graft.

13. To protect and promote the use of the Punjabi language and Gurmukhi script.

14. To work for the strengthening of defence forces by increasing Indian element in the Indian Army and also to work for the progressive Indianization of higher ranks.

15. To work for the modernization of Railway and currency policy, in the interests of agricultural and industrial development of the country.

16. To support the policy of protection in order to encourage indigenous industries.

Rules of the Khalsa National Party

1. (a) The Party shall be called "The Khalsa National Party".

(b) The creed and programme of the Party are given in Appendix.

2. (a) There will be one Central Organisation called the Council of the Khalsa National Party with its headquarter at Amritsar.

(b) Branches of the Party will be established at the district headquarters and at such other places as the Central Organisation may decide.

3. Subject to the general supervision and directions of the Central Organisation, the various branches will be responsible for all Party activities within the respective areas.

Membership

4. Membership of the Party is open to every person above 21 years of age, who subscribes to the creed and policy of the Party.

Funds

5. (a) Members of the Central Organisation will pay an annual subscription of Rs. 50/-

(b) Donations or contributions.

(c) Subscriptions from members of the District Organisation.

(d) Any other sources.

Functions of Different Branches

6. (a) To carry out the Party programme and instruction of the Central Organisation.

(b) To educate the people for the proper exercise of votes.

(c) To hold meetings in rural and urban centres for explaining the party programme.

(d) To submit reports of their work to head office.

Executive Committee

7. (a) The Central as well as the District Organisation will have an Executive Committee.

(b) The Central Executive shall consist of not more than 41 members; five of whom will be nominated by the President; the remaining 36 being elected by the Central Council of the Party.

(c) The quorum of the Central Council will consist of 15 members and that of the Executive Committee of 7 members.

8. The Executive Committee of the District Organisation shall consist of 5 members, elected by the District Organisation. Till such time any District Organisation does not begin to function properly, the Central Council will appoint District Executive Committee.

9. The Executive Committee of the District Branches will work under the general supervision and control of the Central Organisation.

Office Bearers

10. The Office-bearers of the Central Organisation will consist of-

(1) President

(2) Two Vice Presidents

(3) One General Secretary

(4) One Joint Secretary

(5) One Treasurer

(6) One Assistant Secretary

(7) One Propaganda Secretary

11. The President, the Vice President, the General Secretary, the Joint Secretary and the Treasurer will be ex-officio members of the Executive Committee.

12. The Executive Committee and the office bearers will be elected every third year.

13. Office bearers of the District Organisation will consist of a President and a Secretary to be elected every third year.

Meetings

14. (a) The meetings of the Central Council of the Khalsa National Party will be held atleast every six months.

(b) The meetings of the Central and Branch Executive Committee will be held atleast once a month.

15. The President will have the power to call a meeting of the Central Councilor of the Executive Committee whenever he may think it fit or when requested in writing by five members.

16. Notice for ordinary meetings will be one week. Emergent meetings can be called with two days' notice.

Parliamentary Board

17. The Central Organisation will set up a Parliament Board for the purpose of selecting candidates and organising elections to the Punjab and Federal Assemblies.

18. Any amendment of the rules or of the creed of the Party shall require atleast one month's notice in writing and shall have to be carried by 2/3rd majority of the members of the Central Council of the Khalsa National Party present at the meeting.

19. Two third majority will be required for taking disciplinary action against a member whose retention in the Party is considered injurious to the Party's interest[@]".

Success of Khalsa National Party

In the Punjab Assembly elections held in 1937, the Khalsa National Party won 16 out of 33 seats allotted to the Sikhs. Sir Sundar Singh, the founder-President of the Party himself contested from Batala constituency against Akali Dal's nominee Jathedar Tara Singh Akarpuri whom he defeated with a margin of 625 votes after a bitter 'war of propaganda' carried out by both the parties. The remaining 17 seats of the Sikhs were also divided among four different groups representing different schools of thought; thereby preventing a common strategy to safeguard interests of their community in the wake of impending period of turmoil and turbulence.

[@]Personal Papers of Sir Sundar Singh Majithia: (Nehru Memorial Museum & Library, New Delhi).

In this context, it is relevant to quote here an article titled "The Sikhs and the New Punjab Assembly" by S. Nahar Singh, M.A. in "Khalsa & Khalsa Advocate", Amritsar dated March 11, 1937:

"New Cabinet of the autonomous Punjab is formed. Formal notification by the Government will be made soon. Sir Sundar Singh Ji Majithia is taken in the new Ministry. To hazard an opinion or make any conjecture about the political future of the Sikhs is, if not impossible, rather difficult.

"They hold only 33 seats in a house of 175 and that too only in one province. But the said aspect of the picture is that no other community is so keenly divided among itself as the Sikhs are. These 33 members are divided into 5 groups. The Khalsa National Parliamentary Party possesses solid strength of 16 members. Master Tara Singh's party whose leadership in the Assembly devolves on the shoulders of Sardar Sampuran Singh has about 8 members. There is one Congressite, 4 Independents and 5 Socialists. The success of the 5 Socialists at the elections among the Sikhs shows that peasantry of the Punjab is treading a way ruinous to sacred religion of the Gurus. Not a single Mohammadan or Hindu socialist Member is elected. What sort of Socialism those members represent, perhaps the Members themselves cannot define. If they profess the system of popular socialistic Government of today, that is Soviet, they shall openly have to renounce or denounce the Sikh religion. For religion and intellect are banished together; where socialism of the workers and peasants reigns.

"Had all the Sikh members, leaving aside their angular differences and petty jealousies united together in the manner of their Muslim colleagues, perhaps, they would have benefitted themselves individually and collectively as a community in a worthy manner. A solid strength of 33 votes could upturn the scales and the members of the minority community would have proved themselves a deciding factor in the political life of the Punjab. But, most of the Sikh members elected by the Sikh voters have neither the good of the Sikh community at heart nor they look forward to the interests of their voters.

"The leader of the Khalsa National Party has rendered a great service to the cause of Sikhism and the Sikhs by making an agreement with the leaders of the majority Party in the

Punjab Legislative Assembly. The need of the hour required it and it was the only wisest course ....

"A member has two-fold duties to perform. He has to safeguard the rights of his community and further he has to represent his constituency, ventilating the hardships under which his electors suffer and to do his best to get their grievances removed.

"The Sikh community has its very knotty problems. The first and foremost is that it wants its full representation in the Legislative Bodies, in Government and Municipal services on the basis of land revenue and other taxes which the community pays towards government treasury. Decrease in the land revenue is another demand. Owing to the increase in the population of the Sikh cultivators and their holdings becoming petty, the agriculturists require more lands. On the economic stage, where the Sikhs stand today, the abolition of Land-Alienation Act would greatly profit the whole community. There are many other demands of the community. There are local difficulties in every constituency, which ought to be removed ...

"Every Sikh is welcome to have his ideals, ideas and programmes, which according to his schemes should raise the community to highest summits of glory. But before cherishing for such attainments, he must also think that he has to work for and to work with the millions of other people, who are to all intents and purposes, illiterate, ignorant and backward as compared with the political idealist.

"Selfish motives if unfulfilled, should not be brought forward to poison the body politic of the Sikh community. The division of the Sikh members in the new Assembly is more dangerous for the interest of the community than their open declaration to join the opposition in a body. Cooperation of the Sikh members as a body can bring fruitful advantages for the Sikhs. Opposition, neither aggressive or offensive and nor defensive as it will be in the new Punjab Assembly would rather lower the high prestige and honour of the Sikhs in the eyes of the Congress as well as the Government.

"The elected Sikh members of Master Tara Singh's party should think twice before they join the Congress or opposition, whether by doing so they would be serving the cause of Sikhism and the Sikh community or not. They should not do it in haste, thinking that no other way is left for them. Even worst of enemies come to terms, make agreements, forget and sweep the past and work together. The political aims of Khalsa National Party and Master Tara Singh's party nearly coincide. The programmes differ according to the means, resources and circumstances of each Party. And now, when the election excitement and temporary bitter feelings have subsided, there is every possibility of a compromise among the brethren of the Tress-knot. I have still a fervent hope and earnestly wish, that all the Sikh members of the Assembly, should sit together and find out a way which would lead the community to the sunny sites of political cliffs[14]".

However, the eternal war of fratricide, accentuated by such divisions, continued. Unsure about their objective and political future Sikhs were caught unprepared during the worst carnage and displacement from their hearths and homes in East Punjab at the time of the great divide of the Indian sub-continent.

That there was nothing wrong with the policy of participation in the Provincial Government of Punjab, as adopted by Khalsa National Party of Sir Sundar Singh Majithia, is also endorsed by none else than Pandit Jawahar Lal Nehru who describes the reasons for Congress decision to accept ministerial responsibilities in States under the Government of India Act, 1935 which provided for limited provincial autonomy and a 'Federal Structure', despite its earlier declared opposition. Pandit Jawahar Lal Nehru gives the following reason for the Congress to join the State Cabinets:

"It had thus a dual policy: to carryon the struggle for independence and at the same time to carry through the legislatures constructive measures of reform. The agrarian question especially demanded immediate attention[@]".

While the Congress had considered to form coalition Governments in the States in which it had clear majority, the Akali Dalled by Master Tara Singh, could not come to an understanding with the majority Party of Sir Sundar Singh even for the minimum programme to safeguard the interests of Sikh community besides common object of attaining 'Swaraj' due to various reasons. "Khalsa Te Khalsa Advocate" (July 5, 1938) gives the impending Gurdwara

[14] "Khalsa Te Khalsa Advocate", Arnritsar. March 11, 1937, p. 6.

[@] Pt. Jawahar Lal Nehru-Discovery of India, p. 372.

elections and Master Tara Singh's determination to win them besides avenging defeat in the Assembly elections as two major factors which forced him to criticise Sir Sundar Singh and his Party for participating in the Provincial Government, terming them as 'Sardar Bahadur Party'. A cartoon which appeared in 'The Hindustan Times' on July 19, 1937 illustrates the nature and extent of criticism these Ministerial colleagues in the Unionist Party had to face during that period.

The cartoon depicts Sir Sundar Singh playing Tabla'; on his left is Sir Sikandar Hayat Khan accompanying him on harmonium and on his right is Chaudhry Sir Chhotu Ram along with other ministerial colleagues.

Khalsa National Party and Demand for Pakistan

Sundar Singh Majithia's Khalsa National Party was opposed to the demand of Pakistan as raised by a Resolution of the Muslim League. Khalsa National Party, in a Resolution passed in its meeting of March 29, 1940, described the demand as extremely harmful. The Resolution said:

> "...As a result of this demand, the Sikhs would be fully justified to demand back the independent Government of Punjab which the British Government had taken over as a trust when Maharaja Duleep Singh was a minor. It will be adventurous on anyone's part to think that the Sikhs would tolerate even for a day the communal domination of any

community in the Punjab, which is not only their house but their sacred land[15]".

The Resolution further warned the Sikhs that "considering the dangers of the situation, this meeting appeals to the Sikhs that they should dissolve their differences and work unitedly for the service of their 'country and the community[16]".

Sir Sundar Singh's Perception of Sikh Rights

The perception of Sir Sundar Singh Majithia and his associates in Chief Khalsa Diwan regarding the protection of their community's interests in the process of Constitutional Reforms undertaken by the British Government is evident from the contents of the two memoranda"—one in the handwriting of Sir Sundar Singh presented to the Governor General, and the second Address presented to the General, Phillip W. Chetmode Bart, new Commander-in-Chief of India presented on 8th July, 1931.

"(A) **Address in Sir Sundar Singh's Handwriting:**

1. **Organisation Which We Represent:** "The deputation appears on behalf of the Chief Khalsa Diwan and the Sikh Associations as representing the Sikh community as a whole. The memorandum was unanimously adopted by a representative meeting of the Sikhs held in Amritsar—the religious and secular centre of the Sikhs in the Punjab.

"The demand of the Sikhs as embodied in the memorandum has been supported in various meetings held in the different parts of the province and outside it. Even the Sikh League has very recently supported a similar demand by an overwhelming majority in an open Session of the League held at Gujranwala. Only a few Sikhs were found who supported the Nehru Committee Report. I, therefore, believe that demand of 30% of representation of the Sikhs on the local Legislature and on similar proportion on the Central Legislature has the general support of the community.

2. **Chief Khalsa Diwan:** "The Chief Khalsa Diwan which was established in 1902 and is a representative body of the Sikhs registered under Act XXI of 1869, has nearly 100 official Singh Sabhas scattered in different parts of the country. The Educational Committee of the Diwan has 275 educational

[15]"Khalsa Te Khalsa Advocate", Amritsar, April 6, 1940, p. 5.

[16]Ibid.

[17]Papers of S. Sundar Singh Majithia: (Nehru Memorial Museum & Library, New Delhi).

institutions affiliated to it. These institutions for boys and girls comprise of 93 Secondary Schools (43 High and 50 Middle Schools) and 182 Primary Schools 102 for boys and 80 for Girls). These schools are managed and run by local efforts of the Sikhs who generally maintain these institutions. The Diwan's Educational Committee has given these institutions Rs. 3,32,366/- in grants-in-aid. The Central Sikh Association has its branches in different parts of the Province and our demand has its support. When *the Montague-Chelmsford Reforms.* were being considered, the Chief Khalsa Diwan took up the cause of the Sikhs.

3. **Importance of the Community:** "While we form only 1 % of the whole population of India, our strength in the Army is 20% and our proportion of the Indian Army raised in the Punjab has been maintained at about 1/3rd of the awards made for the distinguished and gallant services. On the field of battle in the Great War, Sikhs won 1/3rd of the total awards and one half of these were won by the Punjabis. The number of the Sikhs in the Army is believed to be from 80,000 to one lac, a proportion far higher than in case of any other community.

Land Revenue and Canal Rate: "We pay land revenue and canal rate about 40% of the total.

Sikh States and Aristocracy: "We have Sikh States, and the Sikh aristocracy is 2/3rd of the total number of hereditary Chiefs.

Stake in the Country: "We have a very large number of Sikh Gurdwaras and shrines in the Province and outside it in distant places.

"We sent a deputation to England. One of your colleagues on the Central Committee (the Hon'ble Sardar Bahadur Shivdev Singh) and Sardar Ujjal Singh on the Provincial Committee, were members of this deputation. Unfortunately, our deputation reached somewhat late when the question was before Parliament but our demands were considered to be reasonable and hopes were held out that on the next occasion our claims would be duly considered. The report of the deputation appears on the annexure of our memorandum. We hope, Sir, and trust that this time our claims would receive due consideration at your hands.

"We are the third community in the Province and before the advent of the British, we were its rulers. We are essentially the fighting arm of the Government and ever since our connection with the Government, the services rendered by the community in the various fields of battle are so well known that they were

rewarded with fairly large landed grants and landed property attached to them. Though we are chiefly to be found in Punjab, but being free from prejudices of caste and creed, we are to be found in other parts of India and even outside it as well. We are not hard-bound by the caste shackles and are imbued with non-conservative spirit.

4. **Literacy:** "Of the boys attending the educational institutions, we compare as follows:

Mohammadans	533367	8%
Hindus	377314	9%
Sikhs	133633	10%

In female education, our percentage compared with others is—

Mohammadans	1.1%
Hindus	1.5%
Sikhs	1.4%

5. **Sikh Representation:** "If communal representation is altogether abolished either by separate electorates of reservation of seats throughout India, we do not press for any weightage for our community, and in such a case, we are prepared to stand on our merits. But, as this bane of communalism is kept either open or cleverly concealed, then we are not prepared to sacrifice ourselves merely for the sake of show. But if this is not done, then we claim special weightage for our community. We should be given 30% of the elected and nominated seats. The percentage suggested by the Diwan is—

Mohammadans	40%
Hindus	30%
Sikhs	30%

The reason for this is—

(i) We are mainly in Punjab and outside it we are very small in number-Punjab being our Home.

(ii) We have large Gurdwaras with endowments attached to them.

(iii) We have capacity for the defence of the country.

(iv) Our military services in the past and our strength at present.

(v) We were rulers of this Province.

(vi) No minority community should be at the mercy of any majority community and no majority community should be in a position to tyrannise any minority and in such a contingency, the minority should be able to defeat such an attempt.

6. **Joint Electorate:** "We are for joint electorates and this has been accepted by the Diwan in its memorandum. Thus, percentage be conceded and worked out by any method that might be devised. In case this is desired to be put up, then we can later on put up a scheme in which this would be worked out. Such working requires time.

7. **Second Chamber:** "The Diwan has suggested safeguards of a Second Chamber but if the Government be prohibitive, we do not press for it.

8. **Legislative Council**

Social Constituency: We would not disturb the existing constituency to any great extent but special constituencies should remain. However, Zamindar's constituency is an anarchism with 10 voters in the constituency. We want to merge it to Landholder's constituency and throw open the seat to election.

Rural/Urban: We are not for this distinction as it is not present anywhere else in the country. The size of the present constituencies is too large. This will tend to reduce the size of the constituency.

Number of Punjab Legislative Council: We would suggest 100 as the number with percentage for the different communities as suggested above.

Public Service Commission: We are for the establishment of such a Commission in our Province which will see that all the classes of population are fairly represented in *theseroices but the criterion of appointments in all cases to be merit and efficiency* for the work expected to be done.

Local Bodies: In these, joint electorate be tried and communal representatives to be removed from these. The system of proportional representation by a single transferable vote or single vote system be tried in elections to these bodies.

"These are smaller areas and will afford good ground for training and if the working of the system proves satisfactory then there will be a better chance of the extension of Legislatures. So, we would first have the experiment tried in these bodies.

9. **Cabinet:** "We are for proper representation of our community in the Executive and we do not approve of a Chief Minister and his nominees on the Cabinet as this would not work under the system of communal electorate. Such a thing may be an ideal one but it could only be attempted when communal electorates go and joint and open election system is

introduced. The representatives on the Cabinet should be one who have the backing of the majority of the members of minority community in the Council.

10. **Provincial Autonomy:** "We are generally for it, but we want residuary powers to remain with the Central Government.

B. **Address Presented to Viceroy and Governor General of India**

"May it please Your Excellency,

It is with feelings of deep respect that we have the privilege of extending to Your Excellency and the Countess of Willingdon a warm welcome to the Punjab on behalf of the Sikh community. We feel that in welcoming Your Excellency and the Countess of Willingdon we are welcoming two old and tried friends of India. Your Excellency's former connection as a Governor of two Provinces added to distinction of being Governor General of one of the self-governing dominions of the Empire, and your great experience combined with the confidence of the people is likely to be of great service to India in placing her in a position to realise nationality and to achieve self-Government.

"Your Excellency, India is about to enter upon a new era, and we can assure Your Excellency of our steadfast support to any scheme which would help India and particularly the Punjab to attain self-Government.

"We realise that in the early stages India will need all the cooperation and assistance that England can give her, and we have faith that out of this spirit of mutual helpfulness will be borne a deeper understanding and unity for the peace and prosperity of the world.

"We can with some pride express that democracy is not new to us and we are aware both of its perils and its potentialities in making a better life of our' people. Weare no less aware that democracy can only establish itself on foundations of nationality. We cannot conceal from Your Excellency our apprehensions that if disruptive factors, such as separate electorates which put the communities in water-tight compartments from the start, are introduced in the constitution they may imperil the growth of nationality and success of constitutional Government. *We affirm that we claim no special privileges if the new constitution is founded on purely national lines, but if special privileges are extended to other minorities, we respectfully submit that our interests require adequate safeguards to protect our position. To achieve this object, the Sikh community after giving due thought to the present political situation in the country has unanimously arrived at certain conclusions.* We respectfully beg to submit to Your Excellency the 17 points of our claim, and express our determination so far as lies in our power to stand by them, not with any selfish communal object, but to safeguard our position and economic interests, which we have built up after generations of effort; and to save our Province from ruin. We can affirm without violating any cannons of modesty that we have fought in the farflung battlefields of the Empire and the prosperity of the Punjab owes not a little to our efforts. The Central and Colony districts contribute in revenue more than twice the amount of all remaining districts taken together. Your Excellency will undoubtedly agree that those who pay the bulk of taxation are entitled to have an effective voice in its administration.

"We trust Your Excellency will forgive us if we venture to mention another standing grievance. No member of our community has so far found a place in Your Excellency's Cabinet: and in this period of transition we are apprehensive that in the absence of our representative, our legitimate claims may fail to receive proper attention. The Government of India despatch on Reforms came to us as a surprise in its calm acquiescence to the proposals made by the Punjab Government and which were declared as unacceptable with one voice by our community. We have not only interests in the Punjab but our interests in the Army as well as in other Provinces are to us of paramount importance. We, therefore, earnestly pray that Your Excellency will be so good as to put us in a position to safeguard our interests. *We may also respectfully draw Your Excellency's attention to the fact that no Sikh Judge has yet been appointed to the Punjab High Court. Our representation on the Sandhurst Committee and the Round Table Conference* is *also inadequate and we have had yet no representative on the Public Service Commission. In the I.C.S. Examination, Punjabi—our mother tongue-has not been recognised as one of the vernaculars* in *spite of our repeated requests and representations.* In this connection, we may mention that in the Punjab University, Punjabi has been given an equal status with Urdu and Hindi up to B.A.

"Before we conclude, we cannot help referring to the economic distress which is telling heavily upon the Punjab peasantry. It is a situation which requires a careful and sympathetic handling and demands early adjustment of agricultural debt and the Government demand on the basis of current prices.

"In conclusion, we beg to assure Your Excellency of the desire of our community to keep bright its traditions of loyalty to the Crown and service to the Motherland, and we beg to offer our loyal cooperation in support of policies initiated by Your Excellency in the interest of India and the Empire."

The Sikhs and the Future Constitution of India and Punjab

1. The Sikhs are anxious to secure a National Government and are therefore opposed to any communal majority by statute or any reservation of seats by law for a majority community.

2. The Sikhs occupy an unrivalled position in the Punjab as is reflected by their sacrifices in the defence of India and in the national movements and their stake in the province and therefore demand 30 per cent representation in the Punjab Legislature and Administration.

3. In the Punjab Cabinet and the Public Service Commission, the Sikh community should have a one-third share.

4. If no agreement is reached on the above basis, the boundaries of the Punjab may be so altered by transferring predominantly Mohammadan areas to the Frontier Province as to effect communal balance. In this re-constituted Punjab, there should be joint electorates, with no reservation of seats.

5. If neither of the above alternative is acceptable, the Punjab may be administered by the newly constituted responsible Central Government till mutual agreement on the communal question is arrived at.

6. Punjabi should be the official language of the Province. It should be optional with the Sikhs and others to use Gurmukhi script if they so desire.

Central

7. The Sikhs should be given 5 per cent of the total number of seats reserved for British India in each of the Upper and Lower Houses.

8. There should always be at least one Sikh in the Central Cabinet.

9. In case an Army Council is constituted, the Sikhs should be adequately represented on it.

10. The Sikhs have always had a special connection with the Army and therefore the same proportion of Sikhs should be maintained in the Army as before the War.

11. The Sikhs should have effective representation in the! All-India

Services and should be represented on the Central Public Service Commission.

12. All residuary powers should vest in the Central Government.

13. The Central Government should have special specified powers to protect minorities.

Other Provinces

14. The Sikhs should have the same weightage in other Provinces as is accorded to other minorities.

General

15. The Provincial and Central Government should declare religious neutrality and while maintaining existing religious endowments should not create new ones.

16. The State should provide for teaching of Gurmukhi script where a certain fixed number of scholars is forthcoming.

17. Any safeguards guaranteed in the Constitution for the Sikhs should not be rescinded or modified without their express consent.

Separate Identity of the Community

Sir Sundar Singh's interview with the Viceroy of India on 7th October 1939 at 11.30 AM and his following letter dated 11th October 1939 to Viceroy's Office, confirmed his views about the identity of the Sikhs as a separate religious community:

Lahore,
11th October 1939

"My dear Laithwaite,

After my interview with His Excellency on the 7th of September, I had some conversation with you, and now that further developments may take place on account of the interviews His Excellency is granting to different leaders, both of the Congress and others in India, I wish to bring to the notice of His Excellency that in any scheme for the step forward in the Reforms of this country, the rights and claims of th~ Sikh community as an important community may not be ignored. *We have a separate identity as a community given to us by our Gurus and we will not be prepared to merge it into any other community.* This attitude of the community in the past has led the Hindus (who wanted to absorb us in themselves) to call us by the name of "neo-Khalsas" and even big Hindu leaders, both of Congress and other communities, have done their level best to ignore the Sikhs in the past. The Nehru (Pandit Moti Lal Nehru) Committee Report and the views expressed by Mr. Jinnah, Pandit Madan Mohan Malviya and Mr. Sriniawas Shastri are proofs positive of this.

"The Sikh community, as, you know, has not stinted in any way in the service of the Empire and has not hesitated to spill their bluest blood in the service of British Government wherever they have been called upon to serve. You must have noticed in the Resolution passed in a meeting of the Sikhs in Amritsar on the Ist of October, a copy of which was sent to you by the Chief Khalsa Diwan, that when the last Reforms were introduced in the country, we did not receive the due recognition as a minority community. So far, we have not received any representation on the Central Executive Council, and this omission from the Centre is a point which the community is feeling very strongly.

"Although His Excellency is sure to safeguard our interests, but we feel that without a representative of the community at the Centre, our needs and requirements would not be brought to the notice of His Excellency and the Home Government in time, and thus we go unrepresented and our claims remain unrecognised.

"I trust and hope that whatever scheme His Excellency is pleased to introduce in the best interests of the country, *the recognition of the Sikh rights and consideration for their feelings, sentiments and demands will not be ignored,* and that His Excellency will be pleased to give the Sikh community their rightful place in the future administration of this country. I am taking the liberty of bringing this to the notice of His Excellency because on the occasion of my interview, my talk was confined chiefly to the consideration as to how best the Sikhs could serve the Government in the present world-wide crisis.

"It must be noticed from our Resolution that our offer of service was not *in any way traditional and that it was a voluntary offer of service from a community with loyal traditions behind them* in the service of the Empire.

"I request you to kindly bring this to the notice of His Excellency, so that our claims may not be ignored."

Yours sincerely,
(Sd) Sundar Singh Majithia

J.G. Laithwaite, Esquire, C.S.I., C.I.E.
Private Secretary to
H.E. the Viceroy,
New Delhi.

8

Sir Sundar Singh and Other Important Events

While the role and contribution of Sir Sundar Singh Majithia during his tenure as Revenue Minister of Punjab in economic and agrarian reforms is discussed in the subsequent Chapter, it is pertinent to briefly refer to his activities and role in some other important events related to his community during the period under review.

Shahid Ganj Affair

Gurdwara Shahid Ganj was situated in the premises of a Masjid in Lahore and it was the sacred place where thousands of Sikhs had been executed during the 18th century. There arose a conflict between the Sikhs and Muslims when the Gurdwara Committee of Lahore wanted to demolish the old building for its re-construction and there followed an agitation by both the communities. There were allegations and counter-allegations between Sir Sundar Singh Majithia's Party and Master Tara Singh's Party. In reply to Master Tara Singh's statement of March 30, 1938 about the Shahid Ganj affair, Sardar Sundar Singh Majithia said:

> "...I am not incharge of any Gurdwara; so, it is not my conduct of the management of the Gurdwaras that is being condemned by the Sikhs but of the present head of the SGPC.... As a Sikh, all the Panthic Gurdwaras are as sacred to me and I will not hesitate in doing my humble bit by way of any sacrifice that is demanded of me by my community in safeguarding the sanctity of my holy places of worship but as a member of the Government, it is my duty to see that peace and tranquility is established in my dear province[1]".

[1]Papers of Sir Sundar Singh Majithia: (Nehru Memorial Library, New Delhi: File No. 73, p. 2).

Sir Sundar Singh Majithia and his Khalsa National Party adopted a strong attitude towards the Government, in spite of the fact that Sundar Singh was its member. When the Shahid Ganj affair began to take a serious turn, Sundar Singh Majithia threatened to resign and lead an agitation and this made Sir Sikandar Hyat Khan prevent Malik Barkat Ali's Bill in the Assembly. This was a great victory for the Sikhs that the Bill was dropped in spite of Muslim majority and the credit for it goes to Sundar Singh Majithia.

Gurdwara Mal Tekri (Hazur Sahib)

Gurdwara Maltekri, Hyderabad (Deccan) is a historical Gurdwara in the sacred memory of the Tenth Guru, Gobind Singh. Some Muslims had demolished the 'Manji Sahib' in it and constructed a tomb of one Hyat Khan along with two or three other tombs. The conflict between the Sikhs and Muslims continued for a long time. The territory carne under the Nizam of Hyderabad. The Chief Khalsa Diwan undertook to fight the case and made sincere efforts to secure the rights of the Sikhs.

Sundar Singh Majithia worked with great sincerity and enthusiasm for the Sikh rights and exercised his influence over the Nizam of Hyderabad by writing to him on several occasions. He also visited the site of the Gurdwara and met the Nizam personally. The honourable Bhai Kahan Singh of Nabha, Sant Jawala Singh and Akali Kaur Singh gave evidence before the court which was constituted to decide the case. The result of all these efforts was that the case was decided in favour of the Sikhs.

Sundar Singh Majithia who was making every possible effort for the cause and who was in touch with the progress of the case received the following telegram, No. 293, dated December 17, 1929 from Mr. S. Kalyaranam, Vakil High Court, Hyderabad, Deccan:

"Judgement pronounced. Maltekri Gurdwara Established. Ordered Disinterment of Hyat Khan's body within one month. Adjacent Building Declared Mosque. Letter follows[2]".

It was a great victory for the Sikhs in which Sundar Singh Majithia had played a significant role.

Question of 'Jhatka' Meat

There was a strong resentment among the Sikhs on the prohibition of 'Jhatka' meat in various institutions and cities. The Sikhs are

[2]"Khalsa Te Khalsa Advocate", Amritsar, December 14, 1929.

religiously prohibited from taking any other form of meat than the 'Jhatka'. The Khalsa National Party in its resolution, No.3, at its general session on August 15, 1937 declared:

"Khalsa National Party strongly believes that in Government schools, other educational institutions, hospitals, jails, Police Lines and Railway Stations, restrictions on 'Jhatka' meat should be withdrawn, because religiously, Sikhs cannot take any meat except 'Jhatka'[3].

Speaking on an adjournment motion in the Punjab Legislative Assembly, Sundar Singh Majithia declared:

"...We will not slacken our endeavours and I will go on pressing this view point on my colleagues till our legitimate grievances in this respect are removed[4]".

The restrictions on 'Jhatka' meat were later on withdrawn gradually from various places.

Sundar Singh and Other Gurdwara Agitations

Sir Sundar Singh Majithia, although dubbed by his opponents as one of the 'yes-men' (Sardar Bahadur Party) of the Government, was never found lagging behind whenever his community was suffering difficulties. He was always working in the spirit of a true Sikh to get the grievances of the Sikhs redressed by exercising his great influence with the British. He was the Executive Councillor of the Punjab Government when the tragedy of Nankana Sahib took place. He was greatly shocked when the news of the great massacre perpetrated by Mahant Narain Dass's goondas reached him. He sent a telegram from Rawalpindi to S. Kartar Singh Jhabbar and others asking them not to cremate the martyrs since he was bringing the Punjab Governor so that he could witness the tragic scene. On February 23, 1921, Sundar Singh Majithia along with the Governor and other English officials and Councillors reached Nankana Sahib and showed them the tragic scene. It had a great effect on the Governor's heart who was shocked. The British Government, later on, handed over the Gurdwara to the Sikhs.

Similarly during the 'Guru Ka Bagh' Morcha in Amritsar, he took the British officers to the scene of merciless beating of the

[3]"Khalsa Te Khalsa Advocate", Amritsar, August 17, 1937, p. 9.

[4]Papers of S. Sundar Singh Majithia. (Nehru Memorial Library, New Delhi: File No. 66, p. 1).

Sikhs and influenced them to withdraw the prohibitory orders.

While his strong views are evident from his Note submitted to the Government (reproduced in the earlier Chapter), he spoke about the Jaitu tragedy while presiding over the 'Sikh Educational Conference' at Patiala. He said:

> "We have been brought up in difficulties and odd situations and they have made us fearless and lions. I am very much sorry and shocked over the tragedy and loss of lives[5]". He further asked the Khalsa to be fearless because true Sikhs neither coerce anybody nor do they fear from anyone."

Reservation for Sikhs in Military and Civil Services

Sir Sundar Singh had always endeavoured to secure more rights and reservations for the Sikhs in Military and Civil Services which, in his opinion, would lead to social and economic advancement of the Sikh community and their prestige as a militant and brave community would be established again. In pursuance of his effort, he continued correspondence with the Governor-General of India, and sent him Notes and suggestions for the recruitment of more Sikhs in the Army. In this connection, he had an interview with the Viceroy on October 7, 1939 at 11.30 AM and discussed a few points including the percentage of the Sikhs in the Army which he gave as 39.6% of the total Indian troops which went to War[6]. While asking for the maintenance of this percentage, he requested that the percentage should be raised in Army Headquarters and other Military Departments. He also requested for starting a military training class for the students of the Khalsa College, Amritsar. The following memorandum subsequently submitted by Sir Sundar Singh to the Viceroy indicates his deep concern for employment opportunities for Sikhs in the Army.

"May It Please Your Excellency,

> "I have to thank Your Excellency for the important discussions we had on the 7th morning regarding many points concerning Sikhs. I am putting these points in detail for Your Excellency's careful consideration:

[5]"Khalsa Te Khalsa Advocate", Amritsar, April 24, 1924, p. 5.

[6]Papers of S. Sundar Singh Majithia. (Nehru Memorial Library, New Delhi, File No. 86, p. 17).

1. (a) Position of the Sikhs in the Army

Your Excellency will be pleased to note that the Punjab used to supply nearly half of the Indian soldiers in the Indian Army before the War but of this supply Sikhs contributed 39.6%. In other words, Sikhs provided nearly double their fair share of recruits. So, my request is that present strength to be brought up to that percentage now which has been very much reduced after the War.

(b) The same percentage (as in 1(a)) may be raised in the Army Headquarter and other military departments.

2. (a) Military training class to be started at Khalsa College, Amritsar.

(b) The sons of military men will be given preference in joining this class.

(c) Military trained students from this class, if found fit, be encouraged by providing them service in the regular Army and certain posts be reserved for these students.

(d) Once donations were given to Khalsa College by various Sikh regiments, similar arrangement may be made now for the purpose of military training class at Khalsa College.

(e) Once various Sikh regiments contemplated to construct Soldiers' Home at Amritsar and funds were provided for the purpose; a similar arrangement be made to provide funds for this military class at Khalsa College.

(f) We understand that there are Gurdwara funds in the various Sikh Regimental Gurdwaras under the control of their respective C.Os. Contributions from these funds be provided for the military class at Khalsa College.

3. There were separate Regiments composed of Mazhabi Sikhs which have been disbanded. My request is that these be reconstituted again. Allow me to point out to Your Excellency that during the last War these Mazhabi Sikh soldiers reached a very high standard so that they deserve to be encouraged.

4. In order to secure good recruitment for the military, it is very essential to announce:

(a) that rewards in the shape of lands and 'Jagirs' will be given to those who enlist and serve in the Army during the present crisis or to the relations of those who happen to be killed in the War.

(b) that the relations and dependents of those who go to War will be looked after by the Government and protected during their absence.

5. (a) His Excellency, the Commander-in-Chief's speech the other day in connection with the War material factories to be started in India: my suggestion is that a private enterprise under Government supervision will be less costly and should be encouraged.

(b) A certain percentage in these factories be reserved for martial class in capital, management and labour."*

Sardar Surjit Singh Majithia, Flying Officer, Madras

*Ibid.

He also encouraged his youngest son, Surjit Singh Majithia to join the Air Force during that period. S. Surjit Singh Majithia later joined Pt. Jawahar Lal Nehru's Cabinet as Deputy Defence Minister of India after Nation's freedom. His grandson Dalip Singh son of S. Kirpal Singh also joined Air Force. Both of them became Sq. leaders before quitting for domestic reasons.

In Civil Services

Sundar Singh first got 20% quota for the Sikhs in Government services in 1920. Again on October 8, 1938, when he was Revenue Minister of the Punjab, he was responsible for a declaration of 20% reservation for the Sikhs. The Home Department issued a Notification No. 7929-L-2643-S.G.38/33386 on behalf of the Punjab Government which gave 50% to Muslims, 30% to Hindus and 20% to the Sikhs.

Thousands of Sikhs got services in Military and Civil services with his help. He, thus, secured economic and social advantages for the community.

In a letter marked 'Personal & Confidential' dated October 1939 addressed to Diwan N. Gopalaswamy Iyengar, Prime Minister of Jammu & Kashmir State, Sardar Sundar Singh Majithia complained about the low percentage of Sikhs in the State services. Then he wrote:

> "If you permit me to say, the Sikhs being an important minority deserve some weightage as has been granted to them in the Punjab ....[7]".
>
> He further added, "The fact that the Sikhs were the rulers of the Punjab and Kashmir State before the present Government, gives them a stronger claim for a suitable representation on the services, particularly in the State[8]".
>
> He demanded: "If you could be pleased to see your way to appoint suitable Sikh Officers as Heads of Departments or on other similar key positions, perhaps, they could look after the interests of the Sikhs ....[9]".

Anand Marriage Act

Anand Marriage or marriage according to Sikh customs was an essential item on the social reform programme of the Chief Khalsa Diwan, but due to opposition it was not widely accepted and practised and those practising it were teased and ridiculed. There were legal difficulties also. It necessitated preaching of Sikh principles on the one hand, and performance of marriage on the

[7]Papers of S. Sundar Singh Majithia. Nehru Memorial Library, New Delhi, File No. 88, p. 1.

[8]Ibid.

[9]Ibid.

other hand. In respect of Personal Law, Sikhs were regarded as part of Hindus and, therefore, unless and until an Act was passed to this effect, all marriages performed in this manner were invalid. When Sardar Sundar Singh Majithia became member of Indian Imperial Legislative Council in 1909, he piloted the Anand Marriage Bill moved by Tikka Ripudaman Singh of Nabha and got it passed in spite of the opposition of the Hindu Members and the Sanatani Sikhs. Speaking on the Bill, he said:

> "Sikhism is a faith believing in unity of God and brotherhood of man. Persons of all castes and religions are free to join it. Guru Amar Dass had made it a principle that those who wanted to see him must dine irrespective of caste and creed in the Langar. Guru Gobind Singh emphasised more on it and initiated 'Amrit' in one untensil... The teachings of our Gurus call upon us to give up caste distinctions. I believe that His Excellency (Governor-General) and other Hon'ble Members would agree with me that a religion like Sikhism, which accepts people from all castes and religions cannot remain forever within the domain of the principles of 'Shastras'....[10]"

Freedom of Kirpan

'Kirpan', which is one of the five sacred symbols of Khalsa, had been banned by the Government in various Provinces. Sardar Sundar Singh Majithia did valuable service for the community by securing freedom of the sword from the clutches of the Law. The 'Kirpan' Movement was first started in 1912-1913 when some arrests were also made. The Majithia Sardar, by exercising his influence, got the Law prohibiting the carrying of 'Kirpans' revoked in the Punjab on June 25, 1914; in Delhi on July 17, 1914; in Burma on October 27, 1914; in U.P. on February 26, 1917, and in N.W.F.P. on January 26, 1917[11]. He still was continuing his efforts for its freedom in other Provinces when the Government withdrew the ban on May 19, 1927 from all over India.

[10] Sir Sundar Singh Majithia: Editor S. Mehar Singh 'Rawel', p. 27.
[11] Ibid, p. 44.

The Punjab & Sind Bank Limited

Sardar Sundar Singh Majithia* proved himself to be a great economist as well. In 1908, his efforts along with those of Tirlochan

Painting courtesy 'Sikh Heritage in Paintings' published by Punjab & Sind Bank (sitting Left to Right) S. Tirlochen Singh, Bhai Vir Singh and Sir Sundar Singh.

*The Majithia Sardar, who was the Founder of the Punjab & Sind Bank Ltd. had close association with S. Tirlochan Singh whom he always referred as "Leo Ji" in his personal letters and references, and together with Bhai Vir Singh Ji, this famous trio of friends actively worked for the development of this Bank and performed opening ceremonies of many of its Branches. He continued to work on its Board of Directors till 1934 when he resigned because of his pressing political engagements. The following references from his personal diaries indicate attachment which he had for the Bank:

(i) Jan. 24, 1928: Myself and S. Tirlochan Singh went by car to inspect the building (under construction) for Punjab & Sind Bank.

(ii) Dee. 7, 1934: Today, Ludhiana Branch of PSB Ltd. was opened after 'bhog' of Sri Guru Granth Sahib. Had food at the house of Bhai Sahib Ji (Arjan Singh) Bagrian. Tirlochan Singh Ji and Bhai Sahib Vir Singh Ji went back to Amritsar and I started for Ambala.

(iii) Dec. 29,1934: Attended the Board Meeting of the PSB Ltd. and resigned from its Directorship, which *Leo Ji* felt very much and he became emotional.

Singh and Bhai Vir Singh resulted in the establishment of the Punjab & Sind Bank Ltd. allied with the Chief Khalsa Diwan, with the aim to facilitate economic development of their community. With Rs. 7609 crores of deposit and Rs. 3186 crores of advances, employing 12167 staff members and having 809 branches including extension counters, as at the end of March 1998, the Punjab & Sind Bank which was nationalised in 1980, has become one of the pioneering banking institutions of the country, assisting thousands of businessmen and entrepreneurs. That the growth of this banking institution, has been phenomenal, due to the vision and administrative capability of its founders and subsequent leadership provided by late Dr. Inderjit Singh, is also evident from the following business figures of the Bank as appeared in the Khalsa Te Khalsa Advocate Amritsar on Dec. 8, 1928:

"Punjab & Sind Bank Ltd.,

Offices: Amritsar, Lahore, Layal (pur), Gujranwala & Rawalpindi.

Capital: Rs. 10,00,000

Paid up capital: Rs. 7,75,000

Call money: Rs. 3,87,500

Deposit: Rs. 4,05,040

Reserve Fund: Rs. 14,00,000

Interest on Current Account: 2.25% p.a.

Interest on Savings Bank Account: 4.5% p.a.

Fixed Deposits: 4 to 5% p.a.

depending upon period and amount which could be agreed in writing; special concessions for widows and dividend to share holders @15% p.a.

Humble servant: Tirlochan Singh, M.A., L.L.B., Managing Director".

Imperial Bank of India

His professional acumen as a Banker was further recognised with his appointment on the Board of Governors of Imperial Bank of India, which he gladly accepted as is evident from his notings in personal diaries:

January 20, 1928:

"Reached Amritsar from Patiala. Letter from Sir Basil Backet had already arrived. I was asked whether I was prepared as nominated Governor of Imperial Bank of India in place of late

Sir Ganga Ram. Letter was dated 14th January 1928 and was waiting for me at Amritsar. Sent a letter of acceptance with thanks.

January 28, 1928:

Notification of Government of India about my appointment as Governor of Imperial Bank of India was received today.

A copy of letter dated 11th May 1929 informing Sardar Sundar Singh Majithia about the proposed Central Board Meeting is reproduced hereunder:

IMPERIAL BANK OF INDIA

Central Office
Bombay
11th May 1929

Sardar Bahadur Sir Sundar Singh Majithia, C.I.E.
Majithia House, Albert Road
Amritsar

Dear Sir,

Central Board Meeting

"We beg to inform you that we propose to hold a formal Meeting of the Central Board on Wednesday, the 5th June 1929 immediately after the Weekly Meeting of the Committee of the Central Board to be held on that day, and to enclose a copy of the Agenda of the Meeting.

"2. In this connection, we enclose for your information a copy of a Memorandum which was circulated to the Governors when. a similar formal Meeting was held in May, 1925. We propose to hold the Central Board Meeting at which the half yearly accounts are to be submitted etc. early in July. The first Agenda for this Meeting will be issued shortly.

"3. As explained in the Memorandum, your attendance at this Meeting will not be necessary, but should you propose to attend please inform us of your intention to do so."

Yours faithfully,
Sd/-
Managing Governor

Sugar Factory

He established a big sugar factory at Gorakhpur in 1909 and proved his capability as a good industrialist. He took keen interest in development of his Saraya Estate in U.P. despite his political and administrative pre-occupations in Punjab—a fact that was well-known among the politicians and even the British officers, as obvious from the following letter dated October 23, 1928 from Sir W.H. Hailey, Governor of Punjab, who while replying to Sir Sundar Singh's plea about Raja Ripudaman Singh of Nabha, also refers to prospects of good sugar crop at Gorakhpur:

Governor's Camp
United Province
October 23, 1928

My dear Sundar Singh,

"1 have just had your letter of the 18th, and am sorry that you are still troubled about the affairs of the Khalsa College. 1 asked Mr. Cunningham to get H.E. the Viceroy to look again into the question of the *Nabha endowment; but my understanding was that the Viceroy would not take the question up himself, but would allow you a further opportunity of representing the case* to *him in order that he might be in a position to determine whether there were any grounds in his mind for reopening it.* I am not sure if you asked for this opportunity, but I know that Mr. Cunningham would be glad to secure an interview for you if you would ask him to do so. I think that the re-opening of the question depends on the result of that interview, for I would not think it possible for either Sir Geoffrey or me to make a definite recommendation to the Viceroy in the matter in view of the fact that he has already once considered it. I think that it must be left for him to re-open it if he sees good ground for doing so; and it was this which I intended to secure by speaking to Mr. Cunningham. *"I am afraid that the shortage of rain will affect the sugar crop a good deal, but* it *seems to me that you have been luckier in Gorakhpur than elsewhere,* and I hope you will ultimately find that there is not any real shortage of material for your factory[12]".

With best wishes,

I am,

Yours sincerely,
(Sd) Sir W.H. Hailey

That he took a keen personal interest for the development of his Estate and Sugar Factory at Sardar Nagar in Gorakhpur (United Province) is also evident from the letter dated 27.7.1936 by Shri Charan Mall from Jhelum:

Jhelum,
27.7.36

Respected Maharaj Ji,

"I had just a conversation with you on telephone. Your telegram of 24th reached me at Murree on the morning of 26th and I wrote a letter to you. I would have complied with your wishes at once but for the fact that I was on leave at Murree and. my Deputy Commissioner was away on tour. The only hitch in my way was that certain Sikh gentlemen and later on S.S. Bhagwan Dass son of Sardar Tola Ram Singh of Cambellpur, while discussing the question of next elections remarked that there would be a meeting at your house at Amritsar on the 2nd August and I was afraid that we may not cross each other on the way. Your letter of 24th reached me on 27.7.36 at Jhelum.

"2. Major General Steward, Director Supplies & Transport India, is busy with scheme representation of fruit and meat and I expected him on tour when rain had fallen in the plains. I discussed the whole case with him in December last. He is keen to purchase everything for the S.T. without intervention of a middleman. In this

[12]Personal Papers of Sir Sundar Singh Majithia: (Nehru Memorial Museum & Library, New Delhi).

connection, I suggested it to him that he should purchase sugar direct from the factory owners. He asked me definitely the advantage the S&T would have and I replied that he would have the right quantity, the right quality, the S.T. will have to pay the cost atleast less by the amount which the contractors make over it. In this connection, I suggested definitely your sugar factory at Saryaa and the name of your goodself. He remarked that he would not have any hesitation in making direct purchases if he were to get sugar of standard type. I got your samples and went to see him at Delhi again before his move to Simla but unfortunately he was out in camp. As soon as I know that he is definitely at Simla, I would take the samples which I have already got and show them to him. Possibly, the only obstruction in our way is that S&T contracts date every year from 1st April and usually the tenders for the next contracts are taken in the months of January or early February. There is thus a lot of time to definite understanding with the military department.

"3. I wrote to S. Kirpal Singh Ji on the 2nd of May what I thought of the future of Indian Sugar adding that I expected trouble in sugar matters, as the stocks of sugar would be very high and rates must go down. I had no reply to this letter.

"4. The future of Indian sugar depends mainly on the control of sugar on the lines of cement. Mr. Davidson, General Manager, Bird & Co. discussed the whole situation with me at Jhelum and I suggested to him and to other manufacturers the following two solutions:

1. Sugar Control Board (fixing all-India Prices).

2. If two or three companies join together, they could purchase the sugar of the important factories. The Russian Government has entered into an agreement with Afghan Government for articles including, of course, sugar. There are more consignments from Java also corning and Russian sugar gaining popularity in Afghanistan.

"5. Some sort of understanding will have to be arrived at between sugar manufacturers and sugar dealers and it would be by no means easy for sugar dealers to make a large sum by way of commission without any trouble."

6. Your agents, Messrs. Mool Chand Mohan Lal have been in correspondence with me recently and I told them that I have not that least hesitation to take up the work on fairly reasonable terms.

"7. Re-organisation in remote corners and monopoly of sugar in Indian States is both difficult and expensive and it would not be possible for me to carry out this work on the rate of commission which is generally given to brokers. Time has now come when the sugar manufacturers will have to take the sales in their own hands, for there is a little good in leaving this article in the hands of selling agents. You would excuse me if I repeat my old suggestion that you may discontinue the present agency system for sale and re-organise under your direct care and control the sales of your sugar. You also realise that success in your case is mainly the result of your direct supervision and schemes in these days of hard competition. I will discuss this case when I come to Amritsar on the 2nd or 3rd of August to see you.

"8. Is Sardar Mangal Singh Ji standing for elections? I shall be grateful for a reply on this point for reasons known to him. I believe, this point may arise at the meeting at your house but again I will be there on that day.

"9. I hope, you have sent a reply to the Trade Commissioner, Bombay. But, now the case is to be forwarded by Trade - Commissioner Bombay and the Director General of Commission Intelligible Calcutta to the Trade Commissioner at London. It is most unfortunate that Sardar Bahadur Sardar Mohan Singh got his leg fractured when he was arranging to get the work for my son Mr. P.N. Kayshap. Sardar Mohan Singh is keenly interested in the well-fare of my son for whom he has very high opinion. The Trade Commissioner has made enquiry from several banks also and the reports so far as I know are very favourable.[@]"

[@]Personal Papers of Sir Sundar Singh Majithia: (Nehru Memorial Museur & Library, New Delhi).

9

Sir Sundar Singh's Role as Revenue Minister

During his first tenure as a Member of Punjab Legislative Council with effect from 23rd February 1921 to early 1926, Sir Sundar Singh Majithia did his best to protect the interests of agriculturists, even in the face of severe criticism. Despite Government's pre-occupation with other pressing issues pertaining to the ongoing movement leading to the enactment of Sikh Gurdwaras and Shrines Act, 1925 and other important issues, Sir Sundar Singh took initiative in some important legislations to protect the interests of agriculturists along with undertaking some important development projects in the State besides setting high standards of working of his department. His subsequent tenure as Revenue Minister of Punjab under the Prime Minister, Sir Sikandar Hayat Khan was equally remarkable as farmers' champion in the company of his other ministerial colleagues like Chaudhary Sir Chhotu Ram, B.A., LL.B., Minister of Development (who represented Jhajjar General-Rural seat), Hon'ble Mr. Manohar Lal, M.A., Finance Minister (who represented University Constituency), Nawabzada Major Khizar Hyat Khan Tiwana, Minister of Public Works, and, Mian Abdul Haq, Minister of Education.

Sir Sundar Singh's first term as Revenue Member of Punjab Legislative Council in 1921 was marked by lower crop out-put, as per the report of Mr. H.W. Nicholson, Executive Engineer, On Special Duty, who prepared. following reports about Punjab:

> **Character of the Seasons:** "The year 1921-22 started under conditions unfavourable to the sowing of Kharif crops and the monsoon came too late to enable any large addition to the Kharif sowings to be made. But full advantage was taken of the monsoon to sow as large an area of Rabi crops as possible. Although there was no rain during November, December and

January, river supplies were well maintained with the result that the Rabi area irrigated exceeded that of the corresponding season of the previous year by about 1,000,000 acres. The rain which fell in February and March was well distributed, benefited the standing Rabi crops, and assisted the early Kharif sowings of the following year. In April and May of the year 1922-23 the weather was much drier than usual and the rainfall in moderate to large defect. The monsoon was fitful till about the end of August when it strengthened and continued to be vigorous during the first half of September, giving good and general rainfall throughout the Province. It ended on the 22nd September and the total rainfall during the period June to September was slightly in excess of the normal. The September rains were followed by light showers in the first and second weeks of October which enabled good rabi sowings to be made, and the rains which fell during the winter proved useful for the maturing of the crop, the rabi irrigation being a record. In contrast to the previous two years the year 1923-24 opened with favourable conditions for the Kharif crop while the early Rabi sowings were greatly helped by good and general rainfall during the months of August and September, followed by light rain in March which benefited the standing crops.

Results: "The average area irrigated in the Province by Government works of all classes was 10.5 million acres as compared with 9.25 million acres, the average of the previous triennium. In addition to this, an average of the previous triennium. In addition to this, an average area of 695,000 acres was irrigated from channels, which although drawing their supplies from British canals, lie wholly in Indian States. The area irrigated in 1922-23 was the largest on record and exceeded the average of the triennium ending 1918-21 by 1,454,964 acres.

"Taking productive works, only, the area irrigated during each of the three years showed an improvement on the figures of the previous triennium and the average of the triennium was over a million acres more than of the previous period. This increase was shared by all the canals without exception and was due to the favourable climatic conditions obtaining and to the steady development on the canals of the Triple Project, especially the Lower Bari Doab.

"The canals in operation (Productive and Unproductive) paid 14.5 per cent in 1921-22, 15.75 per cent in 1922-23, and 17.5 per cent in 1923-24 on a total capital expenditure of Rs. 2,327 lakhs incurred on them.

Works completed: "The remodelling of the headworks of the Lower Jhelum canal at Rasul and the construction of a subsidiary weir at Tajawala, the headworks of the Western and Eastern Jumna canals, were completed[1]".

Sir Sundar Singh Majithia along with his colleagues in the Legislative Council worked for the review of the Land Revenue System to provide relief to small land-holders. On a resolution to constitute a Committee to examine the assessment and land revenue policy and to ensure that no new settlement is started until the report of the proposed Committee is published, he spoke in the Punjab Legislative Council debates in July/August, 1921:

"....My friend while dealing with the grievances of Zamindars referred to the assessment of income-tax and said that as in the case of income-tax people are required to show their accounts, similar action is not taken in the matter of land revenue assessments.

"I am afraid, there is a very great difficulty experienced by income-tax assessors in finding out the true income of an assessee. An endeavour is always made on the latter's part to hide facts and not to give true statements of their accounts. I presume and I think it is only natural that a Zamindar also would be very chary in giving true accounts of his income and expenditure. I do not mean to say that accounts are kept by Zamindars. I know Zamindars do not keep accounts, but all the same, one has to depend upon some sort of assessment or valuation of all those factors in corning to a conclusion on the subject ....

"He also mentioned as an example the Multan settlements ... I hope our friends will understand that assessments of revenue are only to be taken on the lands which are actually under cultivation and on which crops have matured. For the rest of the area, particularly those parts which are irrigated by wells, only a sort of assessment is made on parts actually irrigated and brought under cultivation from wells and not the whole area of a Zamindar's holding."

[1]National Archives of India, New Delhi.

"I remember one passage particularly in the speech of my friend, Mr. Shah Nawaz, in which he said that more land was lying waste in olden times on account of the policy of the officials of the East India Company. I would ask my friend to picture to himself the condition of the country some years back before colonization operations of various areas was started in Lyallpur, Montgomery Bars,. Perhaps, my friend will remember that it was impossible to obtain in those barren tracts either water or any other commodities. Beyond a little milk, it was impossible to obtain any thing else and least of all water. And what have those tracts now become by the bringing of water from the rivers of the Punjab which before the colonization went unharnessed and to waste? I do not ask him to look at it from a scientific stand point because, of course, there is no waste in nature; whatever water is drawn up by the Sun is brought back by the clouds in the form of rain. Independently of Nature's aid, I would ask him to consider what the result has been of irrigation.

"He mentioned also something about permanent settlements. I would simply point out to him the condition of the tenantry in the permanently settled areas of Bengal. 1 do not think, it is enviable. The tenants in those parts are always complaining about the exactions of the landlords who take advantage of their position under the permanent settlement. 1 think, the present tendency in England is also against a permanent fixity of land rents. Mr. Lloyd George is not very much in favour of permanent land laws, and he is perhaps going to benefit from a study of the conditions prevalent in this country and will introduce land laws there not on permanent basis but probably on fluctuating terms ...

"I am thankful to Raja Narendra Nath for the points he has mentioned for enquiry, and 1 can assure him that all these points will be duly considered by the Committee which is to be appointed. But as regards prices, he said that it was for consideration whether those now prevailing would become a permanent feature of the economic conditions in future or would go down to pre-War levels. I am reminded in this connection of the wages of labour previous to the earthquake of 1905 when coolies employed on construction work were paid no more than 4 annas to 6 annas, or at most 8 annas a day;

but after that catastrophe their wages went up to 12 annas and instead of coming down have now risen to one rupee. Similarly, the wages of artisans have gone up a great deal and though there is a possibility of the prices of foodgrains falling to some extent, I believe, that they won't fall to the pre-War level. If they do, I should be happier because it will alleviate the sufferings of the middle class people who are feeling the pinch of the high prices very much. Now, coming to the Resolution I have given an undertaking that Government is prepared to accept the first portion of the Resolution of my friend in its amended form. I am glad, an opportunity has been given to Government to accept this part of the Resolution. As regards the Report of the Joint Committee, the matter has been under consideration of the Government. I may inform the Council that small committees composed of the Legislative Council Members have been formed in connection with the different subjects, whether transferred or reserved, and that they have received the consideration of His Excellency the Governor. It is to be hoped that Government will be in a position to announce the formation of these Committees shortly, and that some of these Committees will help to lighten the work which falls to my lot, and that I shall receive the help and advice of the Hon'ble Members of the Legislative Council from the people's point of view on subjects such as land revenue, etc., and that their advice about settlement operations will be of great help to me."

Resolution Regarding Land Revenue Assessments

"This Council recommends to the Government, first, to appoint a Committee consisting of officials and non-officials to examine its present assessment and land revenue policy and to report what changes should be made in it, and secondly, to start no new settlement until the report of the Committee is published and has been discussed in this Council."

"Continuing in the discussion, Mr. P.J. Fagan said: Sir, the Hon'ble Sardar Sundar Singh Majithia has already explained to the Council the position which is taken up by Government in connection with this Resolution and I do not propose to touch that aspect of the question in debate at all except to make a few remarks towards the end of my speech. I am more concerned to deal with the somewhat vehement attack which has been pressed by the mover of this Resolution against the general settlement policy of Government.

"So far as that attack embodies the suggestion or the insinuation that a settlement as carried out now-a-days is the occasion for pernicious operations of an oppressive and tyrannical nature calculated to compass permanent injury to land revenue payers, that aspect of the matter has already been sufficiently dealt with by the previous speakers. I do not intend to follow them into that part of the subject except to enter a comprehensive and unhesitating denial of the charges and insinuations which have been made. Government entirely repudiates the very exaggerated and highly coloured picture which the mover drew as in no wayan accurate representation of the nature and course of settlement operations as at present carried on[2]."

Bhakra Dam Project

Sir Sundar Singh's keen interest to push forward the work on the scheme of Bhakra Dam Project on Sutlej along with the on-going Thal project on Chenab river, prompted Chaudhry Sir Chhotu Ram, who represented South-East Rohtak (non-Muslims) to demand additional irrigational facilities for Hisar and Rohatak districts and he moved amendments to Government Resolution on February 28, 1924 leading to a debate in which Sir Sundar Singh gave a detailed reply about the proposed Bhakra Dam Project*, as follows:

"Sir, I take an early opportunity at this stage to put forward certain points before this House, the consideration of which, I believe, will facilitate the decision of this Resolution. The Members of this House will, perhaps, remember that not very long ago this question was raised when my friend, Mian Shah Nawaz, put forward a proposal about the construction of the Thal Canal. This House will perhaps remember that after a full discussion of the question and after I had put forward both the sides of the schemes, both the Thal and the Bhakra Dam

[2]Punjab Legislative Council Debates, Vol. II, July to November 1921. (National Archives of India, New Delhi).

*Bhakra Dam Scheme was supposed to irrigate nearly two millions of acres of land comprised within the erstwhile States of Patiala, Jind, Bikaner and districts of Rohtak, Hisar and Karnal.

Projects, this House adopted the Resolution of Mian Shah Nawaz. This House has to bear this in mind when we are coming to a decision on this question that Government will have to give full consideration to the views expressed by this House: My friend, Chaudhri Chhotu Ram, has referred to the promises made by Sir Michael O'Dwyer in his Durbar speeches and has also mentioned the conditions as regards famine both in Hissar and Rohtak and also the services rendered by men of those districts to Government during the War and he has, like an ingenious lawyer, appealed to Members of this House, both Sikhs and Muhammadans, to support his cause. I do not in any way give the question of the conditions of this tract less consideration because it is subject to famines, but this House will remember that on that subject, the Revenue Secretary in his speech on Mian Shah Nawaz's Resolution explained to the House that the Government had practically abolished famine from this Province. On the other hand, I have got the fullest sympathy with the people of these districts in their troubles and shall be delighted if the scheme which my friend has in view comes to fruition. This House probably will bear in mind that before Chaudhri Sahib's proposals could be accepted by Government, the matter has to be fully discussed in this House. This House has to vote grants for the purpose and the scheme has to be fully looked into from the financial and engineering points of view and the proposals have to be submitted to the Government of India for sanction and possibly for the sanction of the Secretary of State. Unless these formalities are observed, it is not possible for the Government to bind themselves to any action in the matter.

"I should further like to bring to the notice of this House the remarks made by the Inspector-General of Irrigation on the Thal Project and I think it will be right if I tell this House what these remarks are. With your permission, Sir, I will take this opportunity of reading a few quotations from the note of Mr. Gebhie, the Inspector-General of Irrigation with the Government of India. He says:

"I made enquiries regarding the present position of the Bhakra Project and it seems to me it will be some years before a satisfactory project can be submitted. I understand, the political difficulties especially in the case of Patiala are likely to be serious; but even if these can be readily and speedily overcome, there are certain technical points which will have to be very carefully investigated before the Project can be submitted to the Government of India for consideration. I have seen the project estimate for the Dam and in this a most elaborate description is given of how the foundations of the Dam are to be made water-tight."

This House will realise that in the Valley where the Dam is proposed to be erected, Government will have to make a fairly high dam to impound the water in the dam. That will be, I may tell you, something like 400 feet in height because the depth of water in the dam will be 400 feet or so. This wall or dam will have to be made water-tight and to lay the foundation for this purpose, we will have to see that the rock underneath is firm. About this point, the Report goes on—

"But, as a matter of fact, nothing whatever is known about the nature of the foundations beyond what is revealed by two trial pits and an examination of the surface by a geologist. The Bhakra Dam is to hold up 400 feet of water and no dam has ever yet been attempted to deal with more than two-thirds of this depth. The pressure on the foundations will be much greater than engineers have hitherto had to provide for and the nature, not only of the foundations but of the sides of the Valley, must be carefully determined before the plans of the dam can be sanctioned. Bore holes at close intervals and over the whole area of the foundations should be sunk to a depth of at least 30 feet below the bottom of the dam. If the rock should not prove satisfactory, it may be necessary to sink the bore holes to a greater depth. This investigation will take two, if not, three working seasons and will cost a considerable sum of money. Drilling is not cheap because experts must be employed and they mostly come from America. It will also be necessary to divert the river in order to drill in its present bed."

This is the position, Sir, as regards this dam. But on the other hand, as I have very great sympathy with the objects of this Resolution I would be willing to do all that is possible for the Government to. do in the circumstances and to meet the situation, I am prepared to propose with your permission an amended Resolution in the following form. If that Resolution is accepted by the Honourable mover, I think, Government will be prepared to accept it. Sir, I may be permitted to read the amended Resolution:

"This Council recommends that the construction of the Bhakra Dam be taken in hand as soon as the construction of the Thal Project is sufficiently advanced to admit of work on this project being undertaken subject to the proviso that the Council votes the money and that the project should be found suitable from an engineering and financial point of view and has received the sanction of the Government of India[3]".

Bhakra Dam Scheme continued to have Sir Sundar Singh's keen personal interest as he pursued it vigorously during his next term as Revenue Minister under the premiership of Sir Sikandar Hayat Khan, as obvious from his response to criticism in the Punjab Legislative debates in March, 1939 by various members about the delay in implementing the project. Responding to Pandit Shri Ram Sharma about the delay in acquisition of the proposed land from the Raja of Bilaspur, the Majithia said:

"Sir, my Hon'ble Member over there smells rats in everything which this Government does and approaches every matter that comes before this House with a prejudiced mind. Quite naturally, jaundiced eyes must see everything yellow. Let me tell him that I am myself most anxious to see the Bhakra Dam scheme completed because it was in my time when I was Member of the previous Government that this scheme was conceived... Again, the Hon'ble Member has urged the Government the desirability to put undue pressure on His Highness the Raja of Bilaspur. He wanted us to coerce him in a agreement.... Let me tell the Hon'ble Member that we are not in favour of coercive or forcible methods .... *If I continue here for some time longer, I shall try my utmost to see that this scheme matured.* (Interruptions?) *Do you think that I am going to leave the office very soon?* No *doubt, I am an old man and you want me to go away.* But, let me tell you that I am not prepared to be bamboozled by you. (Laughter). We are trying to have the matter amicably settled."[@@]

However, Sir Sundar Singh was, indeed, unfortunate for he could not live to see Bhakra Dam Scheme being finally implemented

[3]Ibid. January to March 1924.

[@@]Ibid.

when Pt. Jawahar Lal Nehru, Prime Minister of Indian Republic, laid the foundation of the Project, after India's independence.

Working of Revenue Department

Speaking on the general discussion of the budget on 6th March, 1924, Mian Mohd. Shah Nawaz, who represented Lahore. (Mohammadan-Rural) spoke highly about the working of Revenue Department under the leadership of Sir Sundar Singh Majithia. He said: .

"...With your permission, Sir, I now desire to make a few observations on the income and expenditure of our Province. The five principal items of revenue are: Land Revenue, Irrigation, Excise, Forests and Stamps.

"The Revenue Department has done exceedingly well this year. It has given us 39 lakhs more than we anticipated. Special thanks are, therefore, due to my esteemed friend, the Honourable Sardar Sundar Singh Majithia and the Honourable Mr. King for realising more revenue and recovering back big arrears. We have budgetted for 1924-25 under this head two crores and eighty-six lakhs instead of three crores and twenty-lakhs, the revised figure for the current year, because we are told that we should not count upon any bumper season and because the arrears have to a very large extent been already realised. In this matter, I beg leave to differ. In my opinion, we are almost sure to realise 15.or 20 lakhs more than your present estimate unless our hopes are frustrated by some unforeseen events.

"I will now pass on to irrigation. All praise is due to the Irrigation Department and I do pay a tribute of praise to the Honourable Sardar Sahib and to my esteemed friend Honourable Mr. Sangster, who have done all that they could do for the benefit of the Department as well as for the province. I have had the honour of sitting on the Canal Committee for the last 3.5 years and I can confidently say that the working of the Department under the wise guidance of the Sardar Sahib and Mr. Sangster has been very satisfactory. All controversial subjects were fully discussed before the Committee with the greatest frankness, and the decisions arrived at were acceptable. It is gratifying to know that the Irrigation Department is going to give us 30 lakhs more than the actuals of 1922-23, and 25 lakhs more than the budget of the current year, and 13 lakhs more than the revised figures. I rejoice to see that the Punjab loan was over-subscribed within a few hours. This is due to the fact that we are going to complete our Sutlej Valley Project as soon as possible and we intend to take the Thal Project in hand in October 1925. As long as we have. some irrigation project in hand and the Crown waste lands to sell, our credit is sure to rise. I, however, want to sound a note of warning to the Government. We are entering upon a very serious competition and rivalry with the Bombay Government who desire to profit at our expense. They have been lodging protest after protest against our Irrigation Projects in the Punjab. Therefore, always beware of Bombay Government.

"I now come to the Excise Department. This is a money-making Department but we must continue, though I am very sorry to say so, we must continue to shower our blessings on the heads of Bhangis and Shirabis, because they come to our help in the hour of need. There is practically no change in the income and expenditure of this Department. It is a great pity that we cannot close up all the liquor shops even within a few years because our financial conditions do not permit us to do so[4]".

Irrigation Facilities

While Sir Sundar Singh was deeply concerned with the irrigation facilities for the farmers, based on his own experience as an agriculturist, he had simultaneously to ensure as Revenue Member reasonable receipts of income from these canals against the capital expenditure on expanding the canal irrigation facilities. His speech regarding the new schedule of Occupiers' Rates for the chief canals in the Punjab is interesting and reflect his deep in-sight of the subject. He said.

"Sir, it has been said here in this House that water of the rivers belongs not to the Province as a whole but to a certain class of people. I must say that this commodity belongs to the Province as a whole and not the irrigators alone should derive benefit from it. Ninety per cent of the population of this

[4]Ibid. 6th March, 1924.

Province is agriculturists. Out of the total area of 40 per cent is irrigated by canals. The total crop area in the Province is 27 million acres, out of which 11 million acres are irrigated by canals. Our friends would, therefore, see that 36 per cent of the population of Zamindars derive benefit from canal irrigation and the rest of the people of the Province who are agriculturists, that is 54 per cent of the total number, do not derive benefit from canal irrigation. Therefore, Sir, my point is that any benefit that accrues to the canal irrigators is not shared by the Zamindars of this Province as a whole.

"Then, Sir, wild statements have been. made as to the income which has been derived by Government from the canals. My friend, Mir Maqbool Mahmood, has gone to the length of saying that from 16 per cent to 22 per cent has been the income from canals. I will now give the House the exact figures. In doing so, I will give the total capital outlay which has been incurred on the canals of the Province and I will also give the gross direct receipts from canals, then the working expenses of these canals, and then the net revenue and last of all will give you the percentages. Upto 1918-19, Rs. 22,45,11,551 was the total amount spent on canals, and in 1923-24 (I will skip over the intervening years), the total expenditure on canals was Rs. 23,21,02,392.

In 1918-19 we received ... Rs. 2,77,10,675
In 1919-20 we received ... Rs. 3,22,49,503
In 1920-21 we received ... Rs. 3,32,61,564
In 1921-22 we received ... Rs. 3,25,81,799
In 1922-23 we received ...Rs. 3,60,06,328
In 1923-24 we received ...Rs. 3,55,72,288
as gross revenue." ....

"I will give the Honourable Members the charges in pre-British India and in other countries. The first time the rates were imposed was in the time of Feroz Shah who dug the first canal in India. He took one-tenth of the gross produce as water rates, that is to say, in addition to the land revenue that was taken from the irrigators. The same was continued in the Moghul period. It must also be remembered that the canal which was constructed by Feroz Shah was an inundation canal which as such supplied water precariously. Our canals are perennial ones where water is given practically throughout the year except when the canals are stopped for repairs, etc. It must further be remembered that Feroz Shah never borrowed a pie to build these canals. What I mean to say is that he had not to pay a 'kauri' by way of interest charges on the borrowed capital. Mr. Strange, an authority on irrigation, who has written a book called "Irrigation, Buildings and Roads" makes a certain statement from which it appears that in America, the' water rates are one-fifth to one-sixth of the produce of land. Coming to Egypt, I will take the opportunity of reading a letter from Mr. Strickland, who has just come from those parts. I would not read the whole of his letter but I will read only a portion. He writes: "In Egypt in rich districts it is 22 to 23 rupees an acre". This I may say includes land tax also but it must be remembered that this rate is taken on all crops without any distinction. Different rates are taken here for different crops. We charge one rate for wheat, another for cotton, a third for oil-seeds and so on; while in Egypt there is only one rate." ...

"Now coming to a little bit of comparison between the cost of water by well and by canal irrigation, I will give some of my experience which I have in the United Provinces. I take the example of the United Provinces because the labour there is cheap and the level of water in the wells is lower than what it is in the Punjab." ...

"One has to bear in mind that in the well irrigation, one has to bear a good deal of initial expense, first, by sinking wells, secondly, in procuring a pair of bullocks, thirdly, in the up-keep and repairs of his persian wheels. All this expenditure is borne by the irrigator while in the case of canals, water is let into the field and the cultivator has to take no trouble about it. Of course, people complain about the alleged illegal gratifications exacted by Patwaris and others, but if this be the case, they have to thank themselves, for if they do not pay these illegal gratifications, no body is going to trouble them. Besides, I may assure this House that if any information in regard to these illegal gratifications is brought to the notice of the Government, Government is prepared to prosecute their corrupt employees who take illegal gratifications. (Hear, Hear)[5]".

[5]Ibid.

Interests of Agriculturists (Zamindars)

In view of the fact that Sir Sundar Singh and Sir Chhotu Ram under the premiership of Sir Sikandar Hayat Khan took keen interest in safeguarding the interests of agriculturists, there was widespread criticism by the opposition which dubbed them as the 'Government of the Zamindars'. While Sir Chhotu Ram sometimes could not restrain himself from using offending language against the opposition parties and non-agriculturists, *Sir Sundar Singh was more inclined to parliamentary language of logic and humour while pushing through many legislative bills,* some of them like Land Alienation Act, Money Lenders' Bill and Punjab Restitution of Mortgaged Lands Bill were landmarks in protecting the interests of the agricultural community.

Speaking on the Punjab Restitution of Mortgaged Lands Bill, which was moved by Sir Sundar Singh on 23rd June 1938, Rai Bahadur Mukand Lal Puri (representing Rawalpindi-General Rural) said:

> "The Act confers certain economic disabilities on the so-called non-agriculturists regarding purchase of land realization of their debts. According to the census, the population of the Province belonging to the non-statutory agricultural tribes is 56% or more ... "

Replying to the debate on the Bill on 18th July, 1938, Sir Sundar Singh said:

> "Before 1901, there was no distinction between an agriculturist and non-agriculturist. Every body could purchase land without let or hindrance. The people who were notified as non-agriculturists at that time are now raising a hue and cry that they may also be notified as agriculturists so that they may be able to deprive the petty Zamindars of their lands. That is why the Hon'ble Members opposite are making' persistent efforts to oppose the proposed Bill. Sir, the Land Alienation Act was passed during the regime of Lord Curzon and proved a boon for the petty Zamindars. Before that, a Zamindar could mortgage his land with a non-agriculturist, but after 1901, only agriculturists were permitted to purchase and that is why they are opposing the proposed legislation ... Again, my friend Dr. Sir Gokul Chand Narang advanced another argument that the 'bania' has not got a 'lathi' in his possession by which he can compel the ministerial party to

accept his view-point. The Zamindars, in his opinion, have a 'lathi' and they get everything done if they so desire. But, I may submit that that 'bania' has such a 'lathi' which can break all other 'lathis' and that is his 'Behi' (account book). The 'lathi' of the Zamindar is powerless to save him from the 'lathi' of a 'bania'.

"I may submit that once a poor jat questioned someone as to how 'banias' make money. He was told that he made it by the 'Pasku', i.e. a 'bania' weighs less by binding a small stone with his balance and thus he earns much. The [at also conceived the idea of opening a shop of'Lun' 'Tel' (salt and oil). He opened the shop and sat on the shop and attached a big stone with his scale as 'Pasku' .... The [at sat in his shop waiting for someone to come to him and buy from him. After a short while, a small girl came with some com in her lap and asked the Jat shop-keeper to give her oil in exchange (interruptions). The Jat shop-keeper put the whole of the grains in one pan of his scales but on account of the weight of the stone which he had tied with his scales as 'pasku', the pan did not come down. When· the girl asked for oil in exchange for her corn, he remarked how could he give her oil, her corn was not sufficient to adjust even the poise of the scales. So, Sir, is the case of my friends on the opposite. They are crying because their 'pasku' is being adjusted[6]".

After a long debate and hot discussion, the Bill was finally passed on 21st July, 1938.

Zamindara Conference, Layalpur, *September 4, 1938*

His concern for the living conditions of the poor farmers and their exploitation is also evident from his following speech of Sir Sundar Singh while presiding over the said Conference at Layalpur on September 4, 1938. He said:

"Out of the Four Bills which have been formulated to safeguard the interests of the Zamindars, two are my contribution ... Within the powers vested with us, we have tried to do whatever we could for brethren. The extent of success is a different matter, but in the capacity of servants of the

[6]Punjab Legislative Council Debates: National Archives of India, New Delhi.

people, we have tried to eradicate the ills affecting the poor farmers, as a result of which the treatment which we received is well known to you. Dr. Gokul Chand Narang tried to befool me and Raja Narender Nath by naming us as 'foolish and innocent' Sardar and Raja respectively.... But, we could not never forget the difficulties of those who had elected us as their representatives and made us Ministers ....

"I am known for collecting money and, more importantly, one who keeps strict control over such deposited money. I cannot give up anything unless it has the consent of all concerned because it is a question of joint responsibility. Other Ministers are responsible for my work and I am responsible for their performance. Since 1930, concessions in revenue have been given to the tune of Rs. One crore, ninety lac and twenty-five thousand... Those who do not like our efforts, they will appreciate us after some time. *I am being taunted that what effect the recitation of 'Gurbani' and lives of the Gurus had on me if I sacrifice the interests of one section over the interests of the other. I do not know what effect the recitation of 'Gurbani' had on me, but I know that the meaning which Guru Gobind Singh derived from the sacrifice of his four beloved sons was that he pointed towards Sikhs and said thousands of them are alive. Of course, his beloved sons were not of less importance* to *him, but in the interest of the Nation, he could make any sacrifice. The money-lenders and non-agriculturists brethren are, similarly, not of lesser importance or lovable for us but in the interest of the country, there was no other way to save* it *except to restore the lost right of the poor and hardworking peasant. Guru Sahib, pointing towards the Sikhs had told the Pandit, "that it* is *only with the blessings of these that I occupy this position; otherwise there are crores like me*[7]".

That he had no hesitation to admit about his agriculturist background which enabled him to appreciate the difficulties of the farming community is also obvious from the excerpts of his following speech which he delivered at Amritsar on April 11, 1937 in reply to an Address of Honour which Sikh Youth League presented to him. He said:

[7]"Khalsa Te Khalsa Advocate", Amritsar, September 8, 1938.

"I am myself a Zamindar and very well know the difficulties of the farmers ... [8]".

Alienation of Land (Amendment) Act

Sir Sundar Singh moved on June 21, 1938, the Punjab Alienation of Land (Amendment) Bill whose object, in the words of the Majithia Sardar was:

"Certain defects which had arisen as to the interference of the Civil Courts in the decision regarding the caste of the people who were affected by the Alienation of Land Act, may be removed. It was considered that this matter was to be decided by the Deputy Commissioner in his capacity as Revenue Officer and Financial Commissioner also considered that it was only the Deputy Commissioner who had to decided on this. But, it so happened that in certain cases people went to Civil Courts and the Civil Courts decided that they were not bound by the decision of the Deputy Commissioner in the matter....

"The object of the Bill is that we must remove the jurisdiction of Civil Courts, and secondly, we must check the evil of 'benami' transactions.

Replying to an interruption by Dr. (Sir) Gokul Chand Narnag, who complained that he could not follow the Minister, Sardar Sundar Singh said:

"I am very sorry, my friend has not been able to follow me. He will follow only one thing, i.e. protection of non-agriculturists against the agriculturists. (Loud Cheers)..."

There was a long discussion in' which the following prominent Members took part:

1. Dr. Gokul Chand Narang
2. Rai Bahadur Mukand Lal Puri (Rawalpindi General-Rural) who vehemently opposed the amendment.
3. Raja Ghaznafar Ali Khan.
4. Malik Barkat Ali.
5. Pandit Muni Lal Kalia.
6. Premier, Sikander Hyat Khan.

The Bill was later passed by the House[6].

[8]"Khalsa Te Khalsa Advocate", Amritsar, April 17, 1937.

[9]Punjab Legislative Assembly Debates: National Archives of India, New Delhi.

The Punjab Tenancy (Amendment) Bill ***June 1929***

Lala Duni Chand (Ambala-Simla: General-Rural) moved The Punjab Tenancy (Amendment) Bill and said:

"Under the existing Tenancy Act of 1887, the occupancy rights can be granted only under three sections, viz. Section 5, Section 6 and Section 8. It is only in exceptional cases, as these sections show, that occupancy tenancy rights can be established... Since the Punjab Tenancy Act was passed about 50 years ago, conditions have changed greatly in regard to the rights of the tenants and the landlords.... What I want is that those tenants who have been continuously in occupation of land for 20 years on 31st December 1941 should be granted the right of occupancy, subject to the payment of the rent either in kind or in cash and subject to the payment of any customary rights that they were paying on the last day of completion of the 20th year."

Sir Sundar Singh strongly opposed the Bill and said:

"Sir, my friend has been very eloquent in showing kindness and sympathy to poor tenants. I do not know whether he has studied the whole situation. What would be the effect of this Bill in the Provincer May I say, Sir, with your permission that this Province and the adjoining Province of the United Provinces are slightly different from each other. There they have a large number of landlords and here in Punjab, we have petty landlords, and big landlords according to that scale are hardly 13 in this Province. (A voice: an unlucky numberl). Yes, it may be an unlucky number (Lala Duni Chand, why are you applying the same analogy here?). I must apply the same analogy of the United Provinces because things have happened there, of which I am personally aware. In the time of Lord MacDonald and previous to that, landlords and tenants lived happily for ages together... Then the question of occupancy, tenant came in and the landlord's interest and tenant's interest were there separated from each other. The landlord wanted the tenant not to acquire occupancy rights; while the tenant wanted to have occupancy rights. The period of acquiring occupancy rights in the U.P. at that time was 12 years. My honourable friend is very kind and sympathetic to the tenants here and wants 15 to 20 years... The solution of the difficulty has been found in the U.P.; in that once a tenant, then a tenant for life, and for five years after his death, his son will be the tenant and no landlord will be able to turn him out. This is the fixity of tenure that has been given to the tenants in the U.P ... May I point to this Honourable House, through your Sir, what will be the effect? As soon as this Bill is allowed to be introduced, there will be thousands and thousands of ejectments of those tenants who have been living on those lands for years together...

"As I have said, the Punjab is a land of peasant proprietors. One man keeps a small piece of land to make his living and makes the tenure a sort of economical holding. He has his own land, gets some land from the landlord of the adjoining holdings and cultivates it and goes on cultivating it. If this is the sympathy that my honourable friend has that this man should be ejected, I am afraid, I cannot see eye to eye with him in this matter...[10]".

The motion was lost in the din of the House:

The spirit of Sir Sundar Singh to work for the protection of the farming community despite criticism within and outside the Punjab Legislative Council is illustrated from his reply to the debate on June 27, 1938 over the supplementary demands in respect of irrigation works. He said:

"Criticism is quite all right provided it is made with responsibility, but if criticism is simply for criticism's sake and not for constructive purposes, it is not a desirable thing. My honourable friends have said that I am under the thumb of other Ministers (Opposition cheers), I am trying to do my duty according to my rights and I will soon be doing my duty in spite of what my friends on the Opposite benches say. I will try and do my duty to the best of my ability (Hear, hear from the Ministerial benches). These are the things that require consideration. My friends know very well that this sort of criticism is not to be found in the provinces where responsibility has been placed on the shoulders of the Congress in spite of the fact that Section 144 is being applied and there are lathi charges, and other things are being done in the name of the Congress."

[10]Ibid.

"Chaudhri Krishan Gopal Dutt: "Only against the landlords".

"Sardar Sundar Singh Majithia: I will come to the landlords later on. If your are a landlord, I will deal with you. Let my friends say anything that they like, I am not going to mind and listen to them and I will go on doing my duty and let the caravan pass. (Here, Hear from the ministerial benches)[11]".

Dr. Gokul Chand Narnag confirms his strong opposition to the above legislations as illustrated from the following excerpts of his interview with Dr. Hari Dev Sharma:

"Sharma: What was the policy that was followed by the Party called the National Progressive Party under the leadership of Raja Narendra Nath?

Narang: That was not a political party, really. The only thing was that people worked together in opposing those various destructive Bills that Chhotu Ram introduced. That is all. Otherwise, there was no separate programme. They had no important measures to bring to the Council. They knew that they would be defeated by the Muslim officials. The Punjab Government was dominated by Muslims and Muslim sentiments. They knew that the Hindus were in a minority and you know, the British Government had hardly any sympathy with the Hindus, particularly in provinces where they were in a minority. They could not have any sympathy worth the name with the Hindus. Thus, the Progressive Party could exert little influence.

Sharma: If you put up the relative programmes of the two parties: the Unionist Party and the National Progressive Party, and if you look at their programme as also the leaders who represented both the parties, it would appear that the Unionist Party, in spite of its being communal in its approach to problems some time, was more progressive. For example, its attempt to restrict the encroachment rights of the land-owners or to safeguard the interests of the tenants. What do you say?

Narang: It was certainly progressive in the sense that it wanted to favour the agriculturists at the expense of non-agriculturists. And, every act that they did was influenced by

[11]Punjab Legislative Council Debates: National Archives of India, New Delhi.

this consideration, to favour the agriculturists. The Money-lenders Act was passed for this purpose and the rate of interest was reduced and the detenues suffering imprisonment were exempted from certain restrictions. All these things were, from their point of view, to favour the underdog. All the money-lenders were Hindus and they were better placed from the economic point of view and, therefore, they were anxious to crush them, as far as possible. All this was meant to favour the agriculturists-the poor agriculturists as they called them."

Sharma: Don't you think that the backbone of the Unionist Party was the economic discontent?

Narnag: You are right. It was, on the face of it, economic. To favour the poor, to favour the underdog, as I said, and on this pretence they went on. But, it had a communal tinge. All the 'Shahukars' in the Punjab, almost without exception, were Hindus, and the majority of the agriculturalists in the Punjab were indebted to Hindus. And, therefore, they wanted to help the poor people and we opposed them because we thought they were going too far. That was our reasoning. It did have a certain communal tinge because the Party that was being affected by these measures consisted of Hindus.

Sharma: Do you think that behind the introduction of these measures, men like Fazl-i-Hussain had an intention to hit the Hindus?

Narang: No, no, I should not say that.

Sharma: That was too incidental?

Narang: That was the result. They wanted to help the have-nots, the poor[12]".

That sincere efforts of the Unionist Party to safeguard farmers' interest led to the division of the Society into agriculturists and non-agriculturists and subsequently divided the Sikh community into Jats* and non-Jats and other sub-castes is also clear from the apprehensions of the citizens of Rawalpindi who presented the following Address in the honour of Sir Sundar Singh Majithia:

[12]Nehru Memorial Museum & Library, New Delhi.

*Ironically, this is the anti-thesis of the teachings of the Sikh Gurus, particularly the spirit of Khalsa which Guru Gobind Singh enunciated to put an end to the discrimination on the basis of caste, colour or creed.

"It is our proud privilege to welcome you in our midest and to congratulate you heartily on your selection as a Member of the first Punjab Cabinet under the reformed Constitution. Your success and that of your colleagues in the recent elections augurs well for the community and means a vote for a constructive programme that you propose to follow.

"Honoured Sir, with a valuable experience of politics and social service, you combine unequalled learning and ability. You are not only progressive in thought and creed, but are most illustrious representative of the ancient culture of this land. Profoundly learned as you are, you possess rare gifts of political sagacity and clarity of vision. It was this trait of your towering personality that enabled you to see clearly through the spreading mists of political controversy and to formulate a programme that the Congress has only been recently driven to adopt. Whatever may be the value of civil disobedience and non-cooperation, there is no doubt, that this policy of barren obstruction breeds hatred and acrimony. But, you Sir, as the accredited leader of Sikhs have correctly realised the need of the hour and given us a great lead. We are confident that the ship of the community is in the hands of an experienced pilot and it will steer clear of all difficulties. Your whole life has been a veritable and willing sacrifice for the community. The educational institutions of the Sikhs owe their all to your unceasing efforts and keen interest in the education of the community. By your educational activities, you infused within us a life which has enabled us to live up in the face of numerous hardships with heroic fortitude. The fact that many of our youngmen are occupying high positions of trusts and responsibility redounds to your credit.

"Respected Sir, you have been fortunate in having among your colleagues men of great parliamentary experience like Sardar Ujjal Singh and gentlemen of Sardar Uttam Singh's character and ability. They, we are confident, will. give their unflinching support to you in safeguarding the interest of the community. It is a matter of pride for us that one of your able lieutenants, Sardar Uttam Singh belongs to this place and is held in great esteem by all the inhabitants of the district.

"There is at present an unwholesome distinction between Jats and non-jats. We, who are residing in this part of the province, have always done our little but in our own way to ameliorate the conditions of Sikhs. On account of our meagre and inadequate representation in the provincial legislature, we might have a cause to be anxious about our political existence but our confidence in you impels us to believe that our legitimate rights will be safeguarded and that your personality will cement the differences between these two political sections of Sikhs.

"We do also firmly believe that you will be an ornament to the Cabinet and your versatile genius and unrivalled experience will enable you to win support of your colleagues in promoting the interests of the community. We are confident of the fact that at great personal risk and inconvenience, you have accepted the command of the community to lead it, but we are sure that you will acquit yourself bravely and earn the gratitude of all, who. look upon you for leadership and guidance[13]."

Appreciation

Sir Sundar Singh's tenure as the first Revenue Member of the Punjab Legislative Council (from 1921 to early 1926) won him high appreciation from all sections of the society, despite the fact that it was one of the most challenging periods for any Government, or for any representative of a community undergoing a period of unprecedented agitation for Reforms and turbulence accompanied therewith. That he did his assignment in the Government in a commendable manner besides living up to the expectations of his own community, is evident from the extracts of speeches of the President and other Members of the Punjab Legislative Council who, cutting across party lines and communities they represented, spoke highly of Sir Sundar Singh Majithia who along with Sir John Maynard, the Finance Member, were to lay their respective offices after completing their respective terms. Following are the excerpts from the 6th Session of the Second Punjab Legislative Council on Saturday, the 12th December 1925 bidding farewell to Hon'ble Sir John Maynard and Sardar Bahadur Sundar Singh Majithia:

"Mr. President, it appears that this is the last day of the sittings of the Council and that, in all probability, it will not have

[13]Ibid. File NO. 105.

to meet again before the Honourable. Finance Member and the Honourable Revenue Member will be relieved of their high offices on completion of their terms. The Honourable Sir John Maynard, the Leader of the House, and Sardar Bahadur Sardar Sundar Singh Majithia, have been the two distinguished members of this Council ever since the inauguration of the. reforms. I think, I am voicing "the unanimous opinion of this Hose that Members are very anxious to say farewell to their parting colleagues and friends and express appreciation of their work, good fellowship, pleasant comradeship and sincere friendship for a long period of five years."

The Honourable Rai Sahib Chaudhri Chhotu Ram (Minister for Agriculture) said:

"Sir, it is not long before Sir John Maynard and Sardar Bahadur Sardar Sundar Singh Majithia will be leaving this Council and there will be no opportunity for this Council to express its appreciation of their services to it." ...

"With regard to the Honourable Sardar Bahadur Sardar Sundar Singh Majithia, we have all known him fora considerable number of years. He was a vigorous worker of the good of the Sikh community and took an appreciable interest in the general affairs of his province and country. Having made a name for himself in the general affairs of the province and the country, he was called upon to occupy the high office which he had occupied for five years with conspicuous ability. His courtesy and his politeness are known to one and all of us. He was equally pleasant to work with, and his company was always a source of joy to those who came in contact with him. No doubt, it will be a kind of wrench to us all to part with such colleagues and with such excellent officers, and I am sure, that both the Honourable Sir John Maynard and the Honourable Sardar Bahadur Sardar Sundar Singh Majithia, when they have retired, will look back upon this Council and their connection with the Government and this House with pleasure and will not forget us in their retirement. (Cheers).: "

Mian Muhammad Shah Nawaz (Lahore: Muhammadan-Rural) spoke:

"Sir, I have very great pleasure in associating myself with all that has fallen from the lips of the Honourable the President and the Honourable the Minister for Agriculture with regard to the Honourable the Finance Minister, who is the .Leader of the House, and the Honourable the Revenue Member. With sincere thanks and gratitude, we appreciate and acknowledge their, distinguished and meritorious services to the Province ....

"The Honourable Sardar Bahadur Sardar Sundar Singh Majithia is one of us. Suffice it to say that his appointment as Revenue member has proved a complete success. He has done his work with ability and industry and to the satisfaction of all concerned. *He has given us the Sutlej Valley Canal,* which is nearing completion and which will irrigate nearly one million acres of land in British territory alone and thus add to the prosperity of the Province. Further, he has charted out another irrigation scheme of great magnitude, namely, *the Thal* Project, which is now before the Government of India and which I have every hope will soon be sanctioned by the Secretary of State. His courteous manners and generous disposition have won laurels from members of all communities. I have every hope that these gentlemen will continue to take interest in the affairs of India and particularly in the affairs of the land of Five Rivers. With deep regret, we bid them farewell and wish them both long life, prosperity and all happiness."

Professor Ruchi Ram Sahni, Punjab University, said:

"Sir, I also want to associate myself wholeheartedly with everything that has been said about the Honourable Sir John Maynard and the Honourable Sardar Bahadur Sardar Sundar Singh Majithia..... As the Honourable Minister for Agriculture has said, Sir John is a liberal in politics. He himself told me this not long ago. He also said to me that most of the members of the Civil Service wanted India to get "Swaraj" at the earliest possible moment. Whether that is so or not, I do not know. But, I welcome the assurance that it is so. We do not often see signs of it (Laughter) but I am perfectly certain that Sir John himself is as good .as his word and when he retires to his home, I trust, he will do his best to see that *India gets what is after all her birth-right."*

"Then, Sir, about the Honourable Sardar Bahadur Sardar Sundar Singh Majithia, I need not say much about him for the simple reason that he is not leaving us in the sense in which the Honourable Sir John Maynard is leaving us. We all know how much the Province owes to the Sardar Bahadur not only with regard to the Sutlej Valley Project and other irrigation works which owe their initiation and progress to him but also in various other public activities in which he has been engaged so devotedly all his life.

"His life has been dedicated to public work for the Punjab, and the Sikhs in particular. The great Khalsa College owes a great deal to his selfless labours and there are other activities also in which he has left the stamp of his personality and of his individuality. Sir, I wish to say at the end that we deeply appreciate the work that these two gentlemen have done in this Council as well as outside the Council".

Lieutenant Sardar Sikandar Hayat Khan (Attock: Muhammadan Rural) said..

"Sir, I have great pleasure in associating myself with the previous Speakers. The Punjab owes a great debt of gratitude to Sir John Maynard for many reasons and particularly for putting the finances of this Province on a sound basis. It was particularly through the efforts of Sir John Maynard that instead of the deficit budget which we had from year to year, we have surplus budget now."

"...As regards Sardar Sundar, Singh Majithia, he is leaving this Council, but he will still be with us and we hope he will be useful outside this Council just as he has been here. The Zamindars have been connected with the Revenue Department and as the head of the Revenue Department, he has been sympathetic in their aspirations and has done a great deal to look after their interests. I hope, he will continue to take a keen interest in them when he has left this Council and will be of help and benefit not only to Zamindars but to the whole Province. Sir, we part with a heavy heart and wish them prosperity and good health and bid them God speed."

Sardar Tara Singh (Ferozepore: Sikh-Rural) said:

"Sir, we are always impressed with some' distinguishing features of every individual with whom we mix. I have' always been impressed with the personality of Sir John Maynard, who has worked as a real leader of this House. Sir, I have learnt many a lesson from him in the Council Chamber, one of them being that he had great respect for officials.

Whenever the Hon'ble the President entered the Council Chamber or went out of it, he was the first man to stand in his seat. That is one lesson I have learnt from him. The second lesson I have learnt from him is that throughout the period of two years that I have been a member of this Council he never lost temper..... "

"As regards Sardar Sundar Singh, however much is said will be too little. The present prosperity of the Sikh community, I may say, is due to his popularity. In all departments of life, he has given to his brethren, a leaf out of his own book. He is about the only Sardar who is busy with his work from morning till evening. Therefore, Sir, I am much indebted to his personality on that score. He is not going to leave the Punjab and I am still hopeful that he will be able to continue to help us. With these words, I bid the two gentlemen good-bye."

Diwan Bahadur Raja Narendra Nath (Punjab: Land-holders - General) said:

"Sir, I wish to join in these laudatory references that are being made to the retiring members of the Executive Council. I have had the honour and the pleasure of knowing both these gentlemen for a long time. With Sir John Maynard, I was associated officially and I first came to know him about 15 years ago, though I knew him before too.

"As regards the Sardar Sahib, I have known him longer. I have had the honour of coming into contact with his illustrious father, Raja Surat Singh Majithia. He belongs to a family that has played an important part in the political history of the Province and I am glad that the expectations that were formed of him when he took over charge have been fulfilled. He has proved to be an open-minqed, sincere, honest and frank adviser of Government, putting all his cards on the table whenever occasion required it."

Malik Firoz Khan Noon (Shahpur East: Muhammadan-Rural) said:

"Sir, I heartily associate myself with the previous Speakers in what they have said in connection with the past services of our departing colleagues, the two Executive Councillors. .... "As for Sardar Bahadur Sardar Sundar Singh, we shall have the pleasure of meeting him now and again after he leaves this Council and I hope that the sweet atmosphere of his sugar factory in the United Provinces will not take him away from us for ever. I hope that he may come back to us as an elected Member of this House and help us in our deliberations. As far as his administration of the Revenue Department is concerned, he has been the right man in the right place and all of you will agree with me that he has been very sympathetic to all persons with whom he had to deal with in the discharge of his official duties. Wish them both a very long, happy and prosperous life."

Mr. J.M. Dunnett, Home Secretary, said:

"Sir, I trust that on this occasion, you would permit one from the Government back-benches to say a few words. Our tongues are tied regarding Sir John Maynard by our pride and regret, regret that one so energetic, competent, and in a word so young should be laying down his office at a time when so much is still to be done for the Province and for India. (Hear, Hear). I can only trust that a portion of his mantle, a double portion of his spirit - that spirit of liberalism, affection for India, and respect for Parliamentary institutions and procedure will descend on us.

"Sir, the work of the Honourable the Revenue Member is before you and before this House and before the Province, and has been described, necessarily inadequately in the preceding speeches today. *But, in the hearts of the members of the Government benches, there is a grateful feeling of acknowledgment, a feeling of recognition of that kindliness with which Sardar Sahib has exercised authority over us and the great encouragement which he has always given us* in serving in office and doing our duty in the Council. Sir, the Punjab will never fail to provide competent statsmen-like members, but the first Indian Revenue Member will leave in our hearts the memory of kindliness and friendship and a fragrant recollection. (Hear, Hear)."

Mian Abdul Aziz (Lahore City - Muhammadan - Urban) said:

"Sir, as regards Sardar Bahadur Sardar Sundar Singh Majithia, we need not dilate much because he will not be leaving us in the same sense as Sir John Maynard. The Sardar Bahadur's home is situated some 35 or 33. miles away from here. He will be always with tis and among us. Sir, he is the first Indian Revenue Member and when he was appointed to this office, it was very much doubted whether any Indian would ever be able to discharge successfully the onerous duties of this great office. But, Sir Sardar Bahadur, through his conspicuous ability and untiring energy, has come out with flying colours in the test to which he was submitted. I know Sir John Maynard will leave us for ever but in the case of Sardar Bahadur we have this consolation that we will be able to meet him every now and then. We congratulate him on his splendid success which he has achieved in the performance of his duties connected with the office of Revenue Member of this Province. We also request him to impart the same lesson to his successor on which he himself acted successfully during the tenure of his office. In conclusion, I wish both the retiring honourable Members, long life and good health and hope they would try to make themselves as much useful to this Province as they have proved hitherto."

Dr. Gokul Chand Narang (North-West Towns: Non-Muhammadan - Urban) said:

"Sir, I should have been perhaps the first to get up and express my sincere appreciation of Sir John Maynard's work in this Council and also of the work of Sardar Bahadur Sardar Sundar Singh Majithia. I was a bit late but it does not mean that I am behind anybody else in appreciating the good work done by these two members of the Executive Council. ....

"In Sir John, I *have found virtues which [have not always found* in *a bureaucrat.* His learning and ability are well-established and there may be many others who may be possessed of that learning and that ability and that forensic skill which he so often displayed in this House, but there are few who possess his other gifts. I *was a little surprised that the Honourable the Minister for Agriculture compared him* to *a 'bania' although* it *gave me a little pleasure that a jat Minister for Agriculture had at last found one 'bania' whom he could eulogise. It* is *really a great thing that* in *this Zamindar-ridden Council where the word Zamindar* is *heard more often than the name of God, there was at least one 'bania' who could command the allegiance of the House.* This gives me pleasure.

"...I am sure, Sir John seated on this side of the House would have been a tower of strength to us as he has been to the other side of the House. *We find* in *the Sikh history that after the battle of Sobraon or some other battle, I forget which, a British soldier taunted an old Sikh soldier thus: "Well, you used to boast of your courage and bravery but we have beaten you." The old soldier put his hand on his long beard and retorted: 'Well, Sahib, had we one or two generals like yours, the story of today would have been different.' Similarly, if* Sir *John had been on our side (and there* is *nothing to prevent him now from. being on our side) the story of many a battle fought on the floor of this House would have been different.* (Applause)."

"As regards the Honourable Sardar Bahadur Sardar Sundar Singh Majithia, my honourable friend Raja Sahib, has already pointed out that he belongs to one of the noblest families in this Province, a family which has rendered important services to this Province in the past right from the Sikh times up to the present time. *There are many noble names associated with his family and it may not be known to many honourable Members of this House that not only have they been great soldiers, great landholders and administrators, but at least one member of their family was a great scientist as well as a great mathematician and astronomer - a scientist of a very high order if we take into consideration the times in which he lived. The Sardar Bahadur was our first Revenue Member and as has already been pointed out, I am exceedingly delighted to be able to say today that the first Revenue Member has been a very great success. He has not given cause to any community to find fault with him.* He is as popular today as he was on the day when he first took charge of this exalted office. (Hear, Hear). I wish every body who occupies or is expected to occupy any of the high posts which are now available to the Indians, would keep that great lesson in view. (Hear, Hear). My learned friend, Mian Mohammad Shah Nawaz has spoken of the great schemes which have been launched during the term of the Sardar Bahadur as Revenue Member. But, I may say that when we compare the future of this Province with the material benefit that these two schemes may bring to this country, the latter is of very little importance. His success and his popularity are a guarantee for the future that if larger instalments of self-government are given to the people of this country, they would not necessarily abuse those powers. This is to me of much greater importance and of much greater value than anything else that the Sardar Bahadur might have done. It is a source of great pleasure and great satisfaction to me that the Sardar Bahadur is not going away to Hungary or Austria or to any other country in Europe, and that he is going to stay either in the Punjab or in the United Provinces where he has got a nice sugar mill.

"He may either stay in this Province and be a tower of strength to us; if he condescends to come into this Council as an elected Member, or, if he stays in the United Provinces, I am sure, there also by his example to other Talukdars he will prove a source of material help to the United Provinces of Agra and Oudh. Both of them are in the prime of youth, if I may so put it, because a man is never old if he feels that he is young. Though the Sardar Bahadur has got a grey beard as compared with Sir John, I may apply to him the epithet of *semper juventus* which one of the Congress leaders once applied to another Congress leader. I think, this can be applied to both of them. Both of them are young and they are ever green and I wish them long life and happiness and opportunities of doing service to this country and to England, because by serving this country, they especially Sir John, will be doing great service to his country as well." (Applause).

Sayed Muhammad Husain (Montgomery: Muhammadan - Rural) said:

"Sir, every one of us has to depart from this world one day or other. If a tyrant or an unscrupulous man departs from this world, all the people heave a sigh of relief, but the departure of the righteous and the just and the noble is always a real calamity to the country. The departure from service of two eminent Punjabis - I include Sir John with the Sardar Bahadur as a Punjabi because Sir John has spent the prime of his life in the uplift of this Province - is really a great calamity to this province and their loss is really irreparable."

"As regards my honourable friend Sardar Bahadur Sardar Sundar Singh Majithia, I *have been associated with him in many ways. He is the most senior student of the institution to which* I *and several other members of this Council have the honour to belong. He is the senior most student of the Atichison College, an institution which has saved several large families from ruin. It gives me very great pleasure* and pride to see one of the senior most students of the Atichison College at the helm of affairs in the Government. *The Sardar Bahadur has always been trying his level best to uplift the*

old families and Zamindars' cause here. He is leaving us soon and he would have been very glad had the Land Revenue Bill been pushed through in his Council life time. I know it very well that it is due to no fault of his that the Bill is not yet an accomplished fact. Who does not know with what zeal he championed the cause of the Land Revenue Bill in the proper quarters and he has been trying his very best to see the Bill passed before he lays down his office? *Needless to say how anxiously every Zamindar of this Province is looking forward to this legislation which was promised by the Select Committee of both Houses of Parliament.* Sorry, it is that it has not been ordained for the Sardar Bahadur to see the most cherished measure of his being put permanently on the Statute Book; his is not the role to pilot this Magna Carta of the Zamindars through this Council.

"At the same time, let us hope that he will come back to us at no distant date as an elected member and see that the Bill which he was trying to evolve in his official capacity is passed through the Council to the everlasting benefit of the poor Zamindars of this Province.

"Sir, these two eminent Punjabis are soon to lay down the reins of their high office, but their memories shall ever remain green in our hearts. Every man who belongs to this Province will honour their names and cherish their memories in his heart of hearts."

"Then as regards our Sardar Bahadur, I hope that when he shall have managed the sugar factory in the United Provinces, he will come back to us and see that his most cherished object, namely, the Land Revenue Bill, is pushed through this Council and we all trust that he will be a tower of strength to us, the non-official side, when he comes back to us as an elected member.

"Once more, I wish them long life and happiness." Mr. Owen Roberts (Non-official, Nominated) said:

"Sir, I feel it an honour to associate myself. with the appreciation which has been expressed by other Speakers. If anything can contribute to confidence in the future, it is the standard of administration which has been set up by these honourable gentlemen whom we are now bidding farewell. On behalf of those whom I am here to represent, I thank them and bid them God speed".

Rai Bahadur Sir Gopal Das Bhandari (Non-Official, Nominated) said:

"Sir, it is too difficult for me to give expression to our feelings of gratitude to Sir John Maynard and Sardar Bahadur Sardar Sundar Singh Majithia." ...

"I shall be considered to be right in saying that in Sir John Maynard and Sardar Sundar Singh, we shall be missing two luminaries, two bright stars from the firmament of this Province as well as of this Council. They have made a deep impression on our minds which it will be too difficult for time and distance to efface. I can say as regards Sir John Maynard that in him, elements are so combined that even Nature standing here could say that he is a man. As regards Sardar Sundar Singh, I have known him for a very long time and I shall not stand the charge of being partial to him if I say that it is really the proudest day for me to say that Amritsar has produced a man who wherever he was placed did his work and did it to the satisfaction of all concerned. I shall have more occasions to meet him than other honourable Members, but it is the prayer of each and everyone of us that they may have the rest which they have so fully earned, that God may give them a long lease of life and that they should enjoy this rest in happiness and prosperity."

Rana Firoz-ud-Din Khan (South-East Towns: Muhammadan Urban) said:

"Sir, I feei I shall be failing in my duty if I do not associate myself whole-heartedly with everything that has been said about the Honourable Sir John Maynard and the Honourable Sardar Bahadur Sardar Sundar Singh Majithia, by the Speakers who have preceded me."

"Dr. Narang is glad that after all the Honourable Minister for Agriculture has a good word to say about one 'bania' at least. I say, this shows the true Zamindar mentality. His quarrel is with fleecing 'bania' spirit and not with the word 'bania', and that he is not slow to acknowledge good qualities even in a 'bania'.

"As regards Sardar Sundar Singh Sahib, I have no personal knowledge of his services other than those which are connected with the office of the Revenue Member. My friend, Sardar Tara

Singh, has just remarked that our Revenue Member has been long associated with the public life of this Province and has done his best to forward the progress of this Province. His one quality which I admire is that even during the tenure of his high office, he lost no· opportunity of helping the cause of the nation. I hope, Sir, that even now he will associate himself in doing good to the Province in the same manner as before. I need not say much for the simple reason that he is not leaving us in the sense in which the Honourable Sir John Maynard is leaving us. Sardar Sahib will remain in this country, whether in this Province or in another. He is old but he is young at heart."

"Dr. Gokul Chand Narang intervened to remark: 'He is not so old. Only his beard is grey.'

"To the above remark, Rana Firoz-ud-Din replied: **'I** stand corrected."

"Sir, in concluding my remarks, I beg to say that both these honourable gentlemen have discharged their onerous and responsible duties with conspicuous ability, integrity and fair-mindedness and I hope that their successors will also keep in view the traditions which they have established during their office tenures."

Chaudhri Duli Chand (Karnal: Non-Muhammadan - Rural) said:

"I thank you, Sir, for having allowed me to express a few words of tribute to the most valuable services of the Honourable Sir John Maynard and the Honourable Sardar Bahadur Sardar Sundar Singh Majithia.

"Sir, the previous Speakers have touched upon all the points on which I intended to speak and I do not propose to reiterate any of them, lest Sir John Maynard should rise to a point of order, because he knows so many points of order. Anyhow, I wish to say one or two things more.

"As regards Sardar Sundar Singh Sahib, I may say that he is one of the most popular officers of cheerful disposition. Cheerfulness is one of the special traits of his character and I must admit that I have learnt from him that one should always be cheerful in one's dealings with others. Sir, it is a matter of common knowledge that when Government officials go on tour they consider themselves, perhaps for keeping the prestige, super-human and do not mix with people. The poor people get frightened and cannot express themselves truthfully. I may be allowed to refer to a recent tour of the Honourable Sardar Sahib. When he came to our district, people thought him like other touring officers but when Sardar Sahib was found sympathetic and genial to everybody, they were astonished and some of them remarked to the effect that Sardar Sahib was also a human being like themselves. Sir, it was due to his genial and cheerful disposition that even older men came forward and related the state of affairs quite fearlessly and truthfully."

Sardar Jodh Singh (Sikh-Urban) said:

"Sir, I being the last Speaker on this subject, nothing is left for me to say except to feel the satisfaction that the epithet of 'pucca bania: which I used in reference to the Finance Member during my last budget speech is going to, endure." ....

"As for Sardar Bahadur Sardar Sundar Singh, I need not say much. I have the honour of knowing him for the last 23 years and in a junior capacity I was associated with him in the work that he undertook for the uplift of his community. Sir, I need only say this much that *'I have seen very few honorary workers who drudged* so *diligently for the duties that they took up without remuneration and who perhaps in return for all their sweating may get a bad name instead of fame'.*

"Grief has been expressed by many Members because of his parting with us in this House, but in a way I am pleased because as soon as he leaves his present office, he will turn to the educational activities which are now suffering for want of him. When he comes back to public life, we are not going to allow him, as Malik Firoz Khan Noon has said, to run to his sugar factory in the United Provinces, but we propose to see him at the helm of the affairs of the Khalsa College and see it converted into a University before long. With these few words, Sir, I bid a hearty farewell to both the retiring Members.

Replying to the above encomiums, both Sir John Maynard and Sardar Bahadur Sardar Sundar Singh Majithia spoke respectively as under. The Honourable Sir John Maynard, Finance Member, said:

"Sir, I am touched and made happy by the many kind things which have been said by you, Sir, and by the Speakers who have followed. This is the sort of thing that makes one realise, though I knew it before, how many friends one has. Somebody said that farewells are always sad. It is always sad to be doing a thing for the last time. I feel just now that for the last time I have said in this Council: 'I regret that the answer to this question is not ready. It will be communicated to the honourable Members when ready'. May I say, Sir, what I think I have said before that in the capacity of a Finance Member it is really a satisfaction to me to have been described by that name which I think Sardar Jodh Singh invented and which has now become a sort of tradition. Though a 'pucca bania', I am not a registered one, (Laughter), and I am perfectly prepared to render account to anybody who wishes to have it. I am prepared to provide accounts and provide a memorandum of all transactions to anybody who may desire to have it. In a long official career, somebody has called it 40 years, as a matter of fact it is 39, but that is quite near enough for all practical purposes. In a long period of 39 years of service in this Province, I have enjoyed deeply many most interesting episodes, but I think the crowning episode of all was when I saw this young Parliament coming into existence and when I myself was privileged to take part in its deliberations."......

Sardar Bahadur Sardar Sundar Singh Majithia, Revenue Member, spoke as follows:

"Sir, I must thank you heartily and all my brethren in the Council for the very kind way in which they have remembered me and my humble work in this Council for the past five years. I have also to thank my official friends in the back-benches for the very kind way in which they have made mention of me and my connection with them.

"Sir, when I came to this office, I was not well-versed with the ways of officialdom and I was feeling that in coming to a new place, I was probably coming amongst foreigners and strangers. But, my five years' experience has given me impressions which I shall cherish with fond memory throughout the remaining years of my life. I found my official colleagues not only helpful, not only considerate, but always kind and pleasant to meet with and to talk to and discuss matters. I have had the good fortune of coming in contact with a good many heads of departments and I testify here on the floor of this House to the very great help that I have received in the discharge of my duties pertaining to my office (Hear, Hear) from the members of the Civil Service whom I have had to deal with, either as Secretaries of Departments or Heads of Departments.

"No doubt, in my private life, I had been doing some sort o£clerical work (a little bit of clerical work) for my community, to which I have the honour to belong, but when a man comes to new office, he sometimes feels shy and particularly in a big office like that of the Punjab Government where he has a lot to do with many files. I have had long occasions of having to sit among files throughout the past five years of my service, but I must say that the subject matter contained in the cases put before me had been so well put, or shall I say that the matter had been so well cooked that I had not very great difficulty in digesting what was placed before me and in forming my own conclusions thereon.

"Sir, to the Honourable Members of this Council, I must express my thanks for the uniform courtesy which I received at their hands and I will carry back with me pleasant memories of my five years' life in this House. To the kind brethren and friends in this House, and to my colleagues, I am very grateful for the kind way in which they have remembered me and for appreciating what little I have been able to achieve in this office.'

"Sir, I am growing old (Voice: No, no), though I have a great complaint against my honourable colleagues to my right and this was very vividly testified to me when His Excellency the Governor came for the first time to the Punjab on the occasion of his public arrival. My honourable friend, Sir John Maynard, was sitting in the same carriage with me and I had to sit asa junior member to his left. Some of the outside public who were seeing all of us, said: 'See, there goes a Budha, probably my grey beard gave them that impression that I was old.' Though I must say that the young looks of my honourable colleague to my right belied his years, yet I could not hide my age from the public gaze with my grey beard and though I asked my colleague to exchange places, he would not give his place to me because he was really senior to me in life.

"Sir, it is always a great pleasure to one who is laying down the reins of his high office to carry with himself fond memories and kind treatment such as I have received at the hands of the honourable Members of this House. If I may be permitted to say, Sir, I have throughout my official career kept before my mind's eye one ideal in the discharge of my official duties, and that is the oath that is administered to us on the assumption of our office. *When we take office, we are enjoined not to show any favour to any man but to discharge our duty honestly, straightforwardly and justly. I have always had that oath before me and though by persuasion I am a Sikh, yet as a public servant of the Punjab, I had been a servant of all the communities. (Hear, Hear). I have tried to keep this principle before me, namely, that I am neither a Sikh nor a Muhammadan nor a Christian nor a Hindu, so long as I am a member of this Government and holding this high office, though by belief I am a Sikh, but that* is *between me and my God.*

"Sometimes, Sir, I felt and felt it very strongly and it always pained me to hear of dissensions and differences between the different members of the various communities that inhabit this Province. What is it after all a few loaves and fishes that we are wrangling and quarrelling for? Is that to be the be-all and the end-all of our existence? Surely not. We should work for the advancement of the Province in which we live; official and non-official all alike must join hands in happy concord to carry on the great work that lies before them. We must always learn from those who are able to give us instructions and we must never hesitate to learn things which might go to improve us, whatever be the source from which they come. *If we all cultivate the habit of loving each other, of respecting each other and of respecting each other's religious feelings and sentiments, I am sure, that a good deal of the misunderstandings and differences that we find in this world today would come to an end and not only the Government and Government officials would be happy, but also the whole world would become a peace-loving and a happy family.*

"In conclusion, I thank you all once more from the bottom of my heart for all the kind words that you have said about me. To my friend, Mian Muhammad Shah Nawaz, I must express that I am afraid that I have not done much for his project, but I can take pride in the fact that the scheme about the Thal Project has gone to the Secretary of State for his sanction. Though I am not able to convey to my honourable friend the sanction of the Secretary of State, let me hope that it will come, as it is bound to come, in course of time. No doubt, the scheme has been a little bid delayed but deferred hope is always sweet. (Applause)."[14]

[14]Punjab Legislative Council Debates, Vol.III, part B): National Archives of India, New Delhi.

The zeal with which Sir Sundar Singh & his colleagues like Sir Chhotu Ramworked to safeguard the interests of the agriculturists led them to criticism as 'Zamindar's Government'. While Sir Chhotu Ram is remembered by people of Haryana by way of celebration of his birth anniversary by 'Jat Mahasabha' in Rohtak and other places in January every year, there is no such expression of gratitude by any organization in Punjab despite his great contribution for the welfare of the farmers of his state. Even name of the road leading to the 'Majithia House' at Amritsar, which was named after him, was subsequently changed with that of another political leader.

10

Personality of Sir Sundar Singh

The family traits, education and knowledge acquired, aims and objects of life along with the ways and means adopted to achieve them; the extent of success, observance of moral values and contribution to socio-economic welfare of the society, are some of the characteristics of extraordinary persons who leave their imprint on the history of mankind. Writing about an ideal man, Aristotle wrote:

> "He is of a disposition to do men service, though he is ashamed to have a service done to him. To confer a kindness is a mark of superiority; to receive one is a mark of subordination. .... He never feels media, and always forgets and passes over injuries. .... He does not speak evil of others, even of his enemies, unless it be to themselves .... He bears the accidents of life with dignity and grace, making the best of his circumstances, like a skilful general who marshals his limited forces with all the strategy of war. .... He is his own best friend, and takes delight in privacy whereas the man of no virtue or ability is his worst enemy and is afraid of solitude!".

while Immanuel Kant - the German philosopher, describes the in-born sincerity and sense of duty in a man in the following words:

> "...an action is good not because it has good results, or because it is wise, but because it is done in obedience to this inner sense of duty, this moral law does not come out from personal experience, but legislates imperiously and *a priori* for all our behaviour, past, present and future. The only thing unqualifiedly good in this world is a goodwill - the will to follow the moral law, regardless of profit or loss for ourselves. Never mind your happiness; do your duty. .... It is a hard ethic,

[1] "The Story of Philosophy" by Will Durant, p. 79

you say, this placing of duty above beauty, of morality above happiness; but only so can we cease to be beasts and begin to be gods."[2]

That Sir Sundar Singh Majithia was, indeed, fired with a sense of duty towards his community, the Nation and the Society as a whole, is illustrated by the activities that occupied almost his entire life-span, is evident from the preceding chapters of this biography which, in fact, is the history of the entire community, holding out lessons from the past for the present generation to equip them with clear perceptions about the future.

Personality Assessment

To arrive at a fair and unbiased assessment of the personality of Sir Sundar Singh Majithia, it will be relevant to take a note of the different view-points about him.

Akali view: While dubbing his modus - operandi of 'fruitful cooperation with the Govt. of the day to the extent of community's interests', none of his strong critics ever questioned his integrity as a true & devout Sikh or his concern/ contribution for the upliftment of poor & down trodden, peasants and community as a whole. Even Master· Tara Singh, the great Akali Leader, who was one of his avowed critics, referred to his magnanimity and gentle behaviour in letter dated 28.6.34 which he wrote from Rangoon during one of his self-imposed exiles:

"At this parting, I remember you not only as a friend but also as a person who was kind to me when I was a student*, No doubt, I fell out with you occasionally, but your regard never diminished in my heart[3]" .....However it is a fact these two personalities represented two divergent rather conflicting views of Sikh politics with almost same level of determination as both were men of firm convictions. While one led the popular wave of anti-British and pro-Congress movement, the

[2]Ibid. ps. 276-277

*Bhai Jodh Singh says that he introduced Master Tara Singh as a promising and talented student to Sardar Sundar Singh Majithia, who was Secretary of Khalsa College at that time, and recommended him for financial help. Accordingly, Sardar Sundar Singh extended the financial help to him through funds of Sardar Dyal Singh's 'Samadh' - Interview with Bhai Jodh Singh by the Author on 25.6.78.

[3]"Some confidential papers of the Akali movement" Ed. Ganda Singh, published by SGPC, Amritsar, p. 308.

other worked independent from the Congress, if not always pro-British. The fact remains that both were true Sikhs and sincere to the community they represented and had different perceptions about preservation and protection of its interests.

British View : Despite a general opinion about Sardar Sundar Singh due to his life long cooperation with the British Government in various reforms it introduced in the country and acceptance of his offices and privileges, the report dated 11th August, 1911 of Mr. D. Petrie, Asstt. Director, Intelligence, Govt. of India reflects a different impression about him, "there is' conduct of the Chief Khalsa Dewan leaders, Sundar Singh Majithia and others, who are the controlling centre of the body, who are constantly in the company of such persons as Jagat Singh 'updeshak' and other preachers who are responsible for the type of speeches and writings which have been described.

Sundar Singh's companions are such men as Trilochan Singh, pleader, Vir Singh of the Khalsa Samachar News paper, Jodh Singh of the Khalsa College and others. The disloyalty of these men is notorious, and is admitted on all hands[4]"....

Moderate View: Bhai Jodh Singh, during his farewell speech on the eve of retirement of Sir Sundar Singh as a Revenue Member of Punjab Legislative Council on 12th December, 1925, described his character in the following words:

> "I have seen very few honorary workers who drudged so diligently for the duties that they took up without remuneration and who perhaps in return for all their sweating may get a bad name instead of fame".[5]

Bhai Jodh Singh, one of the contemporaries of Majithia Sardar also felt that although he had come across hundreds of Sikh leaders during his public life, who valiantly led various crusades against oppression and tyranny, but none of them appeared to be as capable, farsighted, sincere, dedicated and selfless as the Majithia Sardar.[6]

Admirer's View: For making an assessment of the personality and contribution of any leader of the community or the Nation, the

[4]"Development in Sikh Politics" (1900-1911) by D. Petrie, published by Chief Khalsa Dewan.

[5]"Punjab Legislative Council Debates" Vol. VII, Part B-P. 1757, National Archives of India, New Delhi.

[6]Interview with Bhai Jodh Singh by the Author on 25.6.1978

Addresses of Honour' which are presented to him at various places during his life time, could be considered as a broadly correct picture, discounting the little exaggeration or extra praise which are natural ingredients for such occasions.

The following Address which the electorates of Batala Constituency presented to Sir Sundar Singh Majithia on March 1, 1937 is reproduced below:

> "During the end of October 1936 when all the communities were having serious consultations for sending best representatives to the Punjab Assembly from their respective constituencies, we, the humble people, were thinking that the person whom we choose as a representative of the Sikhs from Batala Tehsil should be such whose integrity would be trusted, whose heart should be full of love for his community, who should have the capacity and capability to discriminate between good and bad for the community, who steer 'the boat of the community from the present whirlpool' with his political wisdom and statesmanship."
>
> "Lovable Sardar Ji: during repeated deliberations about these qualities for electing our representative, we could not think about any other great personality than yourself because you possess each one of those qualities which the true 'Jathedar' of a community should possess."
>
> "The true dedication, determination and selflessness and the relentless spirit with which you worked for the last 40 years, has changed the entire outlook of the community besides infusing new life in its educational, social and religious spheres. About 450 Sikh educational institutions in Punjab is the result of your hard work and the Khalsa College, which is now approaching the status of a University, is the living example of your love for the community and tireless work. Lakhs of rupees of the community are safe in your hands in every respect. While you have earned the deep affection of the Sikhs for these services to the community, Hindus and Muslims were impressed with your great qualities during your tenure of five years as Member of the Executive Council of Punjab."
>
> "Needless to say that for a great personality like you, the membership of the Punjab Assembly is neither a matter of great attraction nor there is any doubt that whichever place

you had selected, the brethren of that constituency would have considered themselves as fortunate and would have gladly elected you. We are indebted to you that you have acceded to our request and given this honour to us and w.e are not only giving a capable member to the Punjab Assembly but also a 'Jathedar' to other Members of the Council who would protect the interests of their community besides safeguarding Hindus and Muslim brethren, who' would consider you as their true friend[7]".

Humility

Perhaps, one of the greatest qualities and characteristics was the humility of the magnetic personality of Sir Sundar Singh which made even the stoutest hearts bend in reverence before him, as borne out from some of the speeches and events narrated below. Replying to the Addresses of Honour in the villages Murrer and Ghania-ki-Bandar in Batala Tehsil when he was honoured on March 27, 1937 on the eve of 'Hola Mohalla', Sir Sunder Singh said:

"The service which you have entrusted to the humble servant is not easy to perform in the present circumstances. It is different from what I performed earlier. The composition of the Council was of different nature and the governance was not by the elected representatives of the people. In the new system, the responsibility of Government lies on the shoulders of the representatives elected by you. You give blessings to your representatives and help them with your consistent affection and confidence. ... *When this humble servant had appeared before you before the elections, I had submitted that the motive of the Party whom* I *am going to represent in the Assembly, is to act upon and take maximum advantage from the new system of Government; thereby reaching the final goal of 'Swaraj'. You have honoured me by making me your representative and I have confidence that you endorse the aim, object and programme of the Khalsa National Party*[8].

During the second Conference held by Sri Guru Nanak Dharam Parchar Diwan, U.P. at Gorakhpur on November 1-3, 1940, Sir Sundar Singh presided and expressed the following sentiments:

[7]"Khalsa Te Khalsa Advocate", Amritsar: March 3, 1937, p. 5.

[8]"Khalsa Te Khalsa Advocate", Amritsar, March 30, 1937, p.l.

"I realize my weaknesses and must have made some mistakes in the performance of my duties, but I have faith in the benevolence of the Guru and the Almighty Father who, I trust, shall accept me whatever I am and I shall consider myself most fortunate if I get place among the shoes of the holy congregation. I know that it is very difficult to be a true Sikh, but if the Guru accepts this body and bowed head, no body would dare to lift his head from the feet of the 'Sat Guru'. I am reminded of Tulsi Dass who loved Shri Ram Chander who refused to prostrate himself in the Mandir of Sri Krishan and said:

(Tulsi will bow his head only if Thou have the Arrow and the Arch in Your hands).

"I, once again, thank you for the honour which you bestowed upon me by making me President of this Conference. So *long as we are together and owe allegiance to the Guru, I am yours and you belong to me, no body can come between us to divide. Let us unite and remain united to work for the mission of the Sat Guru and for the glory of the community. Let us do our best for the service of the community and the Nation and I have complete faith that if we make united efforts, success will be ours*[9]....

Other important political Resolutions" which this Conference passed were as follows:

"1. Condemnation of the scheme of Pakistan.

2. Sikhs should be given the status of minority in United Provinces with 5% reservations.

[9]"Khalsa Te Khalsa Advocate", Amritsar: November 14, 1940, p.19

*The above political Resolutions and his speeches a few months before his death as also the declared object of the Khalsa National Party, i.e. attainment of complete 'Swaraj' as also the unification of all the communities into a "United Indian Nation" besides promotion of 'communal concord as a prelude to development of Nationality', as also the fact that he had not only developed his own industrial estate in U.P. but was also honoured by the Government of United Provinces by making him Honorary Munsif of District Gorakhpur as early as July 1906, clearly indicate his staunch nationalist, broad and secular approach while simultaneously working to ensure that his own community was able to secure maximum constitutional safeguards and adequate representation in the inevitable changed system of governance in all the Provinces where they had pockets of population.

3. There should be no restriction in U.P. on 'Kirpan' - a religious symbol of the Sikhs.

4. Proper recording of population of the Sikhs during the census and the Sikh officials to be associated in adequate number during the census.

5. Every 'Nanak-Panthi' should register himself as a Sikh.

6. Government holidays on the 'Gurpurabs' of the Sikh Gurus.

7. There should be atleast one representative of the Sikhs in the Legislative Council.

8. Organized preaching of the Sikh religion in U.P., etc.[10]"

Some Incidents

Apart from the above speeches, deep humility of the Majithia Sardar is also illustrated in some of the incidents/' events which would have normally evoked a strong reaction from any ordinary person. Once, Sir Sundar Singh went to 'Akal Takht' to attend a 'Panthic' meeting at the invitation of the Shiromani Gurdwara Prabandhak Committee. A few persons, having difference of opinion, uttered a few words against his personality. But enlightened and wise people in that very meeting moved a Resolution expressing resentment and hatred against those who had attacked the Majithia Sardar. Sir Sundar Singh, who was present in the meeting, stood up as soon as the Resolution was moved. With a heavy heart and tears in his eyes, he said:

"Khalsa Ji! Whatever you are going to do is intended for my respect, but if you have my respect in your heart, please put this Resolution in my lap[11]".

He kept on standing with his stretched shirt till the Resolution was withdrawn.

How Differences Are Resolved

Sardar Jodh Singh wrote in the daily 'Ajit' on October 3, 1978:

"The religious head of the Roman Catholic Christians is called the Pope. His selection is conducted unanimously. At the time of his election process, the senior Bishops lock themselves in a specified hall. As long as black smoke comes out

[10]Ibid.

[11]Sir Sundar Singh Majithia: Ed. Mehar Singh Rawel, p.30

of the chimney of that hall, people outside understand that unanimity has not been reached. When white smoke is emitted out from that chimney, it is an indication that agreement on Pope has been reached. Those Bishops cannot come out without deciding on one name."

"When agreements take place in the wake of some common danger and differences of years are resolved within a few second, selfless and persons of love do not quarrel at all, but if there is a misunderstanding, the true love brings them together again. This kind of agreement is not dependent on any argument, force or compulsion[12]".

He refers to one such incident involving Sir Sundar Singh Majithia and Sardar Harbans Singh Attari, who were both working together in the service of the community in the spheres of Chief Khalsa Diwan and Khalsa College, Amritsar having inherited virtues and values from their great ancestors connected with the Sikh kingdom of Maharaja Ranjit Singh. Despite the material richness - around them, their magnetic personalities were embodiment of high moral values whose simplicity, sincerity and dedication were the hall-mark of their lives in the traditions of true Gur Sikhs.[13]

"The residents of Palaces had love and respect for ordinary Sikhs in their hearts. Recitation of their daily prayers (Nit-Name), listening to hymns and reading of 'Gurbani' was part of their daily activity. Throughout his life, Sardar Sundar Singh Majithia had been going to the Golden Temple, Amritsar, to pay his obeisance. After having seen Sardar Harbans Singh Attari serving shoes at the Sikh Educational Conferences, persons like Diwan Chuhar Mal and other Sindhis became beloved Sikhs of the Guru. During the course of this service to the community, some misunderstanding developed between the two. Sardar Sundar Singh Majithia lived in Majitha House, Amritsar, while Sardar Harbans Singh Attari lived seventeen miles away at Attari Nagar."

"Mutual contacts stopped due to some misunderstanding. Besides interruptions in the service to the community, this physical separation became unbearable for the two souls. Both

[12] "The Daily Ajit" (Punjabi): Oct. 3, 1978, p.l.
[13] Ibid.

were selfless. Both were passengers of the same path. The source of inspiration for both was the 'Gurbani' which gives lesson of humility. Then, why they became indifferent to each other? What prevented them from becoming one again?

Longing of love and affection would often make them restless. Their souls might have been meeting between Amritsar and Attari but the chains of ego would prevent their bodies to come close to each other."

"One day, this longing of love became unbearable for Sardar Sundar Singh Majithia. All complaints and misunderstandings vanished. The feeling of age and worldly superiority also went away. The spirit of love activated the body. Driving his car, Sardar Sundar Singh went straight to Attari where Sardar Harbans Singh was also feeling restless since morning. He was also undergoing the same feeling as experienced by Sardar Sundar Singh. Today, he was standing outside his house as if he was waiting for somebody. His feet were also dragging him towards Amritsar. Something was going to happen. Someone was going to come."

"Within no time, the car of Sardar Sundar Singh reached. Sardar Sahib came out. Sardar Harbans Singh moved ahead and a stream of tears rolled down their cheeks. They embraced each other. Tears said everything which silent tongues could not say at that moment. All misunderstandings were removed. The entire bitterness was gone. After fifteen minutes of tearful embrace, their eyes met each other. They were sparkling with a strange brightness. There was a sacred glow on their faces. They became one again and were never divided into two thereafter."

"Differences are also resolved like this. Alas! We could have such reconciliation among our leaders of national level[14].

Despite his general disposition of humility, as stated above, he had clear perceptions of men, events and ideologies besides the interests of the community, about which he had the courage of conviction to express himself fearlessly as elderly statesman and leader of the community would be expected to do, attracting criticism which he would resent and even threats to his life. Referring to a meeting where Sardar Mehtab Singh used some offending words about Sardar Sundar Singh, Sardar Ujjal Singh, then

[14]Ibid.

Member of the Legislative Council, wrote in his letter dated 21.9.1932 to Sardar Sundar Singh:

"Many thanks for your very kind letter dated the 19th instant.

"I fully appreciate your feelings and your just indignation at the treatment of some of the members of the Council of Action. But, believe me, that none of us - atleast I can speak with confidence about myself - was very attentive to what everyone was saying at the meeting. The views of all those sitting were well known and we were all talking with the members sitting on either side. No serious notice was taken of what actually fell from the lips of Sardar Mehtab Singh. I regret very much that he used words which he should not have done. I believe, if it is known to him that his words have given you cause for resentment, he will be prepared to apologize.

"Every Sikh, I am sure, has the highest respect for you, no matter how different views he might hold from you.

"My only justification in repeating the request I made in my last letter is that so long as the method of protest is constitutional, there is no reason why the whole community should not be able to take a united action. Young men and enthusiasts can benefit by your experience and wise head while you can be made to move slightly quicker by their enthusiasm. So far, there is no fundamental difference in the programme proposed by anybody. But, if the community stands divided,* the whole effect of the constitutional protest will be lost.

*That the divergence of views in the community had always persisted and its divided approach has resulted in harming of its own interest; thereby making the task of its well-meaning leaders very difficult, is also borne out from the following comments of Dr. Bhai Jodh Singh: "I feel that the S.G.P.C. was a religious body. In my mind, politics and religion are not the same thing. Even now, I am opposed to this when Akalis say that politics and religion are the same. They refer to the old Sikh times. Then, the existence of the Sikhs depended upon their political life; their religion and politics were same in the times of Baba Banda and Guru Gobind Singh, but not now. Sikhs are now divided. There are some communists, there are some socialists, and there are (similarly) Congressmen. They cannot come together. I cannot visualize that Hindus and Hindus alone will ever govern India. They are also divided into communists, socialists, Congressmen, Jan Sanghis and what not. I cannot imagine that at any time, there will be a Government in India based on religion."

(Interview with Dr. Bhai Jodh Singh by Dr. Hari Dev Sharma: Nehru Memorial Museum & Library, New Delhi).

"I still hope that you will not allow the community to go wild or fall prey to extremism and will give the benefit of your guidance along the right channels[15]".

Sardar Sewa Ram Singh, B.A., LL,..B., Advocate

There is a very typical example of harsh language which Sardar Sewa Ram Singh, one of his many 'friends', had used about the contribution which Sardar Sundar Singh had asked for the Khalsa Orphanage at Amritsar. In his letter, dated Nov. 9th, 1930, Sardar Sewa Ram Singh wrote:

"I am in receipt of your kind letter of the 7th instant. I have already endowed (or, endorsed) four permanent 'langars' in the orphanage, two in the name of my parents and two of my own. I am afraid, 1 am unable to do more at present for an institution which is controlled by a body which is almost dead and defunct.

"As to my joining the band of 40 personal friends of yours, 1 wonder if such a status could be purchased by payment of a sum of Rs. 500/ - to a fund, which is meant to liquidate a debt that should never have been incurred. 1 believe, we have had enough in the Chief Khalsa Diwan, of calling upon 'personal friends' to contribute to such funds.

"The worthless rag of a paper, which was started with a sinister fund of, 1 believe, over 30 thousand, and dragged down the pre-existing English paper, that was doing some humble work with it, is still being nominally carried on, though no body cares to look into it, much less to pay for it. 1 believe that another fund will soon be started from 'personal friends' again to round off its budget. There are many more such things which may be said but I hope this is enough. Under the circumstances, I beg to be excused.

"In spite of this, however, kindly believe me, as I have always believed it and tried to live up to it, as ever and for ever[16]".

The contents of immediate reply which Sir Sundar Singh Majithia sent to Sardar Sewa Ram Singh, vide his letter, dated

[15]Papers of Sir Sundar Singh Majithia: Nehru Memorial Museum & Library, New Delhi.

[16]Personal Papers of Sir Sundar Singh Majithia: (File No. 89): Nehru Memorial Museum & Library, New Delhi.

Nov. 10, 1930, reveal his sensitivity and concern for the service to humanity. He wrote from Majitha house, Amritsar:

"My dear brother,

I have received your letter dated 9.11.1930. You have addressed me as 'My dear Brother'. Age hence entitles me to consider that the letter is being received from the younger brother, to whom the elder has a privilege to tender counsel of experience. As such the least that I could say is that the tenor and tone of your letter have been disappointing. They seem to befit more the Western mundane thought of the present day than the sublime heritage of the Sikh ideal. They may suit a Sessions Judge's snubbing to his subordinates, but I seriously doubt if they could find any place in a friendly communication, unless habit had become a second nature. I should not have expected them from you.

"The Chief Khalsa Diwan has been described contemptibly as "a body dead and defunct" as if yourself have not been and are not a part and parcel thereof sharing the responsibility of what it now is, or is described to be. Even if dead and defunct (with which there is no agreement), it was *alive* sometimes and you and others too, who partook and even now share in its activities and services rendered, should have a kinder thought towards it. The Orphanage building was a necessity. Without it, the orphanage could not live on and I cannot see how the debt for purchase of orphanage building which was incurred by agreement of all concerned who cared to take any interest, could now be described as one, "which should never have been incurred." The worthless rag of a paper, for which thousands were spent, is surely not what it should be but do we not, yourself including, have a share of the responsibility? You say, Diwan may soon start another fund from 'personal friends' again "to round its budget" and that you had enough of such things .and wished to be excused. If you feel happy in this mood and its expression, I should be very reluctant to disturb your happiness, but as one who in the discharge of what I believe to be service to the community have on more occasions than one relied upon you as a colleague and co-worker in the same noble work, would ask you to ponder, at quieter moment which path has one to follow:

(a) To serve the community as part of tile humanity and the Guru, or,

(b) To consider the charitable contributions made as obligations done to friends and even to think them to have gone so low that their friendship could only be purchased by payment of money.

"If your contributions to the Panthic Institutions have to be in the latter spirit, it is right time to call a halt, but I request you not to forget that if the past has changed, the present also has always been and is in all time to be liable to change.

"The subject, however, relates to the contribution of the Orphanage and I should take the letter to be addressed to its "Member Incharge". As such, however strongly I may feel, the language and its purport, I am duty bound to take it meekly and say, brother, the great Guru has been merciful to you, pray do not refrain from being merciful to His Children."

"Wishing you every happiness and with the earnest thought that the "One" to whom we have always to look up may lead us kindly to light[17]".

Therefore, it was surprising that this power of sheer humility had enabled Sardar Sundar Singh not only to win back one of his friends but who also sought favour of nomination as a candidate for election on behalf of Khalsa National Party founded by the Majithia Sardar about six years later. In his letter dated 15th August, 1936, Sardar Sewa Ram Singh wrote from Lahore:

"My dear brother,

I understand that applications of prospective candidates who desire to contest the next elections on the ticket of the Khalsa National Party, are invited upto the end of this month. I, however, read in the last week's issue of the Khalsa Samachar that certain candidates including Sir Jogindra Singh himself, had already been adopted by the Party. I was surprised not to find my name in the list though I had informed both yourself and Sir Jogindra Singh that I intended to contest the election and I expected that you will settle about me with the Giani Party. You had promised to do so.

"It appears to me that though the Giani Party has yet made no official announcement, yet his followers in Pindi are backing up Uttam Singh. Would you please take steps as early

[17]Ibid.

as possible to adjust the matter with the Giani and secure the, Pindi Rural seat for me? If this is not done, our defeat there would be certain, for our votes being divided between Uttam Singh and myself, it might be a walk over for Harnam Singh, the Akali candidate.

"You had also promised that after the formation of the Party, you will declare that the Akali Party refusing to cooperate, use of your name and that of Sir Jogindra Singh by Harnam Singh among his supporters was unauthorized.

"Kindly let me have a reply by return of post as to what action you were taking in the matter, so that I may proceed further in the matter. I am sending a formal application to Buta Singh at Amritsar."

Sardar Sundar Singh wrote back to Sardar Sewa Ram Singh vide his letter dated 19th August, 1936, as follows:

"My dear brother,

Yours of the 15th to hand. I am sorry I was not able to reply earlier owing to other engagements. I have looked up the Khalsa Samahar issue of 13.8.36 which is the latest and I have not come across the name of any person alleged to have been adopted by the Khalsa National Party. It may be that you have read in some other paper. But, so far we have not adopted any candidate on behalf of the Party and no intimation of any such adoption has been issued on behalf of the party. I have noticed, however, that people have been intimating in public press their wish to stand as candidates for coming elections. Our endeavour so far has been to establish District Committees and for this purpose a meeting was held at Ferozepur. We are now going to Ropar on the 30th with the same view. I have noted what you have said about the candidature of Sardar Uttam Singh Duggal. I learn from Giani Sher Singh that they have already promised him their support and he has been going about in the constituency to enlist support. I note that you are also standing for. the same constituency. But I am not sure whether you have started your campaign in this connection. From what I know of Sardar Uttam Singh, I can say that when he was opposing Sardar Mangal Singh in the last election, he was showing great activity; so, unless you are very serious about your election campaign, you will find him a tough competitor and very obstinate to deal with.

"As regards Sardar Haman Singh, there is no doubt about it that on occasion of Sardar Mangal Singh's election, we (myself and Sardar Jodh Singh) did give him a promise of support and I am not sure what attitude I shall adopt now that the Akali Party of Master' Tara Singh is not working with us. This is a matter which shall seriously require anxious thought and delicate handling. Next time when I come to the plains, I will take steps to consult Master Tara Singh about the matter and with the door of adjustment not having been finally dosed, we may be able to arrive at some amicable decision in the matter. At any rate, I would suggest that if you are keen about election, you should start your campaign immediately and without any delay in the matter as the election in this constituency must mean a tough fight for the candidate. Please let me know in what paper you have read about the candidates having been nominated by the Khalsa National Party as I have not sent out any such list of nominations, none having been nominated so far. No such list has been issued so far from the Office; the only person about whom we have committed ourselves is Sardar Dilbagh Singh of Layallpur and I believe he stands as a candidate on behalf of the Khalsa National Party but his name too has not been published on behalf of the Party in any newspaper[18]".

Professor Teja Singh, M.A.

The. contents of following note from Professor Teja Singh, M.A. addressed to Sardar Sundar Singh Majithia reflects the extent of esteem in which he was held even by those who had quite different views on political affairs:

"My dear Sardar Bahadur,

You know my past career. My chief interest has been in religious, academic and literary matters and I have therefore confined my activities to these spheres alone. By disposition, I am incapable of indulging in sedition, and have even avoided politics, so that I might better do my work wherein I am chiefly interested. This is what I want to stick to and I assure you that I don't intend to take part in political agitation.

[18]Ibid.

In the SGPC too I have always tried to keep the right temper and work for reasonableness.

"To you, as one who has taken so much kindly interest in my past career, I write this note to assure you that it would be sheer injustice to rank me as a seditionist or revolutionary. I am confident, that knowing me as you do, you will kindly remove any misunderstanding that may be lurking anywhere about me[19]".

But, he had his share of threats to life, as illustrated from the following note despatched to him obviously during the period of elections to Punjab Assembly in 1936:

"Dear Sir,

I regret to inform you that I am compelled to appoint a special person for you to make you an aim of shooting in coming time on account of your offering a greatest part of this fool Government.

"Dear brother, no more mercy for you, although you have been alarmed a long time ago. Therefore, you may request to Mr. Odvire (head of thieves) and to Mr. Harding (Chief of Pirates) to send some special troops to your protection.

"But of no vain. Anyhow, you should be finished very soon.

Yours faithfully
(Sd) Khan Akber Singh
A Leader of Revolt[20]"

Speeches

Undeterred by such criticisms and threats, he continued to work for the welfare of his community which was always his primary concern. Dismayed as he was over the schism which developed in the Akali Camp after the Gurdwaras came under the Panthic control, he spoke with anguish while delivering Presidential Address at Gujranwala in 1935:

"I pray to Sat Gurus that the path of Guru Nanak and Guru Gobind Singh may alivaysbe in *high spirits and the Sikh brethren should live like brothers as they had been living during the difficult periods of 'Ghalugharas' when mountains and forests were their houses and the horse-cradles were their beds. During those difficult times, they used to bid farewell again and again, for* it *was not sure that*

[19]Ibid. (Personal Diary, 1924).

[20]Ibid.

they would meet again. Whereas in those period, difficulties were a 'boon' for us, now 'affluence' (comfort) has become a 'curse' for us. It is very sad that brother is *indulging in quarrels with a brother*[21]*"*.

Following excerpts from some of his speeches display sense of concern for the 'Panth' and reflect a deeply religious personality.

May 1937 : He said at many places -

"I am a worthless servant. I shall help wherever I can, but I will not oppose where I cannot help. I shall not return abuses with abuses, but with love for those who abuse me are also my brothers[22]".

"If every one tries to understand his religion fully and realize that God is present in everyone, then they will regard each other as brothers and jealousies and differences will cease to exist[23]*"*.

Speaking at Layallpur on September 4, 1938, he said: "My principle is to do work, work, work and never make a pretence[24]".

He said at Sialkot in October, 1938:

"I have regarded as a great privilege and good luck the service which I *could do for the Guru Panth for the last fifty years, not with a. view to get appreciation.* I *am happy that the Panth has accepted this little service. The aim of a Sikh while doing service is to do it for the sake of service*[25]*"* ....

In 1934, Satguru Partap Singh of Namdharis organised a joint conference of all the Sikh sects at their headquarter, Bhaini Sahib, wherein Sir Sundar Singh also participated. Speaking on the occasion, he said:

"Dear brothers who are fortunate to love Guru Nanak! ... You and the Namdhari Darbar have given us an opportunity to sit together with affection and discuss the matters before. The truth over which we have pondered was touching our hearts for quite some time. Which heart who recites Sat Guru's name can tolerate this division in the 'Panth'? Those were the times when journey was difficult; there were no arrangements for preaching when our Sat Guru Nanak Dev

[21]'Sir Sundar Singh Majithia': Ed. Mehar Singh Rawel.

[22]Ibid.

[23]Ibid.

[24]Ibid.

[25]Ibid.

Ji took Bhai Mardana along on the four long sojourns he undertook on the earth to provide spiritual solace by teaching the path of union with the Almighty. He did all this for the betterment of mankind. He underwent all the difficulties while passing through the mountains, deep forests, oceans and if was during these long journeys that he blessed people like 'Kanda the Demon'. How can we, the Sikhs of the Sat Guru, tolerate mutual dissension, division and failure to unite? The great service rendered by Maharaj Partap Singh and Namdhari Darbar in an endeavour to unite us, deserve sincere appreciation and our gratitude. The fine examples of service, the recitation of Gurbani and the opportunity which he has provided to listen to singing of the sacred hymns (Kirtan) was excellent. The practice of singing of Gurbani on the tunes of theatres is becoming more popular among us, which is not in accordance with our tradition as it motivates our mind towards mischief instead of spiritual solace. I have requested Bhai Harnam Singh Ragi to bless us with his presence sometimes at our Orphanage at Amritsar.

"He (Maharaj Partap Singh Ji) has done a great service to the 'Panth' by uniting the gems of the Panth like a necklace. I express gratitude of the entire congregation to him and the Namdhari Darbar. What I have said is on behalf of the entire congregation and I am confident that Maharaj will not be offended at me.

"Simultaneously, I express gratitude to the representatives of all the Sects who have gathered here to resolve the important 'Panthic' matter. I am also grateful to Bhai Sahib Bagrian who has kept his family tradition and has provided leadership in this sacred task[26]".

Verses

The extreme humility of Sir Sundar Singh is also exhibited in the verses recorded in his handwriting in response to a small poem written by Sardar Bakhshish Singh, Assistant Manager of Bhai Ajit Singh Jujhar Singh Khalsa High School, Sri Chamkaur Sahib, who wrote:

[26] "Khalsa Te Khalsa Advocate", Amritsar: Nov. 1934.

" [illegible]
[illegible]
[illegible]
[illegible]
[illegible]
[illegible]
[illegible]
[illegible]

(Translation:

"Thy Name is beautiful and beautiful is disposition, Uniform inner and outer-self of body which is sweet, Adorned with the red colour, thou are overwhelmed in the colour of red in the spirit of Sikhism,

Service of others have been thy work and profession,

Thou have always been a servant of the community,

Thou love has overwhelmed my heart,

As I saw thou what I heard about thee."[27]

The verses recorded by Sir Sundar Singh on the reverse of this poem reveal a rare example of a great but humble personality:

" [illegible]
[illegible]
[illegible]
[illegible]
[illegible]
[illegible]
[illegible]
[illegible]
[illegible]
[illegible]
[illegible]
[illegible]
[illegible]
[illegible]
[illegible]
[illegible]

[27]Personal Papers of Sir Sundar Singh Majithia: (Nehru Memorial Museum & Library, New Delhi- File No. 105).

Translation:
"Christened I have been but my deeds have not been handsome,
Which makes me ashamed in my heart,
Which had influenced me to commit acts so wrong,
Whose thoughts now frighten my mind,
Just see my wickedness and wretchedness,
That despite such deeds I got christened as handsome,
Even then I have faith in the benevolence of the Guru,
That is why I did not get my name changed,
I am red by birth not by deeds,
How should I get my heart painted with the colour of God,
Without seeking the blessing of the Guru Panth,
How can I dive in the ocean of goodness,
The wickedness has prevented cleaning of this body sheet,
Which makes it sink farther in the dirt of heart,
Having always faith in the benevolence of the Sat Guru,
I continue to console myself."[28]

A True and Devout Sikh

The following excerpts from the notings of Sardar Sundar Singh Majithia in his personal diaries provide an insight into a deeply religious and devout personality which he possessed, besides conveying his sense of concern and involvement with his community, family and other socio-political responsibilities:[29]

"*Thursday, Jan. 1, 1903:* (It pertains to his stay at Delhi along with his colleagues of Chief Khalsa Diwan in connection with Coronation Darbar of the King of Great Britaini).[30]

May God's benevolence be there!

'We culprits always commit mistakes, You are full of forgiveness.'*

"To-day, the Coronation Durbar was held. I washed my hair. Wrote to President, Patiala Council about the tents.

"Nit-Name" (Daily Prayer)**

[28]Ibid.

[29]Nehru Memorial Museum & Library, New Delhi.

[30]Ibid.

* " ਹਮ ਅਪਰਾਧੀ ਸਦ ਭੂਲਤੇ
ਤੁਮ ਬਖਸਨਹਾਰੇ॥"

**The baptized Sikhs are supposed to recite atleast five daily prayers ('Paths') which begin with 'Jap Ji' and 'Jap' usually early in the morning.

Japji Sahib - 5 recitations ('path')
Jap Sahib - 1 recitation
Rah-Ras - 1 recitation
Sohila - 1 recitation

"Saw the illumination at the Baroda Camp. It was electric illumination. "LONG LIVE THE KING EMPEROR" appeared again and again in three colours: Red, Green and White."

"*January 2, 1903:* "Could not get up early in the morning. I was asleep at dawn. Daily prayer ('Nit-Name):

Japji Sahib - 3 recitations (two balance).
Jap Sahib - 1 recitation.
Rah-Ras - 1 recitation.
Sohila - 1 recitation.

"Meeting of the Diwan (Chief Khalsa) began at the Cavalry Lines. Went in the evening and met S. Bhagwant Singh on the way whereas further passage was closed. Therefore, reached the fort via' Kashmiri Darwaja (Gate) and saw the Investiture Hall along with Alison. Passage was again closed on way back."

"*January 3, 1903:* "Distributed books and tracts to the Sardars of the Punjab on behalf of Chief Khalsa Diwan.

Daily Prayer ('Nit-Name')

Japji Sahib - 5 recitations (couldn't complete balance of 2nd Jan.)
Jap Sahib - 1 recitation.
Rah-Ras - 1 recitation.
Sohila - 1 recitation.

Attended the meeting of the Diwan. In the evening, S. Bhagwant Singh Ji presented 'Shagan' of One pound and four rupees each to me and Babu Gir Raj Singh Ji.

Boarded 'Darbar Light Railway' from monument station to Kashmiri Darwaja (Gate) thinking that fare for the return journey will not be charged as we had heard. But we had to pay for the return journey. S. Tirlochan Singh, who had come today only, was also with me. Were lost in the way and had to ask for it before reaching home."

"*Jan. 4, 1903:* Distributed some more books and tracts on behalf of the Chief Khalsa Diwan and persuaded Sardars to attend the Gurpurab celebrations.

Daily Prayer ('Nit-Name'):

Japji Sahib	- 5 recitations (2 previous balance)
Japji Sahib	- 1 recitation.
Rah-Ras	- 1 recitation.
Sohila	- 1 recitation.

"*Jan. 5, 1903:* Remained busy with Gurpurab arrangements.

During preparations, it was told that the Viceroy would visit the camps while the Sardars refused to go. Bhai Kahan Singh Ji arranged with the help of Political Agent that Viceroy should allow the Sikh Sardars to go (to attend Gurpurab) and accept attendance at Durbar. Permission was received at 11 p.m.

Daily Prayer ('Nit-Name'):

Japji Sahib	- 4 recitations (2 previous balance and 1 balance today. Total: 3)
Jap Sahib	- 1 recitation.
Rah-Ras	- 1 recitation.
Sohila	- 1 recitation."

"*Jan.* 6, 1903: The procession of Rajas, Maharajas and Sardars passed through Mori Darwaja (Gate) and reached Gurdwara Sis Ganj Sahib. Lord Curzon witnessed it atop his motor. The grand procession reached Gurdwara. Many Englishmen were also watching it. The evening congregation conducted by the Chief Khalsa Diwan was very impressive. Having left in the morning, returned late in the evening. Tracts were distributed.

Daily Prayer ('Nit-Name'):

Japji Sahib	- 6 recitations (Balance 2J
Jap Sahib	- 1 recitation.
Rah-Ras	- 1 recitation.
Sohila	- 1 recitation.

Went to bed at about 1.30 AM.

"*Jan.* 7, 1903: Remained. in Delhi. Performed the daily prayer. Went out with Bakshi Ji. Attended the Diwan. Harcharan Singh had also come.

"*Jan.* 8, 1903: Performed the 'Nit-Name'.

"*Jan.* 9, 1903: Started from Delhi. Brother became sad.

Occupied seat comfortably, Performed the daily prayer. (3 balance).

"*Jan. 9, 1903:* S. Tirlochan Singh got down at Rajpura.

Performed 'Nit-Name' and completed the previous balance of recitations.

At Gurdwara Mal Tekri (Hazur Sahib, Deccan)

While brief reference about the dispute and riots at this Gurdwara has been made in Chapter IV, Sir Sundar Singh has recorded his visit to the place in his personal diaries, as follows:

July 12, 1929: (Hyderabad State)

"Political Secretary to the Resident and his assistant had corne at the Begumpet Railway Station. Stayed at Guest House.

July 14, 1929 (Sunday): "Letter carne from Sir W. Barton inviting me to corne for Lunch. So I went despite indisposition. Had discussions and he explained the entire position about Mal Tekri and outside. He told that the Government would accept the verdict of the judicial enquiry by a High Court Judge ·as the Sikhs are claiming it as a Gurdwara while Mohammadans consider it a part of some mosque. The platform was demolished by the Muslims who have cremated the body of a 'Fakir' at the place. I put up the entire case which he listened attentively. But, he was of the opinion that during theriots, firing was started by the Sikhs which I also explained. He said that I will be asked some questions in the Council. Overall impression created was satisfactory."

July 15, 1929: "Letter carne from Mr. Armstrong, Director General of Police that he had been injured in the knee while playing Polo and in view of his confinement to bed, I should corne and meet him, I shall meet him after the Council. Went to the Full Council Meeting and the situation was discussed for one and half hour. I put up the Sikh view point forcefully. The Council assured me that Mohammadans will never be allowed to forcibly occupy the Gurdwara and the sanctity of the 'Takht' will be maintained. Services of the High Court Judge will be secured on loan from the Government and his decision after judicial enquiry shall he accepted. The corning of 'Jathas' is not appreciated particularly that of Lahna Singh is not good. Justice will be done in the riot cases. There will not be any favours to any body.

"Met Mr. Armstrong and discussions took place for about one hour. He will send the report for reading. Met Mr. C. Trench in the evening and went to Maharaja Sir Kishan Parshad and discussed the matters."

"*July* 16, 1929 (Hyderabad): "Saw the Golconda Fort with Mr. Manohar Lal Puri, who is Deputy Inspector General of Police and Mr. Abnal Hassan, Assistant to the Political Secretary."

"Mirza Sami Beg Jung Bahadur, Chief Judge came to meet me in the evening. Suggested to him to set up a Bench for trial. He will write to Col. Trench after looking into the legal point."

July 17, 1929 (Wednesday) "Went to meet His Excellency the Nizam Sahib at 9 o'clock. Discussions went on upto *10.30* AM. Maharaja Kishan Parshad and Nawab Nizamat Jung, Political Member were also with him. *His Excellency was* so *simply dressed that* I *could not first recognize that he was the Hon'ble Nizam.* I *thought he must be inside and that the members were waiting for him. When he addressed me only then* I realized that I was in the presence of Nizam Sahib. He was very much impressed with my talks and assured that justice would be done. Visit to Punjab was also mentioned and I took leave at about quarter to eleven a.m. In the afternoon, went to the public school for boys and saw their physical drill. Gave Rs. *20/* - for sweets while returning. Sent letter to Nizam Sahib and 'Farman' through Political Secretary and informed that I was not going today.

July 18, 1929: "Went to meet Nizam Sahib at 9 AM and again Maharaja and Nizamat Jang were present who were pleased to meet me. Discussion on different topics went up to 11.15 AM. Nabha - Patiala question was also asked. Explained about marriage ceremony among the Sikhs and baptism ('Amrit'), Took leave at 11.15 AM and was asked that I may meet the Princes and have tea with them at 4.30 PM. Went for tea at 4.30 p.m. and met the charming young Princes. Talked to them for about half an hour. Wrote to His Excellency my impressions about them (Princes) and thanked him for the nice manner in which I have been treated throughout my stay here.

"Left Secunderabad at 11 p.m."

July 19, 1929: ,(At Hazur Sahib Ji) "Mr. Manohar Lal Puri, D.I.G. of Police was with me. Reached Nanded at about 6.30

A.M. Mr. Rahmatullah, Talluqdar, and Mr. Arif Khan, S.P. and other gentlemen were present for reception. Went to Godavri. After bath, went to Gurdwara Nagina Ghat and humbly offered Rs. 5/- and then payed obeisance at Takht Sahib and offered Rs. 51/-. After 'Ardas' (Prayer) offered Rs. 10/ - to the Ragis. Then went to see Mal Tekri.

July 20,1929: "Listened to the singing of hymns (kirtan') at Takht Sahib and came back at about 8.30 AM. Then went to have on the spot assessment of place of riot. Saw few Sikhs who had been injured. One aged person had lost his hand. Then went to the Collector. In the evening listened to 'kirtan' and met 'Pujari Ji', Bhai Hari Singh Ji with whom views were exchanged and he offered milk to me. At the time of winding up of evening congregation, I was honoured with a 'Siropa' (Robe of Honour) and a 'Shawl' while Gopal _Singh was presented with a 'Siropa' and small turban. Choudhary was. presented with the 'prasad of almonds and 'misri' along with 'sacred dust'.

Jan. 31, 1928: "Bhai Kartar Singh Jhabbar came to see me and told me that there was a change in the view point of Akalis, wanted my help for release of remaining 10 prisoners. I told I will consult on my return from U.P. in a month's time. Reached Saraya on Feb. 2, 1928.

Feb. 12, 1928: "Madam Shergill's birthday. Moulvi Fatehuddin, Assistant Director Agriculture arrived at 9 p.m. He was put up in Aunti's room.

Feb. 16, 1928: "Letter from Madam Shergill asking if brother and she were to come to settle certain things. Replied that they were welcome tomorrow.

Feb. 17, 1928: "Brother, Madam and Vani* came at 3 p.m. and he was asking me about income tax notice that he had received and I explained that house occupied has to be shown in rental income."

May 24, 1928: "Kartar Singh Jhabbar came to see me and spoke about the release of Teja Singh Bhuchar, Lahora Singh, Kartar Singh, Bishan Singh who remained in jail for the last 36 months. Others have been in jail for 12 to 14 months. Promised to speak to H.M.F. (Mian Fazl-i-Hussain).

*Satyavan Singh son of S. Umrao Singh Majithia.

"Received invitation and formed a Committee to prepare a Memorandum to be submitted to *Simon Commission."*

May 27, 1928: "Attended 'Bhog' of 'Akhand Path' in the memory of Gopala Ram at Khalsa College at 9 AM. An emergency meeting of Managing Committee of Khalsa College took place at 8 AM. Collection of Rs. 3301/- were made for the help of Mrs. Gopala Ram and added salary up to leaves of Gopala Ram which amounted toRs. 3000/- and a Special Endowment Trust was constituted so that Mrs. Gopala Ram could be helped with monthly income of interest from it. Sardar Narain Singh was appointed Senior Vice-Principal and estimate for repair of the lorry was passed. Meeting from 12 0' clock till evening continued about the representation to Simon Commission and draft was approved after some changes. More funds to the tune of Rs. 5000/- were collected for Mrs. Gopala Ram over and above the College funds.

May 30, 1928: "At Simla with brother (S. Umrao Singh) at his house.

Sept. 15, 1928: "Today, Miss Cregan had brought one Miss Macdoughtall to play but she did not know how to play Tennis. Played one set with her. Surjit and Nayyam Hussain were the other. Nayyam's game was spoiled whereafter Miss Cregan continued to play. In other words, the exercise of the boys was spoiled.

Oct. 7, 1928: "Meeting of 'Sikh Hal<uk (Rights) Rakshak Committee."

Oct. 8, 1928: "Sardar Bahadur Bishan Singh Ji Puri joined as Principal on 3.10.28."

Nov. 2, 1928: "Kept reading Sikh memorandum and connected papers throughout the day."

Nov. 6, 1928: "Went to Lahore today. Bhai [odh Singh was with me alongwith Gurmukh Singh started at 7 o'clock. Went for witness at quarter to 11. Deputation consisted of, apart from me, S. Mohan Singh, S. Raghbir Singh Sandhawalia, S. Sant Singh Layalpur, S. Tej Singh, Advocate, Rawalpindi, S. Man Singh, Advocate, Lahore, Captain Sardar Bahadur Lakha Singh Resaldar, S. Mangal Singh Man from Gujranwala. Witness started at 12 o'clock and broke for lunch at 1.30 p.m. It again started at 2.30 p.m. and finished at 3 p.m. Then met brother and started along with Jodh Singh and S. Raghbir Singh at quarter to 5 and reached at 6 p.m.

Feb. 14, 1929: "Resolution passed regarding Patiala situation in the Managing Committee of Khalsa College."

Feb. 20, 1929: "Met His Highness at Patiala. Liaquat Hayat was also present. Spoke about Sodhi Harnam Singh's case and discussed Patiala agitation. His Highness did not appear to have liked discussion about Sodhi. Ordered reconciliation of my loan account with the instructions that interest should not be charged from the date of loan and that I should re-pay the balance amount of loan in April. Nawab Sahib will issue the instructions."

Feb. 25, 1929: "Bhai Kartar Singh Jhabbar had come to meet today and had food with me. Boarded train for Lahore at 10.40."

March 22, 1929: (Delhi) "At 2.15 p.m., a deputation of the Sikhs waited upon His Excellency the Viceroy and put up Sikh demands. There were a total of 22 persons. I introduced and S. Shivdev Singh read the Memorandum. His Excellency gave a sympathetic but non-committal response. Discussed Khalsa College with Mr. Cunningham and fixed tomorrow for the remaining discussion."

March 23, 1929: "Went to meet Mr. Cunningham, Private Secretary to the Viceroy at 11.30 AM and handed over papers about Khalsa- College and suggested charging of interest henceforth and that decision about the balance interest should be left to becoming major of the new Maharaja. He promised to speak to Mr. Watson and told that he shall meet me at Simla. There was a tea party at the house of Wasakha Singh for the Sikhs who had come from outside.

"A dinner had been hosted for the Simon Commission by the Sikhs in the evening which was attended by about 175 persons. The Commander-in-Chief had also come for the dinner. I proposed for the health of His Majesty the King while S. Daljit Singh proposed for Simon. His speech, though strong, was not in good taste. Simon's response was non-committal."

March 30/31, 1929: "Conference at Sargodha in which presented Resolution on Sikh University."

March 16, 1931: *"Telegram was received from Dr. Ansari informing that Mr. Gandhi is to talk to 'All Parties Sikh Conference' for which I should also reach there at Delhi.*

March 17, 1931: *"In the evening, discussed with friends about the reply to the telegram. Master Tara Singh of S.G.P.C. was also called and he also expressed himself, whereafter telegram was sent: 'Thanks for invitation. Can join only' if invitation extended* to *Chief Khalsa Ditoan representative'.*

This was sent through Express Telegram.

March 18, 1931: *"Received telegram from* S. *Shivdev Singh that* it *was better to go but decision remained not to go unless invitation is extended to Chief Khalsa Diwan. Telegram came from Dr. Ansari at* 8.45 *that Diwan representative is cordially invited."*

March 19, 1931: "Bhai Buta Singh and another person had come in the morning about Nankana Sahib .... Informed Dr. Ansari, Raja Daljit Singh and S. Shivdev Singh about my arrival telegraphically. Had food in the evening and boarded Calcutta Mail. Reached Delhi at 4.30 AM. Raja Sahib's man and S. Shivdev Singh had come at the Railway Station. . .. Recited Japji Sahib, Anand Sahib, Asa-Di-War, 'Chaupai' and Jap Sahib.

"Went to meet Mahatma Gandhi at Dr. Ansari's residence.

Discussed with him about Sikh deputation of Chief Khalsa Diuian, Sikh League and All-Parties Conference. He advised to send the relevant points as he had understood the Sikh position and he will discuss with Mohammadans in *the evening. Came back and wrote points* in *consultation with all."*

April 28,1931: *"Master Tara Singh Ji, President, S.G.P.C. came* to *meet and talked about propaganda for Sikh Rights on behalf of all parties, besides pressing me except him, myself and Daljit Singh etc. should go for the Round Table Conference.* He referred to Minorities Conference about which I suggested S. Dharam Singh's name from Delhi for President.

May 13, 1931 *to May* 23, 1931: "Could not perform 'Nit-Name' (daily prayers) properly because of illness.

June 2, 1931: "Baba Kehar Singh of Patti came in the afternoon and called for his nephew Dr. Randhir Singh. Discussions were held with them about 10 articles published in 'New Era' against Khalsa College. Told them the real position and advised that if the criticism is constructive, then it is useful whereas destructive criticism could not be cared for and has no utility.

1933

Sir Sundar Singh was at Saraya Estate (Gorakhpur) from the beginning of 1933 till March, 1933. He writes about the New Year:

"New Year began with the blessings of God. Recited Japji Sahib, Anand Sahib, Asa-di-War, Chaupai Sahib, Jap Sahib and Sukhmani Sahib. Then' took bath and wrote correspondence and sent New Year cards. Recited 'path' of Guru Granth Sahib upto Page No. 1332 whereafter 'Rag Prabhati' starts from 3rd 'chaupadas'.

"Recited 'Rah-Ras Sahib' in the evening and went to sleep as soon as it was completed."

March 22, 1933: (Wednesday) "I accompanied Surjit to Lahore to stand witness in the Gurdwara Tribunal about the case of 'Bung a Ramgarhia' but I was not required to give witness. After adjournment, helped to arrive at settlement that between the four minarets, the 'Bunga' of S. Mangal Singh would not be alienated. Possession will remain with S. Bishan Singh etc. as existing. However, no practice will be allowed in it against the Sikh traditions. But it remains personal property of the Sardars. Came back after agreement. Reached home at 3 p.m."

April 1933: *"Started for Lahore at* 10 AM. *Met H.E.* 11 AM. *and he asked if I would go to England for Select Committee. I explained my difficulties and told that perhaps I will not be able to go but shall give final reply after consultations. Told Jogi* (Sir *Jogendra Singh) and it was felt that [ogi should go and I shall perform his duties here (without pay)."*

April 9, 1933: (Sunday) "Reviewed speech of Jogi Ji in the Committee."

April 13, 1933: "Left for Peshawar by car with S. Harbans Singh. Stayed for the night with S. Mohan Singh at Rawalpindi."

April 14, 1933: *Sikh Education Conference:*

"Caught train from Nowshera and reached Peshawar at 11.46 AM. Procession of Sir Jogendra Singh was taken out. Had food at the house of Rai Bahadur Mehar Chand Khanna."

April 15, 1933: "Sessions of Sikh Education Conference were successful. Rs. 7700/- were collected for National Fund. Rs. 500/- from my side."

April 16, 1933: "Session concluded."

April 17, 1933: "Started from Peshawar in the morning.

Met on the way Mohammad Amin Khan at 9 a.m. and had tea with him and took his leave and went to Punja Sahib, paid obeisance and made offering of Rs. 21/- for prayer. Met Bhai Tirlok Singh, Manager, at his residence as he was not keeping well. In the afternoon, went to S. Mohan Singh who accompanied me.

April 18, 1933: "Marriage of Joji* with Gurpreet Singh s/o

S. Gurdyal Singh Maan of Nabha. Marriage was solemnized by Sant Sangat Singh Ji. Donated Rs. 500/- to Chief Khalsa Diwan for religious services.

Dowry: Rs. 10,000/- fixed deposit receipt in the joint name of daughter and bridegroom, clothes, utensils of silver and brass. Gave Chrystler 70 Sedan Car also."

May 6, 1933: "S. Harnam Singh, Retired Governor Jammu came to meet and for a job for his son."

May 20, 1933: (Saturday) "Marriage of *Bibi Sumer": In* the dowry, Wolsley Hornet (12 H.P.) car valued Rs, 6700/- was also given."

June 7, 1933: "Reached Simla."

June 8, 1933: "Decided for operation of S. Kirpal Singh by Major Aspinall for a fee of Rs. 500 / -."

June 9, 1933: "Operation of S. Kirpal Singh successful."

June 29,1933: "Went to meet Sir James Fitzpatrick. After tea, talked about Khalsa College. He said he had only advised reduction in grants. I said it was not grants but interest on endowments. He said he will take up the matter with His Highness and we should also approach him. Talking about Nabha, he said that Diwan Dina Nath should be asked to see the case. He told that Anand Marriage Act was stopped by Maharaja Hira Singh. He did not want this Act. But, if there is no order to stop, then our case is strong."

July 1, 1933: (Saturday) "Vani Ji's letter about Simarjit's insistence on a sugar factory at Chauri Chaura."

July 9, 1933: "Reached Bombay. Stayed at Room No. 534 at Taj Mahal Hotel."

July 10, 1933: "Attended Bank (Imperial Bank) Meeting presided by Naoroji."

*Jagjiwan Kaur daughter of S. Kirpal Singh Majithia.

**Granddaughter of S. Umrao Singh Majithia.

Oct. 15, 1933: "Elected President of Khalsa College Managing Council. S. Sewa Ram Singh Rector and His Highness Yuv Raj" of Patiala, the Chancellor.

Nov. 8, 1933: "His Highness of Patiala came to Majitha House to stay for cricket match."

Nov. 9, 1933: "Yuvraj of Patiala made 66 runs. Amarnath of Kapurthala made 108 runs. Watched the match.

Nov. 10, 1933: "Watched the match. Today, MCC were playing. Dinner to His Highness at my residence. Arrangement at Tennis ground. Attended by 73 persons.

Nov. 11, 1933: "Southern Punjab team made 103 runs for one wicket and the match was drawn. His Highness left and gave Rs. 250/- to the servants."

Oct. 17, 1934: "(Attended) installation of Raja Harinder Singh of Faridkot by Sir James Fitzpatrick."

Sept. 13, 1934: "Committee for building of Takht Sri Patrta Sahib was constituted. I was made Vice-President."

Illness and Demise of Sir Sundar Singh

Despite his illness and retreat to his estates at Sardar Nagar, United Provinces, he remained keenly involved in the affairs of the Province by keeping in close contact with his colleagues in the Government, particularly Sir Sikandar Hayat Khan, the Prime Minister of Punjab, as illustrated from the letter dated 17th January 1941 from the Premier, as under:

"My dear brother,

You must have seen in the papers that I returned from my tour of the Middle East on Sunday last. I had a very interesting tour though somewhat strenuous and you will be glad to learn that our troops both in the Western Desert and on the Sudan Front are in good heart and health. Everyone of the Units engaged in the famous Western Desert battle did extremely well including the. Sikh Companies attached to those Units. One Sikh N.C.O. bayoneted 8 or 9 of the enemy before he was shot and there were numerous similar acts of individual gallantry. The reputation and prestige of Indian troops is very high and everybody was full of praise for their courage and discipline.

*Later Maharaja Yadvindra Singh of Patiala.

"I do hope you are better now and are having a quiet and pleasant time there. I am glad to hear from Sir Chhotu Ram that on the whole you stood the long journey to Sardar Nagar quite well and have shaken off its effects. I pray for your speedy and complete recovery and early return to your Province. Kindly remember me to Kirpal and others.

"With kindest regards and all good wishes."

Before that, he was examined by Lt. Col. Amir Chand, LM.5. at Lahore whose report dated 16.11.40 was countersigned by Lt. Col. W. Ross Stewart, I.M.S., Civil Surgeon, Lahore. The report[31] stated as follows:

"There is history of mild diabetes mallitus of several years' standing and of tibial cedema of about one year's duration.

"On return from Simla to Lahore this October, he noticed some distension of the abdomen which went on increasing from day to day. The tibial cedema also gradually increased and became more marked in the evenings. A little later breathing began to get embarrassed especially on exertion. The urine gradually diminished in quantity and became high coloured.

"On 12th November 1940, he was examined by K.B. Dr. Yar Mohammad Khan. The abdomen was very much distended. The tibial cedema was well marked and breathlessness was troublesome. Pulse was 108 p.m. Blood pressure 160/95; heart sounds regular; no brunt; no evidence of pulmonary congestion. Liver and spleen could not be palpated owing to the presence of a considerable amount of fluid in the abdomen.

"I examined him on 14th November. The fluid in the abdomen, the tibial cedema and breathlessness were somewhat less, but otherwise the findings were more or less the same.

"The examination of the urine did not indicate nephritis.

"Diagnosis - Ascites with cedema of legs (cardiac and hepatic).

"Recommended four months' leave."

Sir Sundar Singh forwarded this report to the Prime Minister of Punjab vide his letter dated 17th November, 1940, as follows:

"I am enclosing herewith copy of a letter No. 11013 of the 16th of November from the Civil Surgeon, Lahore to me together with the medical report in duplicate by Colonel Amir

[31] Ibid.

Chand about my health duly endorsed by the Civil Surgeon. I shall be glad if you will kindly obtain the sanction of His Excellency the Governor to the grant to me of four months' leave, as recommended by the Medical Authorities."[32]

The following letter dt. 20.March, 1941 from S. Tirlochan Singh, who affectionately referred to Sardar Sundar Singh as 'Saunders', also expresses concern for the state of health of the Majithia Sardar:

"Dearest Saunders,

Your letters dated 16th and 18th March. It is a happy news in your letter of 16th that in the opinion of Dr. Victor Egans the fluid accumulation was not increasing since the last 4 or 5 days. It would be a matter of great pleasure if further accumulation stops. This happening, the fever likely would disappear. If the present treatment is bringing about satisfactory result in the above said manner, the Vaidic treatment may continue with advantage.

Periodical visits of Vaid Ji surely would be comparatively more inconvenient to him if he has to come to Amritsar than to see you at Sardar Nagar. This, however, is not a difficulty which cannot be overcome. You advised me that on the return of Kirpal Ji to Sardar Nagar, the matter of your shifting to the Punjab will finally be decided and I shall await the advice of that decision. Kirpal Ji has proceeded to Delhi from Nabha. His telegram was received by S. Harbans Singh here asking him to reach Delhi with Bikaner papers. Likely, the Bikaner Minister was there and matters may have been settled with him there. I have, however, no advice from Kirpal Ji on the subject and you might have heard from him direct from Delhi.

The shareholder who proposed the name of Mr. D.N. Kapur, G.D.A. to be elected as Bank's Auditor is L. Karam Chand of Amritsar. He holds 100 shares of the Bank.

In your letter dated 18th, you have referred to the expected third tapping. The first was done at Lahore and the second subsequently at Sardar Nagar. If the fluid accumulation has stopped as stated in your letter of 16th, does Dr. Victor Egans consider a third tapping desirable so soon after the last. The daily in-take of liquid and of discharge of fluid approximately

[32]Ibid.

equals, and your weight is also not increasing. It seems to have come down from 155 lbs. to 154 and later to 152 lbs.

My best Sat Sri Akal to Bibi Ji and love to children. Vir Ji (Bhai Vir Singh) sends you his best wishes.

With love,
Yours Affectionately,
(Sd) Trilochan Singh,"*

However, he could not survive despite the best possible treatment and the end came on April 2, 1941 at a time when the community and the Nation required the presence of his towering personality, his sober outlook and saner advice in the most difficult period to come.

If some students of history were to analyze the balance sheet or profit & loss account of his life from Banker's point of view, it would appear that the net worth or the actual contribution to his community was not only remarkable but unprecedented when compared with such balance sheets of other contemporary Sikh leaders who although fired with loyalty to their community, had their own style and approach -. sometimes aggressive and provocative expression of dissent** - while trying to project their

*S. Trilochan Singh, who was Managing Director of Punjab & Sind Bank Ltd .., had a life-long friendship with Sardar Sundar Singh.

**It was early January 1947. The Muslim League's demand for creation of Pakistan had by then become so vociferous and that under its extreme pressure, the Khizar Hayat Khan's Ministry had to bow out of office. This surcharged high emotions and excerbated feelings of distrust and animosity amongst the communities. Then, in the Punjab Assembly, a momentous incident occurred which rapidly cast its frightening dark shadows on the developments that were to follow immediately in its wake. Master Tara Singh, the Akali leader, deeply incensed at the sudden turn of events, reportedly brandished his sword in the Assembly. This sent wrong signal to the Muslims. The news instantly spread in the old city of Lahore. Enraged, some Muslim elements targetted and stabbed three Sikhs the same evening inside Lahori Gate Bazar, setting in motion an adverse chain-reaction which later on escalated into open hostilities between Muslims and Hindus/Sikhs. Though leaders of both communities made attempts to bring in sanity but they were so feeble as not to show any tangible impact and arrest the worsening situation. By late March 1947 onwards, the old city of Lahore was engulfed with large scale incidents of stabbings, arson, loot and killings, forcing Hindu and Sikh families to flee to safer places elsewhere. From Lahore, the trouble soon travelled fast and spread to other cities. The rest is history.

(Recollections of Datt, D. - at the age of 19-originally resident of Kucha Balian, Mohalla Sathan, Inside Bhati Gate, Lahore. He has worked in various sensitive Departments of State and Central Governments (1947 - 1986).

viewpoint. His practical and positive contributions in the socio-economic, religio-educational development of his community, his genial character, sober and moderate approach and high standard of life as a true Gur Sikh*, performance as an Administrator, sincerity of purpose, clarity of perception about community's interests and its future safeguards made him one of the tallest personalities of his community whom the British, Mohammadans, Hindus and, of course, the Sikhs also held in high esteem despite inevitable differences of opinion. Even while working for the betterment of his own community, he would rarely hurt or offend others as his approach was peaceful, logical and constitutional which carried a lot of weight because of his unassailable personal character and courage of conviction.

Next Generation

Besides recording his own birthday, i.e. 17th February 1872, Sir Sundar Singh also recorded the following dates of birth of his children in his personal diary:

Kirpal Singh	- 17th June, 1891
Narain Singh	- August 1893 (Died)
Surinder Singh	- 5th March, 1895
Mohinder Kaur	- 6th December, 1896
Bhagwan Singh	- 30th November 1898 (Died 11th June, 1918)
Surjit Singh	- 8th August, 1912 (born at Simla)

Dates of birth of S.Kirpal Singh's children:

Bibi Jagjit Kaur	- August 1911. (Died 6.3.34)
Bibi Jagjiwan Kaur	- July 1913
Gurnihal Singh	- 22nd Nov., 1917
Dalip Singh	- 27th July, 1920
Bibi Tejinder Kaur	- Oct., 1921

S. Kirpal Singh Majithia

While Sardar Kirpal Singh had started assisting his father in various social engagements besides looking after their estate at Sardar Nagar (Gorakhpur), illness also cut short his life span; thereby

*Besides strict observance of 'Rahat' of a 'Gur Sikh and performance of his daily prayers ('Nit-Name'), he abstained from liquor ever since the age of 20 as confirmed by him during one of the debates. in Punjab Assembly while speaking on the 'prohibition policy' of the Punjab Government.

preventing him to take over the mantle of the great legacy which Sir Sundar Singh had left behind him.

Before his untimely demise in 1944, Sardar Kirpal Singh had proved his skill as an excellent administrator in the management of Saraya Sugar Factory besides his extra-ordinary mobility and capacity to-provide leadership in other socio-political organizations like Chief Khalsa Diwan, Khalsa College, Amritsar, Khalsa National Party, Punjab & Sind Bank Ltd., simultaneously looking after the establishments at Amritsar and Simla also. His son Sardar Dalip Singh Majithia, who also had an excellent career in Air Force where from he retired as Sq. leader, flew the first aircraft to Kathmandu in April 1949 besides assisting the Government of Nepal in selection of site for an aerodrome while his uncle Sardar Surjit Singh Majithia was India's ambassador to that Country.

S. Kirpal Singh Mahithia
(1891-1944)

Sir Surendra Singh Majithia

Sir Surendra Singh was the second son of Sir Sundar Singh, who not only inherited many qualities of his father but also had the inclination and opportunity to inter-act with spiritual personalities whose influence led him to observer his faith more religiously. However, this did not deter him from assisting his elder brother

S. Kirpal Singh in establishment and development of Sugar Factory at Saraya Estate. In fact, he was a gifted engineer whose technical skills helped to make Saraya Mills one of the biggest Sugar factories of the country producing excellent quality comparable to the business giants from U.K., France and Jawa.

Sir Surendra Singh Mapthia
(1895-1984)

Continuing the mission started by his father, he contributed to promote education in the state of Uttar Pradesh. Many institutions like Lady Prasan Kaur Inter-College Bardilla, Budha Inter and Degree College Kushi Nagar, Maharana Partap Degree College Gorakhpur and establishment of science block at Gorakhpur University bear testimony to his love for education.

He was a keen sportsman and patronised many events besides playing gracious host to a large number of dignitaries at his estate. Like his father, he was a devout Sikh who strictly followed tenets of his religion while respecting and understanding other faiths. He was very sincere, innocent and affectionate person who revered his parents and loved his brothers. He died in 1984 without any issue.

Sardar Surjit Singh Majithia

Sardar Surjit Singh was the youngest son of Sir Sundar Singh Majithia. He was a excellent sportsman, particularly in tennis and cricket and played in the Ranji Trophy and practised with the best players of his times when he volunteered to join Air Force when war broke out, subsequently proving his mettle as an outstanding Fighter Pilot. He was squardon Leader when he had to leave Air Force at the time of untimely demise of his elder brother S. Kirpal Singh.

Sardar Surjit Singh Majithia
(1912-1995)

His diplomatic career, starting with his appointment as India's first Ambassador to Nepal in 1947, was marked with unprecedented assistance which the Government of Nepal provided by sending 10000 troops to man the Indian border while the Indian Army was engaged in action at Hyderabad. His tenure was one of the finest periods of friendly relations with Nepal kingdom when the traditional friendly ties which the Majithias enjoyed with the Ranas since the period of Maharaja Ranjit Singh, proved to be very helpful.

In 1950, he successfully contested the first parliamentary election from Taran Taran and got elected from Amritsar area for three consecutive terms. He remained Deputy Defence Minister in the Union Cabinet for 12 years where his background as ex-serviceman facilitated appreciation of the role and requirement of Armed Forces besides better perception about the military threat which the country faced from China.

This led to some difference of opinion with Mr. Krishna Menon who had better of Pandit Nehru's ears. An unusual and honest politician as he was, he decided to quit. He also served Chief Khalsa Diwan and Khalsa College, Amritsar and was President of its managing Committee till his death in 1995.

Like his elder brother he was a deeply religious person and according to his family sources, had predicted his death. Apart from the influence of their farther Sir Sundar Singh, the spiritual inclination of the personalities of the three brothers owed to the religious guidance of their mother, viz, the pious lady Sardarni Prasan Kaur who was granddaughter of Sir Attar Singh of Bhadaur.

Sardar Surjit Singh Majithia was survived by three sons, namely, Satyajit Singh, Gurlabh Singh and Giriraj Singh.

Tributes

SARDAR BAHADUR UJJAL SINGH, M.A., M.L.A., described Sir Sundar Singh as 'Caretaker of Panthic Garden' and said:

> "His life is a history. If you see any aspect of life of Sikh community - spiritual, religious, social, economic, educational and political - you will find the reflection of his great life. Khalsa College, Amritsar, Chief Khalsa Diwan, Singh Sabha movement, Sikh Educational Conference, Central Khalsa Orphanage, Amritsar, etc. are all his own creations. The interest, hard labour and love with which he has developed these institutions cannot be described. The kind of dedication, untiring effort and love can only be found in the great care-takers of the communities. While rearing plants of this 'garden', he never cared about his own comfort and worked with single-minded purpose and dedication during which he went away from us[33]".

[33]S. Sundar Singh Majithia, Ed. S. Mehar Singh Rawel: p.74.

Sir Jogindra Singh

"Sir Sundar Singh selected Amritsar for his residence; for it was romance of religion that ruled his heart. He acquired 'Punjab Patriot' which late Mr. Thapar edited for him, for he believed in patriotism which sought and found its strength in stability. These two tendencies ruled him from the days of his youth to the days of his departure. He remained unswerving in his loyalty to his ideals and often achieved substantial results which of more volatile nature failed to achieve. His tenacity of purpose and love of detail assured success of movements and institutions that secured his supporr[34]".

Singh Sabha Movement

"The early years, he was influenced by Singh Sabha Movement, which was first started in Amritsar and then in Lahore by a group of workers led by late Bhai Gurmukh Singh. The movement aimed at removing outside influences which re-established their hold in Sikh homes and were in direct opposition to the Sikh teachings. He gathered around him a group of earnest minded men, who were ready to devote. their lives to the cause of Sikhism. His brother, Sirdar Umrao Singh, kindled in the hearts of a few of his friends the desire for simple and selfless living and steadfast search for truth. The late Sardar Harbans Singh of Attari transfigured in his own person the devotion of a Sikh, the zeal of a crusader and love of simple living of Tolstoy. In a moment of exaltation, he gave up his high appointment and joined Sir Sundar Singh. The result was "Tat Khalsa Movement" and the formation-of Chief Khalsa Diwan which gradually obtained the control of all the Sikh Organisations[35]".

Tat Khalsa Movement

"The Khalsa seems destined to be never out of trouble. The "Tat Khalsa Movement" had to wage a bitter fight with the orthodox Sikhs who followed Hindu customs and with the leaders of Arya Samaj who saw in it a rival. The promoters of the new Movement were not allowed to offer prayers at the Golden Temple. The battle of restoration of pure Sikhism was fought with unflinching persistence and was won. (They also

[34]Ibid.

[35]Ibid.

planned and fought, gathered round the tennis court of Majithia House in the evening. Bhai Vir Singh, his eyes sparkling with spiritual fire, Sirdar Tirlochan Singh, whose soft word turned away wrath, Bhai Teja Singh Hazuria, whose green turban revealed the freshness of his mind, and young Jodh Singh, ready to devote all his intelligence, knowledge and power to the service of the Panth). Alas! eyes seek in vain for the like of them.

"The Reform Movement which began in Lahore shifted its activities to Amritsar. Some of those who regard Chief Khalsa Diwan's policy as conservative may be surprised that the Diwan was viewed with suspicion by the Government of the day and the leaders of the "Tat Khalsa Movement" received the usual attention. The Sikh community has been always infested with a few self-seekers, who went as they go on today, to the length of inventing things which have no existence, in fact, to serve their own personal ends."

His Dauntless Spirit

"The years that had gone had failed to curb his dauntless spirit. I decided to retire from public life with the coming of provincial autonomy. I thought that with separate communal electorates and low franchise, it would not be possible to work for the good of all the people of the Punjab. Sir Sundar Singh and I formed the Khalsa National party with the main object of bringing all sections together and to help one of our youngerman to take his place in the Cabinet. The attempt was very near success. It only failed at the last moment. Sir Sundar Singh continued to persuade me to the last day to change my mind and when he failed to do so, at the last moment, he decided to seek election himself, which he fought with his usual vigour and unflinching courage. He secured election and entered the Cabinet again as a Revenue Member and worked with loyalty and devotion to his colleagues rarely equalled."

"The advancing years were sapping the power of physical endurance but the spirit remained unconquered and unconquerable. He spent the last ounce of strength without seeking respite from labours, which occupied whole of his life. It was with difficulty that he was persuaded to take rest in his estate at Gorakhpur. Here, he impressed all those who came in contact with him with the gaiety of his spirit without giving any sign that his body could not carry more the burden of a strenuous life. He returned to Lahore. It seems as if he just came to leave his weary body at the feet of the Guru and allow his armour to be unbuckled by others, which he refused to unbuckle himself, it may well be said of him. It is idle to comment for those who have their heart in good. They return to their home, lament only for those who barter away truth for that which is false and untrue[36]".

H.E. the Governor of United Provinces

"Although Sir Sundar Singh Majithia came from the Punjab and the Punjab must inevitably feel the greater personal loss at his death, the United Provinces knew Sir Sundar Singh Majithia welL Indeed, the family estates in Gorakhpur originated in an award given by Government to the family in the recognition of loyal services and Sir Sundar Singh was well known to this Province both as a landlord and as an industrialist. As Governor, I am glad to add the tribute of the United Provinces to this most distinguished son of the Punjab[37]".

Hon'ble Sir Sikander Hayat Khan, Premier of the Punjab "A scion of the renowned and leading family of Majithia Sardars, he was a prominent and respected member of the Punjab gentry., His long and meritorious services to his Province and his community extending over a period of nearly half a century had earned for him the esteem and respect not only of the Sikhs but of all classes and communities.

"His public spirited activities, especially in the field of education, will always be remembered with gratitude by his community and his co-workers. That leading Sikh educational institution, the Khalsa College, Amritsar, owes its inception and existence mainly to his selfless and untiring efforts in the course of Sikh education.

"His genial and affable manners and honesty of purpose won for him the respect and affection of his colleagues in the various spheres of his activities. To me, he was a source of strength not only as an esteemed and honourable colleague

[36]Ibid.

[37]Ibid.

but also as an affectionate friend. Like a true soldier that he was, he died in harness in the service of his country and community[38]".

Honourable Sir Chhotu Ram, Revenue Minister, Punjab

"Sir Sundar Singh had a definite religious turn of mind and was a righteous man in the truest sense of the word. He had very high principles of character and was extremely conscientious both as a politician and as an administrator. His private life was characterised by geniality of manner, generosity of temperament and simplicity of a high order. I respected him as a younger brother and will always keep him in affectionate and reverent memory[39]".

Hon'ble Mian Abdul Haye, Education Minister, Punjab.

"A distinguished son of India', a great patriot, he will be long remembered for his contributions to the educational advance of this Province. ..... It was his intense desire for service, his devotion to duty, which he thought he owed to the Punjab which had prompted him to accept the responsibilities of a ministerial office[40]".

Hon'ble Major Khizar Hayat Khan Tiwana, Minister of Public Works, Punjab.

"The late Sir Sundar Singh Majithia was not only a great Sikh but a great Punjabee also. His death would be mourned by all the communities alike and did no injustice to anyone. He had endeared himself to all. Though an aristocrat by birth, he loved to be associated with the humblest in life and felt proud to serve them.

"The great Sardar was undoubtedly a shining of light of the well-known Majithia family who had played a great part in Sikh History[41]".

Maharajidhiraj of Patiala, Yadvindra Singh

"By Sir Sundar Singh Majithia's sad demise, the Sikh community and the Province have sustained a heavy loss. For over a quarter of a century, he was a leading figure in the

[38]Ibid.
[39]Ibid.
[40]Ibid.
[41]Ibid.

public life of the Province and held high offices with distinction, integrity and industry. His contributions to the cause of Sikh education have been invaluable and the Khalsa College, Amritsar of which he was one of the principal Founders, bears the imprint of his initiative and selfless service. In private life, his simplicity and affable disposition endeared him to all who had the pleasure of coming into contact with him. His death has created a void in the public life of the Province and in the ranks of the Panth which it will be difficult to fill[42]".

Maharaja Sahib Kapurthala

"I was deeply touched and grieved to receive the news of the sad demise of one of my very oldest friends, Sir Sundar Singh Majithia. *He was not only respected by the Sikhs but had won the esteem of all communities by his honest and arduous seroices* to *the Province, extending over nearly* 50 *years.*

"He had been many a time to Kapurthala as my guest and I have always been pleased to talk to him and discuss important current matters. I send my heartfelt and deepest sympathy to his sons and all members in their bereavement[43]".

Raja Sahib of Faridkot, Harinder Singh

"I received the news of the death of Sir Sundar Singh Majithia with the deepest regret not only that he was connected with the ruling House of Faridkot but also because in his death, the Punjab and the Sikh community in particular has lost a trusted leader. It was to his energetic activities throughout his life that the Sikh community owes its present educational and religious uplift. *The two great institutions of the Khalsa College, Amritsar and the Chief Khalsa Diwan are monuments of his zealous interest which he took in befitting the Sikhs of the Punjab* to *be the worthy and true followers* to *their Gurus.* His experience in the field both of administration and business was an asset, of which the Punjab is deprived of by his death. 11te Province is much poorer today and I join with his admirers and friends in mourning the loss which is well-nigh irreparable[44]".

[42]Ibid.
[43]Ibid.
[44]Ibid.

Appendix - I

"The Pedigree Table"

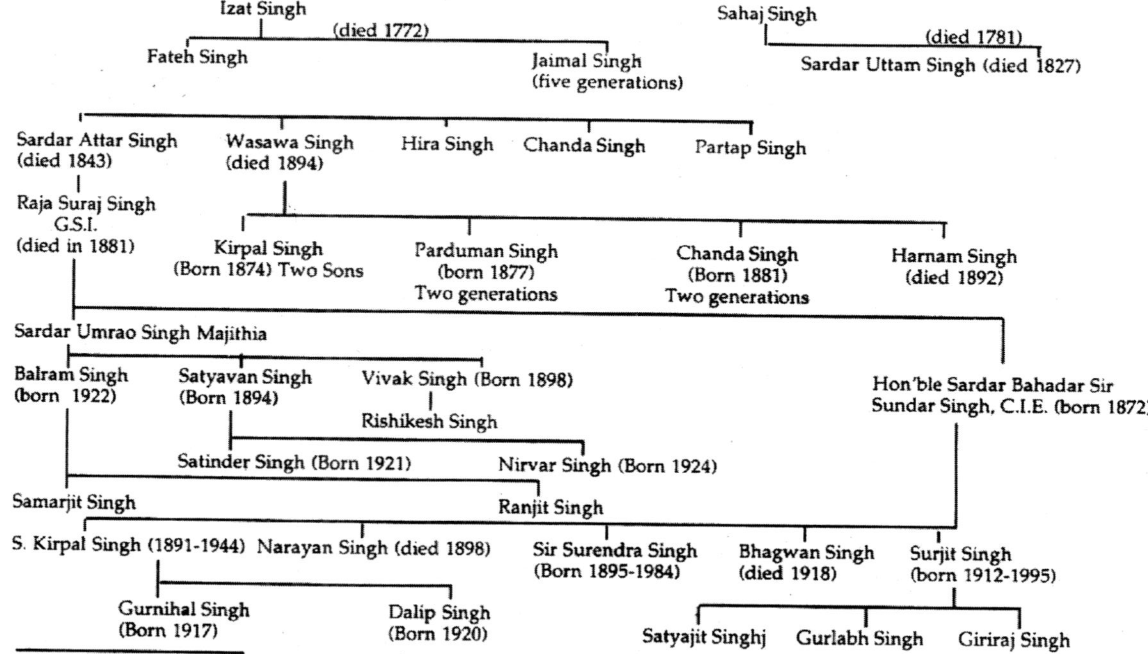

"Chiefs & Families of Note in Punjab" - by Sir Lepel H. Griffin

Appendix-II

Institutions with which Sir Sundar Singh was associated:

Founding of Khalsa College Amritsar	: March 5, 1892
Secretary Sri Guru Singh Sabha, Amritsar	: 1894
Member, Khalsa College Council, Amritsar	: 1895
Founding of Chief Khalsa Diwan	: Oct 30, 1902
Secretary Chief Khalsa Diwan	: i) Oct 30, 1902 to 1920 ii) 1934 to 1937
Secretary, Khalsa College, Council, Amritsar	: 1902 to 1912
Establishment of Khalsa Advocate Paper	: 1903
Central Khalsa Orphange, Amritsar	: 1904
Beginning of Sikh Education Conference	: 1908
Founding of Punjab & Sind Bank Ltd.	: 1908
Member Viceroy's Legislative Council	: 1909
President Khalsa College Council, Amritsar	: 1920 till his death
President of Shiromani Gurdwara Prabandhak Committee, Amritsar	: 1920
Revenue Member, Punjab Government	: 1921 to 1926
Governor Imperial Bank of India	: 1925
President Chief Khalsa Diwan, Amritsar	: 1932-1933
Formation of Khalsa National Party	: 1936
Revenue Minister, Punjab Government	: 1937
Death	: April 2, 1941

Select Bibliography

Primary Sources

A. English:

1. Development in Sikh Politics (1900-1911) - A Report by D. Petrie, Assistant Director Criminal Intelligence of the British Government - published by Chief Khalsa Dewan.
2. Personal Papers of Sir Sundar Singh Majithia (preserved in 105 files) at Nehru Memorial Museum in Library, Teen Murti Bhawan, New Delhi.
3. 'Home - Political', 'Foreign - Political' and other relevant records preserved at National Archives of India Janpath, New Delhi.
4. 'A History of Khalsa College, Amritsar' - Amritsar, 1949.
5. Presidential speech of Sir Sundar Singh Majithia on the occasion of Jubilee Celebrations of the Sikh Educational Conference, Amritsar, 1935.
6. Brief Report on the Educational Committee of the Chief Khalsa Dewan for the year, 1928, Amritsar.
7. The Report of the proceedings of the First Sikh Educational Conference held at Cujranwala. April, 1908.
8. Report of the Third Sikh Educational Conference, held at Amritsar in April, 1910, Chief Khalsa Dewan Amritsar.
9. The work of Sikh Educational Conference by Prof. Charan Singh and Prof. Darbara Singh, Amritsar March 6, 1944 (booklet).

B. Punjabi Publications:

1. Silver Jubilee Book, Educational Committee, Chief Khalsa Dewan, Amritsar, 1945.
2. Golden Jubilee Book, Educational Committee, Chief Khalsa Dewan, Amritsar, 1958.

3. Proceedings of the Chief Khalsa Dewan, Amritsar, Typed and attested copies of the volumes preserved in the Punjab Historical Studies Department, Punjabi University, Patiala in the following volumes:
   Vol. I (1901 - 1910)
   Vol. II (1911 - 1919)
   Vol. III (1920 - 1927)
   Vol. IV (1928 - 1933)
   Vol. V (1934 - 1940)
   Vol. VI (1940 - 1944)
4. Sir Sundar Singh Majithia - edited by S. Mehar Singh 'Rawel', Amritsar, 1942.
5. 'Report' (April 1968 to 1970) Central Khalsa Orphanage, Amritsar.
6. Educational Committee, 'Chief Khalsa Dewan Di Satvin Varshik Report' for the year 1914 - 1915, Amritsar.
7. Educational Committee, 'Chief Khalsa Dewan Di Dasvin Varshik Report' for the year 1917 - 18, Amritsar.

Periodicals:

8. 'Khalsa Advocate', Amritsar, Office Records of the Paper from 1928 to 1943 (Punjabi).
9. 'The Khalsa Samachar', Amritsar, February, 1908 (Punjabi).

Secondary Sources

A. English:

1. Narang, G.C, "Transformation of Sikhism".
2. Bombwall, K.R., "Indian" Constitution and Administration", Ambala, 1971.
3. Harbans Singh, "Heritage of the Sikhs", New York, 1964.
4. Chagla M.C, "Education and the Nation", New Delhi, 1966.
5. Mehta, H.R., "A History of Growth and Development of Western Education in the Punjab", monograph no. 5.
6. Mukherji, S.N., "History of Education in India", Baroda, 1955.
7. Griffin, "Chief & Families of Note", Vol. I, Lahore, 1940.
8. R.N. Cust, Linguistic & Oriental Essays, London, 1891.
9. Kenneth W. Jones - "Ham Hindu Nahin" - The Aryan Sikh Relations (Punjab past & present Vol. XI., Part II. 1977, Punjabi University Patiala).
10. Dr. Ganda Singh - 'Some Confidential Papers on the Akali Movement' - published by S.G.P.C, Amritsar.
11. M.L. Ahluwalia 'Select Documents - Gurdwara Reform Movement", Ashoka International Publishers, New Delhi, 1985.
12. Will Durant, "The Story of Philosophy" Washington Square Press, New York.
13. Jawahar Lal Nehru, "Discovery of India," Allahabad, 1945.

B. Punjabi :

1. Trilok Singh, "Vartman Sikh Itihas", Amritsar, Vol. VI.
2. Jagjit Singh, "Singh Sabha Lahar", Amritsar, 1960.
3. Jaswant Singh, "Master Tara Singh, Jiwan, Sangharsh te Uddesh", Amritsar, 1972.

Index